T0227912

# JAVA
# Programming
# for Engineers

# JAVA
# Programming
# for Engineers

## JULIO SANCHEZ
Minnesota State University, Mankato

## MARIA P. CANTON
Minnesota State University, Mankato

**CRC Press**
Taylor & Francis Group
Boca Raton London New York

CRC Press is an imprint of the
Taylor & Francis Group, an **informa** business

CRC Press
Taylor & Francis Group
6000 Broken Sound Parkway NW, Suite 300
Boca Raton, FL 33487-2742

First issued in hardback 2017

© 2002 by Taylor & Francis Group, LLC
CRC Press is an imprint of Taylor & Francis Group, an Informa business

No claim to original U.S. Government works

ISBN-13: 978-0-8493-0810-9 (pbk)
ISBN-13: 978-1-138-46087-4 (hbk)

This book contains information obtained from authentic and highly regarded sources. Reasonable efforts have been made to publish reliable data and information, but the author and publisher cannot assume responsibility for the validity of all materials or the consequences of their use. The authors and publishers have attempted to trace the copyright holders of all material reproduced in this publication and apologize to copyright holders if permission to publish in this form has not been obtained. If any copyright material has not been acknowledged please write and let us know so we may rectify in any future reprint.

Except as permitted under U.S. Copyright Law, no part of this book may be reprinted, reproduced, transmitted, or utilized in any form by any electronic, mechanical, or other means, now known or hereafter invented, including photocopying, microfilming, and recording, or in any information storage or retrieval system, without written permission from the publishers.

For permission to photocopy or use material electronically from this work, please access www.copyright. com (http://www.copyright.com/) or contact the Copyright Clearance Center, Inc. (CCC), 222 Rosewood Drive, Danvers, MA 01923, 978-750-8400. CCC is a not-for-profit organization that provides licenses and registration for a variety of users. For organizations that have been granted a photocopy license by the CCC, a separate system of payment has been arranged.

**Trademark Notice:** Product or corporate names may be trademarks or registered trademarks, and are used only for identification and explanation without intent to infringe.

## Library of Congress Cataloging-in-Publication Data

Sanchez, Julio, 1938-
    Java programming for engineers / Julio Sanchez, Maria P. Canton.
        p. cm.—(Mechnical engineering)
    ISBN 0-8493-0810-0 (alk. paper)
        1. Java (Computer program language) 2. Mechanical engineering—Data processing. I. Canton, Maria P. II. Title. III. Mechanical engineering series (Boca Raton, Fla.)

QA76.76.J38 S26 2002
005.13′3—dc21
                                              2002025924

Library of Congress Card Number 2002025924

Visit the Taylor & Francis Web site at
http://www.taylorandfrancis.com

and the CRC Press Web site at
http://www.crcpress.com

# Table of Contents

# Chapter 24 - Java Math for Engineers 277

# Chapter 25 - Introducing Computer Graphics 295

# *Preface*

This book about Java programming is designed to address the needs of engineers, scientists, and technology professionals in general. In identifying our target audience we have made several assumptions:

1.  Our readers are not likely to use Java to develop applications of major complexity. Instead, we envision that the programs would be relatively small and specialized towards the solution of a particular problem set of a technological field.

2.  Our audience is more concerned with the solution of numerical problems than with text processing or the crunching of alphabetic data.

3.  The typical development environment consists of a single programmer or a small programming team.

4.  Most of the programs will be used by an individual or by a small technical group.

5.  The programs and applications will not be marketed to the public at large.

Based on these assumptions we have focused our attention on those topics in Java programming that are of greater interest to our audience. At the same time, we have minimized the coverage of topics that are of less concern to the typical engineer-programmer.

On the other hand, Java is a general-purpose programming language; therefore, it cannot be easily partitioned for the convenience of a particular interest group. Java programmers must deal with data types, operators and keywords, methods, classes, input and output, error handling, and a host of other necessary topics. This language core is necessary whatever the purpose of the application.

## Contents

The book aims at a comprehensive coverage of Java 1.3 as a full-featured programming language, using the PC platform. The text assumes no prior programming experience. The only skills expected in the reader are basic keyboarding and user-level familiarity with the PC. The material is sprinkled with short Java programs and code fragments that illustrate the point at hand. The sample programs are stripped of all unnecessary complications and distracting details, however, most of them stand alone as small applications. The purpose of the sample programs is to provide a valid, running sample that can be reused in your own code.

The text covers the following topics:

- Java programming language fundamentals
- Object oriented programming in Java
- Error handling
- Computer number systems
- Fixed and variable precision numeric data
- Numerical primitives
- Computer graphics in Java

The book is divided in two parts. The first one is a description of the Java language, of the fundamentals of object orientation, input and output operations, and error handling. The second part is about Java programming for engineers. It starts with computer number systems, fixed- and variable-precision numeric data, mathematical programming in Java as could be of interest to engineers, and concludes with an overview of Java graphics.

# *Part I*

## Java Language Fundamentals

# *Chapter 1*

# Java Programming

## Introducing Java

Java is a programming language similar to C and C++. Its most characteristic feature is that Java is a platform-independent language. This means that Java programs will run on any machine that supports the language. The slogan "write once, run anywhere" has often been used to describe and promote the Java language.

---
### Incidentally...
---

Java is not without drawbacks, and platform-independency is more a goal than a reality. Often Java programs must be modified before they operate correctly in another system. This has led some critics to rewrite the Java slogan to say "write once, debug everywhere."

---

Java was conceived by James Gosling, in the early 1990s, as a simple and small language to be used in programming consumer electronic devices, such as cellular phones and TV controllers. It was originally named Oak. After a few years of vainly attempting to find a costumer for Oak (also called Green), the design team renamed the language Java and incorporated it into the HotJava browser. HotJava could be used to download and run small programs, called *applets*, from the web. Applets, written in Java, provided a variety of animation and user-interaction features that were not available in a conventional browser. In the summer of 1995, Sun Microsystems released Java as a programming language. It was an instant success. In a few months Java became the preferred programming language of the World Wide Web, and it still is. It also evolved into a popular, general-purpose programming language.

3

Perhaps the most important element in Java's success was its timeliness. The language was introduced at the same time that the World Wide Web was rapidly gaining popularity. The Web is an international network of incompatible computers, made by dozens of manufacturers and having unique hardware characteristics. There is no standard operating system or software environment on the Web.

Java brought a promise of uniformity and compatibility to this diverse hardware and software environment of often irreconcilable differences. Its promise was that a program written in the Java language would execute correctly on any Java-enabled machine. A Java programmer could code a small application, embed it in a Web page, and the program would run on any browser that supported Java.

---

## Programmers note:

---

The language used to create Web pages and other Internet documents is called *Hypertext Markup Language* (HTML). Java code can be embedded in HTML documents in a capsule called a Java *applet*.

---

Java also provides a way of extending the functionality of a Web browser. Using Java, you can create a Web page that does more than is possible with straight HTML. The processing is contained in a Java applet that runs on any Java-enabled browser, including Mosaic, Netscape Navigator, or Internet Explorer. The applet executes correctly on a PC running Windows, on a Macintosh, on a UNIX machine, or on an IBM mainframe. The result is the same if you are connected to the Internet through a high-speed network or a slow-speed modem. This is what makes Java powerful and unique.

## The Portability Issue

In computer talk, the word "portable" describes code that can be moved to various systems with little or no effort. The expression probably relates to a computer connection, called a port, that is used for passing data in and out of a machine. Code that can be made to work in another machine simply by sending it through ports, is said to be *portable*. A programming language, such as Java, that can be easily made to run on various systems is described as highly portable.

Originally, Java's portability was limited to applets intended for the Web. It was soon noticed that Java could be used as a full-featured programming language to develop complete applications. The resulting programs would be portable to any Java-supporting platform. The benefits of machine-independent programming went beyond the obvious problems of hardware incompatibility. In the rapidly-evolving world of personal computers, operating systems were also changing at a fast rate. In the 1990's the same machine could run a half dozen versions of MS DOS, Windows 3.0/3.1, Windows 95, Windows 98, Windows 2000, NT 3.1, 3.5, 4.0, or Windows CE, and Linux. Applications had to be constructed taking into account many variations in the system software. At the same time, many potential customers were lost when an application was limited to a single machine or operating system environment.

Making an application compatible with several machine and software configurations often ends in a programming nightmare. Java promises a simplification of the programming task and a solution to incompatibility problems. No longer does the programmer have to deal with a "moving target" of hardware and operating system software. Instead, Java's "Code once, run anywhere" motto promises that the code can be "future proof" by making it compatible with future machines and operating systems.

## Java as a Programming Language

One reason for Java's success is that if you already know C or C++, Java is easy to learn. By the same token, if you learn Java as your first language, you will later be able to pick up C and C++ without much effort. Java is described as an interpreted, object-oriented, strongly typed language that relies heavily on support libraries. These characteristics of Java are discussed in the following sections.

### Java is object-oriented

An *object* is a program element that contains both data and code. The rationale for objects is that data is useful if there are operations that can be used to transform it. For example, we find it useful to store numbers in a computer system because there are operations that can be performed on these numbers. A computer program stores the hourly wage of a company's employees because it can later calculate the gross pay of each individual by multiplying the hourly wage by the number of hours worked. What use would it be to store numbers in a computer system that cannot perform arithmetic?

*Object-oriented programming* (OOP) views a software system as a collection of classes of objects. Each object class is a self-contained unit of data and the processing operations that can be applied to this data. You can image a payroll program that contains a class called Wage-EarningEmployee. The objects of the class are the individual wage earners employed by the company. In this sense Joe Smith, who makes wages of $18.25 per hour as a carpenter, is an object of the class WageEarningEmployee. The class contains data elements for storing the name and address, hourly wage, number of hours worked, number of dependents, and all other information necessary for managing the payroll. In addition, the class WageEarningEmployee also contains programming routines (called *methods*) for calculating wages, paying taxes, printing checks, and performing other necessary data manipulations. Other classes of the payroll software system may be called SalariedEmployee, AdministrativeStaff, and Executives. Each class would hold the data and processing elements necessary for each employee type.

---
## Programmers note:
---

As an object-oriented language, Java resembles Smalltalk. Smalltalk was developed at the Xerox Palo Alto Research Center (PARC) and first released in 1980. Although Smalltalk has never been very popular, it is considered a model for object-oriented programming languages. Java supports inheritance, encapsulation, and polymorphis, the cornerstones of object-oriented systems.

---

### *Java is strongly-typed*

Java is described as a *strongly-typed* language. This means that all data must belong to a specific type and that the data type cannot be changed while the program is executing. For example, whole numbers belong to one data type and fractional numbers to another one.

To understand the notion of a strongly-typed language you can imagine a data type named int, that is intended for storing integer (whole) numbers, and another type named float, designed for storing fractional numbers. (It just happens that the int and float data types actually exist in Java.) In this language, we could use the int type to store the number of dependents of an employee since this value would always be a whole number; while the employee's hourly wage, which could be a fraction, would be stored in a type float. Now suppose that an employee, for tax purposes, wanted to claim a fractional number of dependents, say 2.5. If the language is strongly-typed it would not be possible to store a fractional number in a data element of int type. A weakly-typed language, on the other hand, would allow storing a fractional number in an integer data type. Java is defined as strongly-typed because each data element must be consistent with the type of the data container that holds it. Strongly typed languages are said to be more reliable.

## *Java is similar to C++*

The basic syntax of Java is identical to C++. However, the designers of Java proposed to solve several problems that had plagued C++ and to eliminate features that were considered non-essential. The most visible difference is that Java is a pure object-oriented language. This means that Java programs must always use OO structures, while in C++ object-orientation can be turned off. The following are some important differences between Java and C++. Do not worry if you cannot understand all the terminology at this time since all of this is revisited later.

- In Java, the size of the data types is the same for all platforms. For example, a Java int data type must be encoded as a 32-bit signed 2s complement representation (more on this later) in every platform to which Java is ported. This is not the case in other languages in which the size of the data types can change from one system to another one. This feature of Java is necessary to ensure portability.

- In contrast with C and C++, Java performs automatic *garbage collection* at run time. It is the language, not the programmer, who takes care of reclaiming storage that is no longer in use. This simplifies the coding and program design.

- Java supports multithreading. A *thread* can be loosely defined as an individual program task. Multithreading allows an application to perform several tasks simultaneously. By supporting thread synchronization and scheduling, as well as the handling of deadlocks, Java makes it possible to develop code that makes better use of system resources and enhances performance.

- Java allows the programmer to deal with error conditions by means of exceptions. This simplifies the code and reduces clutter by offloading the error processing operations.

- Java is a smaller and simpler language than C and C++. It is easier to learn and use and is more reliable.

- Java is free. All of the Java compilers, runtime, and standard libraries are provided by Sun Microsystems at no charge. The software can be downloaded from the Sun Web sites and there are no royalties to be paid for its use. The programs that you build using Java software can be sold without displaying acknowledgments, disclaimers, or other statements of acceptance or recognition.

## *Java uses libraries*

The Java language is quite small. Much of the language's functionality is achieved through libraries. There are two types of Java libraries: the core libraries that are part of the Java Development Kit (JDK), and the optional

library additions. The core libraries must be present in every implementation of Java, while the optional libraries can be present or not. However, if a
feature in an optional library is supported in a particular implementation, it
must be fully supported in the standard way.

The complexity of the Java libraries can intimidate a beginning programmer. In the current version of the Java Development Kit (JDK), there
are 12 core libraries. Table 1-1 lists the core Java libraries.

**Table 1-1**

*Core Java Libraries*

| NAME | CLASSES | DESCRIPTION |
|---|---|---|
| java.lang | 93 | Basic runtime support for the Java language |
| java.applet | 4 | Applets support |
| Java.awt | 298 | Windowing and GUI support |
| javax.swing | 500 | Supplements java.awt and improves GUI support |
| java.io | 75 | Supports input and output |
| java.util | 77 | Utility data structures |
| java.rmi | 65 | Remote method calls |
| java.sql | 26 | Supports Java Database Connectivity |
| java.security | 106 | Supports secure data coding and decoding |
| java.net | 38 | TCP/IP, UDP, IP, and other network support |
| java.beans | 43 | Component software support to promote rapid application development by reuse of existing code fragments |
| java.text | 50 | Support for localized text elements such as dates, time, and currency |
| java.math | 2 | Support for the DECIMAL and NUMERIC types in the SQL database. Do not confuse with java.lang.Math class |
| javax.accessibility | 14 | Supports large text sizes for the visually impaired |

### Java is an interpreted language

A Java program is executed by an application called the Java interpreter
that must be installed in the host system. The Java interpreter is named
Java. The interpreter reads the code contained in a file produced by the
Java compiler, called Javac. This compiler, in turn, reads a source file written in the Java programming language. The result of the compilation step is
a file usually called the *Java byte code*. The Java source file, which serves as

input to the compiler, has the extension .java. The Java byte code file generated by the Javac compiler has the extension .class. It is the file with the .class extension that is executed by the Java interpreter. In Chapter 3, you will learn to create and run a program using the Java software development tools.

## Java Code

A program, in general terms, is a sequential set of instructions designed to perform a specific task. In this sense, the set of instructions that must be followed to start up a particular model of automobile could be described as the start-up program for that vehicle. By the same token, a computer program is a set of logical instructions that makes the computer perform a specific function.

For example, you may write a computer program to calculate the interest that accrues when you invest a given amount of money, at a certain interest rate for a specific period of time. Another program could be used to tell a robot when it is time to recharge its batteries. A third one to help a physician diagnose a childhood disease by examining the patient's symptoms. In all of these cases the program consists of a set of instructions that perform conditional tests, follow a predictable path, and reach a predictable result. A set of haphazard instructions that lead to no predictable end is not considered a program.

### Communicating with an alien intelligence

When we write a computer program we are communicating with an alien intelligence. A computer is a machine built of metal, silicon, and other composite materials. It has no knowledge and no common sense. In a way, a computer is no more than a tin can. If one-hundred years ago someone had found you attempting to communicate and give orders to a tin can, you would have probably been committed to a mental institution.

Our main difficulty is that the tin can never *knows what you mean*. A human intelligence has accumulated considerable knowledge of the world and of society at large. The set of instructions for a human to get me a can of pop out of a vending machine can be rather simple:

```
"Joe, here is fifty cents, would you please get me a Pepsi?"
```

Joe, who has knowledge of the world, understands that he must walk out of the room, open the necessary doors and walk up and down stairs, reach the vending machine, wait in line if someone is using it, then place the coins in the adequate slot, punch the Pepsi button, retrieve the can of pop, and bring it back to me, again opening doors and walking up and down stairs as necessary. Joe has knowledge of doors, of stairs, of money, of waiting in line, of vending machines, and of a thousand other worldly things and social conventions that are necessary to perform this simple chore.

The machine, on the other hand, has no previous knowledge, does not understand social conventions, and has no experience with doors, stairs, people standing in line, or vending machine operation. If we forget to tell the robot to open the door it will crash through and leave a hole shaped like its outline. If we forget to tell it to wait in line if someone else is using the vending machine, then the robot may just walk over the current customer in its effort to put the coins in the slot. The tin can has no experience, no social manners, and no common sense. Giving instructions to a machine is different and much more complicated than giving instructions to an intelligent being.

This is what computer programming is about. It is sometimes considered difficult to learn, not so much because it is complicated, but because it is something to which we are not accustomed. Learning programming requires learning the grammar and syntax of a programming language, but, perhaps more importantly, it requires learning to communicate with and issue commands to a tin can; a task indeed!

### Flowcharting

Computer scientists have come up with tools and techniques to help us develop programs. One of the simplest and most useful of these tools is the *flowchart*. A flowchart, like the word implies, is a graphical representation of the flow of a program. In other words, a flowchart is a graph of the tests, options, and actions that a program must perform in order to achieve a specific logical task.

## Incidentally...

Present-day computers do not have human-like intelligence. Assumptions that are obvious when dealing with human beings are usually invalid when dealing with a machine. Computer programs must leave no loose ends and presume no reasonable behavior. You cannot tell a computer "well... you know what I mean!" or assume that a certain operation is so obvious that it need not be explicitly stated. The programmer uses a flowchart to ensure that each processing step is clearly defined and that the operations are performed in the required sequence.

Flowcharts use symbols and special annotations to describe the specific steps in program flow. The most common ones are shown in Figure 1-1.

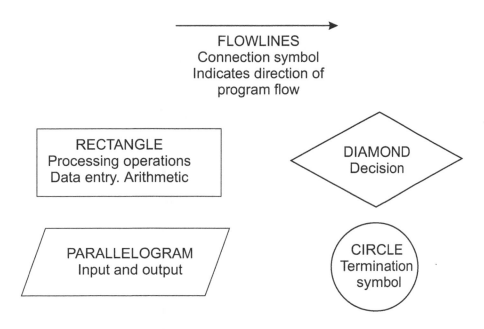

**Figure 1-1** *Flowcharting Symbols*

Suppose you needed to develop a program to determine when a domestic robot needs to recharge its own batteries. Assume that the robot contains a meter that measures the percent of full charge in its batteries, as well as a clock that indicates the time of day. The program is to be based on the following rules:

1.  The robot should recharge itself after 5:00 PM.

2.  The robot should not recharge itself if the batteries are more than 80% full.

The logic for recharging the robot batteries will first read the internal clock to determine if it is after 5:00 PM. If so, then it will read the robot's battery meter to determine if the batteries are less than 80% full. If both tests are true, then the robot is instructed to plug itself into a wall outlet and recharge. If not, it is instructed to continue working. The logic can be expressed in a flowchart, as shown in Figure 1-2.

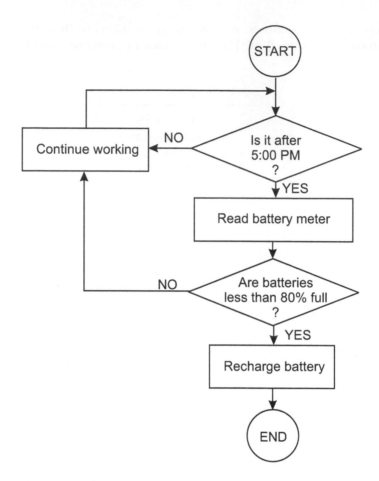

**Figure 1-2** *Flowchart for Recharging a Robot Battery*

Note in the flowchart of Figure 1-2 that the diamond symbols represent program decisions. These decisions are based on elementary logic, which requires that there must be two, but not more than two choices. These possible answers are labeled YES and NO in the flowchart. Decisions are the crucial points in the logic. A program that requires no decision is probably based on such simple logic that a flowchart would be unnecessary. For instance, a program that consists of several processing steps that are always performed in the same sequence does not require a flowchart.

The logic in computer programs often becomes complicated, or contains subtle points that can be misinterpreted or overlooked. Even simple programming problems usually benefit from a flowchart. The logic flowcharted in Figure 1-2 is based on recharging the batteries if it is after 5:00 PM "and" if the battery meter reads less than 80%. In this case both conditions have to be true for the action of recharging the battery to take place. An alternative set of rules could state that the robot must recharge itself if it is after 5:00 PM "or" if the battery is less than 80% full. In this case, either condition determines that the robot recharges. The flowchart to represent this logic must be modified, as shown in Figure 1-3.

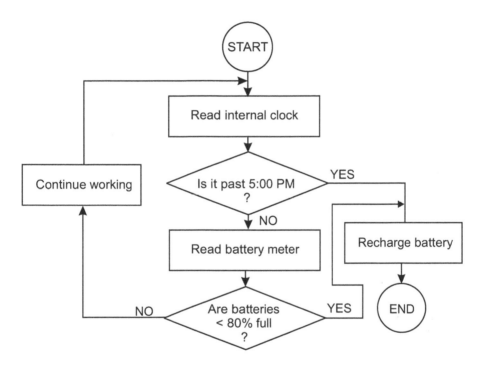

**Figure 1-3** *Alternative Logic for Recharging a Robot Battery*

Now suppose that there are critical functions that you do not want the domestic robot to interrupt, even if it is after 5:00 PM or if the battery is less than 80% charged. For example, if the robot is walking the dog you may not want it to let go of the leash and go plug itself into the wall outlet. In this case, you would have to modify the flowchart and insert an additional test so that recharging does not take place if the robot is currently performing a critical activity. Furthermore, you may decide that a very low battery could damage the machine; therefore, if the meter shows less than 20% full charge, the robot should plug itself into the outlet no matter what. Here again, the program logic and the flowchart would have to be modified to express the new set of conditions that determine which program action takes place. It is easy to see how program logic can easily get complicated and why flowcharts and other logic analysis tools are so important to the programmer.

# *Chapter 2*

# Your First Java Program

## Installing the JDK

The Java software development kit, called the JDK, is available for downloading at the Sun Microsystems Java software Web site at:

```
http://java.sun.com
```

The Java software is free. The Web site also contains useful Java programming information and tools, documentation, demos, as well as answers to frequently asked questions (FAQ). Appendix A contains detailed instructions for loading and installing the Java development software in your system. You must install the Java software in order to do the exercises in this chapter.

## Selecting an Editor

One component that is not included in the JDK is a text editor. You need a text editor for creating the Java source used by your programs. There are several text editors available in a PC. Edit is the MS-DOS editor while Note-Pad and Wordpad work in Windows. Although any one of these programs can serve in a pinch, all three have drawbacks. Edit, the MS-DOS editor, has the disadvantage that it mangles filenames that contain more than 8 characters. This makes it difficult to navigate through typical Windows folders, which usually have long names. In order to use Edit, you may consider placing all your source files in a first-level directory and use short names for the program files.

NotePad and WordPad are Microsoft editors that run in Windows. WordPad is the more powerful one. The main objection to using these editors for Java progamming is that they do not save a file with the extension

.java. Instead, WordPad and NotePad will automatically add the extension of the currently selected text type. For example, if you attempt to save a file under the name Demo.java, either editor will append the extension of the currently selected text type. If the selected file type is a text document, the resulting file will be named Demo.java.txt. The solution is to enclose the filename in double quotation marks when saving the source file to disk. For example, to save the file HelloWorld.java in NotePad or WordPad, you would type:

```
"HelloWorld.java"
```

The quotation marks prevent NotePad and WordPad from appending an extension to the filename. As long as you remember this requirement, you can use WordPad or NotePad in developing Java programs.

The book's CD ROM contains a Shareware editor named TextPad that was especially developed for Java programming. You may want to experiment with TextPad to see if it suits you. If you are going to spend time developing Java software using this editor, you should pay the modest Shareware registration fee.

## The HelloJava Program

In the first edition of their book on C programming, Kernigham and Ritchie listed a simple program that displayed a screen message with the text "Hello World". The Java version of the Hello World program is as follows:

```
//    Java version of the Hello World program
//    Developed for the book "Java for Engineers"
//    by CRC Press
public class HelloJava
{
  public static void main(String[] args)
    {
      System.out.println("Hello World, this is Java");
    }
}
```

### Java language rules

Java follows a few simple rules of syntax:

- Upper- and lower-case letters are different symbols in Java. When typing Java code you must be careful to follow the required capitalization, because *Main* and *main* are different.

- Java ignores white space. White space characters are those that do not appear on the screen, such as blank spaces, tabs, and line end codes. You will soon learn how Java programmers use white space to make the code more pleasant and readable.

- Java uses braces {} as grouping symbols. They mark the beginning and the end of a program section. A Java program must have an equal number of left and right braces. The part of a Java program located between braces is called a *block*.

- Every Java statement ends in the ; symbol. A statement is a program element that generates a processing action. Not every Java expression is a statement.

- Computer programs usually contain text that clarifies or explains the code. These are called *comments*. Comments must be preceded by a special symbol so that the text is ignored by the compiler. In Java, there are two ways of inserting comments into your code:

    The // symbol creates a comment that extends to the end of the line. For example:

```
// This is a single-line comment
```

The // symbol can appear anywhere in a program line.

/* and */ symbols are used to delimit a comment that can span over more than one line, for example:

```
/* This is a
   multiple line
   comment   */
```

## Programmers note:

Multiple line comments are now considered bad style. The reason is that comments that span several lines may force the reader to look up or down in the text for the comment symbols. A much clearer style is to use the double slash symbol to mark each comment line. This is the style we follow.

### The program header

Programs often begin with several commented lines, sometimes called the *program header*, that contain general information about the code that follows. The following elements are usually found in the program header:

- The program name
- The name of the author or authors
- A copyright notice, if one is appropriate

- The date of program creation
- A description of the program's purpose and the functions it performs
- A history of the program changes and updates
- A listing of the tools used in developing the program
- A description of the software and hardware environment required to run the program

   Programmers create their own program headers which they paste into all their sources. The following is a general-purpose program header that you can adapt to suit your needs:

```
//***************************************************************
//***************************************************************
//   Program name
//   Copyright (c) 200? by
//   ALL RIGHTS RESERVED
//***************************************************************
//***************************************************************
// Date:                          Coded by:
// Filename:                       Module name:
//                                 Source file:
// Program description:
//
//***************************************************************
// Libraries and software support:
//
//***************************************************************
// Development environment:
//
//***************************************************************
// System requirements:
//
//***************************************************************
// Start date:
// Update history:
//            DATE              MODIFICATION
//
//***************************************************************
// Test history:
//   TEST PROTOCOL          DATE         TEST RESULTS
//
//***************************************************************
// Programmer comments:
//
//
//***************************************************************
//***************************************************************
```

## On the Web

The listed sample header above is contained in the Chapter 2 folder at www.crcpress.com. The name of the file is Header.java

### The HelloJava code

Let's examine the HelloJava program line-by-line. The program is re-listed below:

```
//    Java version of the Hello World program
//    Developed for the book "Java for Engineers"
//    by CRC Press
public class HelloJava
{
  public static void main(String[] args)
    {
      System.out.println("Hello World, this is Java");
    }
}
```

The first three program lines are as follows:

```
//    Java version of the Hello World program
//    Developed for the book "Java for Engineers"
//    by CRC Press
```

These three program lines are a comment. They are ignored by the compiler and have no other purpose than to document and explain the code. We have used the // symbol to comment the lines individually.

The first non-comment line of the HelloJava program is as follows:

```
public class HelloJava
{
```

Programming languages, Java included, use special language elements called *keywords*. Keywords are reserved and cannot be used in regular expressions. The keyword **public**, called an *access modifier*, determines if other parts of the program can use this code. The keyword **class** is necessary because everything in a Java program exists in a class.

The first class in a Java program is called the *driving class*. The driving class must have the same name as the file in which it is stored. In other words, if you save a Java program in a file named MyHello.java, then the driving class must have the name MyHello. In the sample program, the source file has the filename HelloJava.java, and the driving class is named HelloJava.

## Programmers note:

One of the most common mistakes made by beginning Java programmers is to use a different name for the file and the driving class. You
must also be careful to use identical capitalization in the file name and
the class name.

The left-hand roster symbol indicates the beginning of the class named
HelloJava. At the end of the program listing there is a right-hand roster
symbol that terminates the HelloJava class.

The next statement in the HelloJava program creates a method named
main(). Java code must always be contained in a method. The main()
method is created as follows:

```
public static void main(String[] args)
   {
```

Every Java program must have a method named main. The words public, static, and void are Java keywords that determine the characteristics
of the main method. Static indicates that the method remains active at all
time that is, that it "stays." Void indicates that main returns nothing to the
operating system. The element inside parentheses represent a string
typed by the user when the program is executed. This string is sometimes
called the *command tail*. Command tails are seldom used in Java programming.

## Incidentally...

We use parentheses following the name of methods to make them easier to identify. Hereafter, the method named main appears as main().
This is a common style followed by many programming books.

Program execution always starts at the main() method of the Java
class that drives the application, that is, the class that has the same name
as the application's source file.

The left-hand roster indicates the beginning of the main() method.
Later in the listing you can see a right-hand roster that marks the end of
main(). The following statement is included in main():

```
        System.out.println("Hello World, this is Java");
     }
}
```

The purpose of this program line is to display the message "Hello World, this is Java" on the screen. System is a built-in class that is part of the standard Java libraries, while out is an object of this class. The word println(), pronounced print line, is a method of the System.out stream. The purpose of this line is to display a single text line on the video display. The text to be displayed is contained in double quotes. This is called a *string literal*. A stream can be visualized as a sequence of characters between a source (reader) and a destination (writer).

Figure 2-1 shows the elements of this program line. These elements are discussed in detail in later chapters.

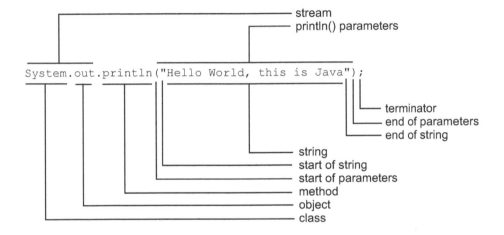

**Figure 2-1** *Breakdown of the println() Statement*

At the end of the program listing we see two right-hand rosters. The first one marks the end of the main() method. The second right-hand roster marks the end of the class HelloJava, which in this case is also the end of the program.

## Creating the HelloJava Program

As a first programming exercise, you should now type, compile, and run the HelloJava program. This will also serve to make sure that your development system is working correctly. Start by executing the editor of your choice and typing in the code. Make sure that you maintain the same capitalization as in the listing. Figure 2-2 shows the program as it appears in the TextPad editor screen.

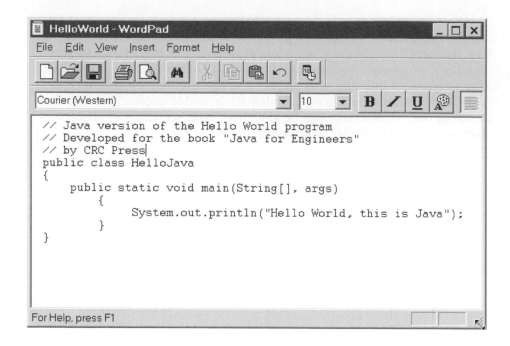

**Figure 2-2** *Typing the HelloJava Program*

Once the program is typed into the editor, it must be saved with the same name as that used in the driving class, in this case, HelloJava. The text file that contains the program code is called the *source file*. In Java, the source file must have the extension .java. Therefore, the program is saved as

```
HelloJava.java
```

Remember that the capitalization must be the same in the name of the source file, as in the name of the driving class. Also note that Java ignores white space in text formatting, but spaces inside a name are not ignored. Hello Java and HelloJava are different names.

The Java program development software that comes with the JDK must be run from the MS DOS command line. If you have correctly entered the PATH and CLASSPATH commands in your autoexe.bat file, as described in Appendix A, the system will be able to locate the development software without having to type in the path specification.

---

## Programmers note:

---

It is usually a good idea to execute the Java compiler from the same directory where the source files are located. This ensures that the system can find the source files.

---

Proceed as follows to compile the HelloJava program:

1.  Open a window with the MS DOS command prompt. If there is no MS DOS icon on your Windows desktop, you can find the MS DOS command prompt in the Programs command of the Windows Start menu.

2.  Log on to the directory where the source file that you intend to compile is located.

3.  Execute the Java compiler from the MS DOS command prompt.

    In the case of the HelloJava program, the command will be:

```
javac HelloJava.java
```

Javac (usually pronounced java-see) is the name of the Java compiler. If compilation takes place correctly, no error message is displayed and the MS DOS command prompt returns to the screen. If the javac compiler produces an error, you will have to locate it in the source code and correct it before attempting to re-compile.

Figure 2-3 shows the MS-DOS prompt window during the compilation and execution of the HelloJava program.

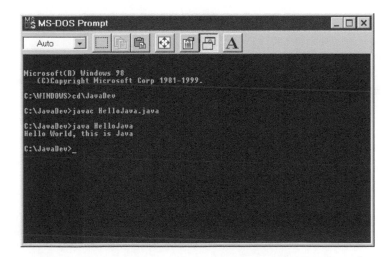

**Figure 2-3** *Compiling and Executing the HelloJava Program*

## Programmers note:

At this stage of your Java programming, most errors are due to typing mistakes. Incorrect capitalization and missing rosters are among the most common ones.

When the program has compiled without error, the compiler creates a file with the extension .class. This is the executable that can be run by the Java interpreter. The name of the java interpreter is java.exe.

Developing a Java application often requires going back and forth between the editor and the compiler. To save time, it is usually a good idea to place the editor in a desktop window, and the MS DOS command prompt in another one. You can then switch between both windows while developing the application or making corrections in the source.

# *Chapter 3*

# How Computers Store Information

## Storing Text and Numbers

A program's work consists mostly of storing, manipulating, and processing computer data. In this chapter we look at how this data is stored in a computer system. To a beginner, some of the topics could be intimidating. Binary and hexadecimal numbers sometimes appear to be a profound and arcane mystery that can only be understood by the gurus of computing. Nothing could be further from the truth. As you will see, binary and hex numbers are used in computers because they are more reasonable and easier to apply than conventional decimal numbers. Furthermore, you cannot be a programmer without a working knowledge of the number systems used by computers. A related topic is how text and numbers are encoded so that they can be stored in a computer, and how these data storage codes are used in Java programming.

## Number Systems

A number system is a collection of rules and symbols that we use for counting and doing arithmetic. The Hindu-Arabic or decimal system has gained worldwide acceptance. We are all familiar with the symbols:

```
0   1   2   3   4   5   6   7   8   9
```

It has often been said that the decimal system of numbers resulted from the practice of counting with our fingers, and that if humans had six fingers instead, our number system would have six symbols.

The first and most important use of a system of numbers is in counting. The simplest form of counting is called *tallying*. We all occasionally resort to the tally system by drawing a vertical line for each object we wish

25

to count. A refinement of the tally system is to make groups of five elements by drawing a diagonal line for each fifth unit. The tally system does not require numerical symbols. The ancient Egyptians used the tally system to count from 1 to 9. Roman numerals probably derived from the tally system since we can detect in some Roman numerals, the vertical and diagonal traces. In the system of Roman numerals there is no symbol for zero, the digits have no positional value, and some digits require more than one symbol. These factors make Roman numerals difficult to use.

The Hindu-Arabic system of numbers was introduced into Europe during the 14th and 15th centuries. These numerals are used in a counting scheme in which the value of each digit is determined by its column position, for example, the number

4   5   7   3

consists of 4 one-thousand units, plus 5 one-hundred units, plus 7 ten-units, plus 3 single units. The total value is obtained by adding the column weights of each unit.

## Binary numbers

The computers built in the United States during the early 1940s used decimal numbers to store data and to perform arithmetic operations. In 1946, John von Neumann observed that computing machinery would be easier to build and would be more reliable if the electronic circuits were based on two states, labeled ON and OFF, and that these two states could be represented by the digits 1 and 0. A system of numbers of only two digits is called the *binary system*. With binary numbers, the two states of an electronic cell are made to correspond to the digits 0 and 1.

---

## Incidentally...

---

John von Neumann, who was of Hungarian descent, insisted that his last name should be pronounced "fon Noiman". In 1930, he was invited to be a visiting lecturer at Princeton University. He later became one of the original six professors at Princeton's Institute for Advanced Study and Research; Albert Einstein was one of the other five. In 1946, von Neumann published a paper in collaboration with Arthur Burks and Herman Goldstein. The paper, titled "A Preliminary Discussion of the Logical Design of an Electronic Computing Instrument", turned out to be a perfect blueprint for building a computer. For this reason, the modern-day digital computer is described as a von Neumann machine.

---

The binary system is the simplest possible set of symbols with which we can count and perform positional arithmetic. Hexadecimal numbers, also called hex, are a convenient shorthand for representing groups of four binary digits. Figure 3-1 shows the relation between a group of four electronic cells and various number systems.

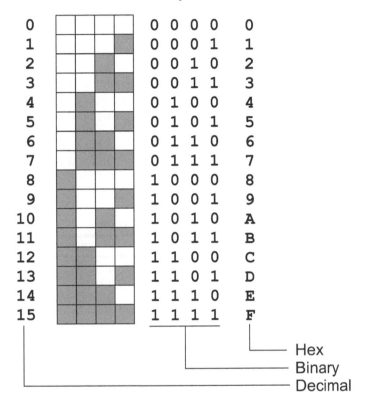

**Figure 3-1** *Decimal, Binary, and Hex Numbers*

If we think of each cell as a miniature light bulb, then the binary number 1 can be used to represent the state of a charged cell (light bulb ON) and the binary number 0 to represent the state of an uncharged cell (light bulb OFF). In this sense, we say that a bit is set if its binary value is 1 and that a bit is reset, or clear, if its binary value is 0.

## Hex numbers

The rightmost column in Figure 3-1 contains the hex numbers. Hex numbers are convenient because they are a shorthand way for representing groups of four binary digits. These groups of four electronic cells are the building blocks of computer systems. In most modern computers, memory cells, registers, and data paths are designed in multiples of four binary digits. In Figure 3-1, we see that all possible combinations of four binary digits can be encoded in a single hex digit.

## Computer memory

Today computer memory is usually furnished in the form of a silicon wafer that houses a package of integrated circuits. Each memory cell is a transistor circuit capable of storing two stable states. One state is represented with the binary symbol 1 and the other one with the binary symbol 0. The memory cells are usually arranged in groups of 8 bits, called a *byte*. In most machines, the byte is the smallest unit of memory that can be directly accessed by a program.

Table 3-1 lists the most common units of measurement associated with computer memory.

**Table 3-1**

*Units of Memory Storage*

| UNIT | EQUAL TO |
|------|----------|
| nibble | 4 bits |
| byte | 8 bits |
|  | 2 nibbles |
| word | 16 bits |
|  | 4 nibbles |
|  | 2 bytes |
| kilobyte | 1024 bytes |
| megabyte | 1024 kilobytes |
| gigabyte | 1024 megabytes |

Memory is organized linearly, that is, memory cells are placed in a single straight line that extends from the first to the last cell in the system. The sequential number assigned to each unit is called the *memory address*. The maximum number of memory units in a particular system depends on its internal architecture. Each memory cell in a typical computer consists of one byte (8 bits) of data. Figure 3-2 shows the numbering of the individual bits within a byte.

## Character data

Computers store data in groups of electrical cells, each of which holds either binary 1 or 0. These patterns of 1's and 0's are the most efficient and convenient way of representing computer information. A group of eight cells, called a byte, stores a number in the range 0 to 255.

**Figure 3-2** *Bit Numbering*

Characters and symbols are stored in computers according to a code in which each character or symbol corresponds to a numeric value. For example, if we agree that the upper-case letter A is represented by the number 1, the letter B by the number 2, and so forth, then the upper-case letter Z is represented by the number 26. Once we accept this scheme for representing letters by numbers, we can encode text messages using numbers instead of letters. In this manner, the letters ACZ would be represented by the numbers 1, 3, 26.

Several schemes for representing character data have been adopted and abandoned over the years. Hollerith code and the Extended Binary Coded Decimal Interchange Code, known as EBCDIC, were popular some time ago. American Standard Code for Information Interchange, or ASCII (pronounced as-key), has gained almost universal acceptance. Java recognizes several character sets, including ASCII; however, the language supports a universal character set named Unicode. While ASCII characters are stored in 8-bits, Unicode is based on 16-bit values. This wider format allows supporting non-English and multilingual environments. Figure 3-3 (on the next page) shows the symbols in the ASCII character set as well as their decimal and hexadecimal values.

You can use Figure 3-3 to determine the decimal and hex value of any ASCII symbol. First, you look up the column value of the symbol, and then add to it the row value. For example, the decimal ASCII code for the letter "c" is 96 plus 3, or 99. By the same token, the value of the ASCII symbol for the number "6" is 36 hexadecimal or 54 decimal.

Characters are stored in computer memory according to the numeric values assigned to them in the adopted representation. In ASCII encoding the name "Jane" appears in computer memory as the decimal values 74, 97, 110, and 101 since these are the ASCII decimal values for the letters "J", "a", "n", and "e." In Hex, the values would be 4A, 61, 6E, and 65. Figure 3-4 shows the binary and hex values for the ASCII characters that form the name "Jane."

| Decimal → | HEX | 0 / 0 | 16 / 10 | 32 / 20 | 48 / 30 | 64 / 40 | 80 / 50 | 96 / 60 | 112 / 70 |
|---|---|---|---|---|---|---|---|---|---|
| 0 | 0 | | | (space) | 0 | @ | P | ` | p |
| 1 | 1 | | | ! | 1 | A | Q | a | q |
| 2 | 2 | | | " | 2 | B | R | b | r |
| 3 | 3 | | | # | 3 | C | S | c | s |
| 4 | 4 | | | $ | 4 | D | T | d | t |
| 5 | 5 | | | % | 5 | E | U | e | u |
| 6 | 6 | | | & | 6 | F | V | f | v |
| 7 | 7 | | | ' | 7 | G | W | g | w |
| 8 | 8 | | | ( | 8 | H | X | h | x |
| 9 | 9 | | | ) | 9 | I | Y | i | y |
| 10 | A | | | * | : | J | Z | j | z |
| 11 | B | | | + | ; | K | [ | k | { |
| 12 | C | | | , | < | L | \ | l | \| |
| 13 | D | | | - | = | M | ] | m | } |
| 14 | E | | | . | > | M | ^ | n | ~ |
| 15 | F | | | / | ? | O | _ | o | |

**Figure 3-3** *The ASCII Character Set*

```
01001010-01100001-01101110-01100101 ————— Binary values
  4AH        61H        6EH        65H ————————— Hex values
  "J"        "a"        "n"        "e" ————————— ASCII characters
```

**Figure 3-4** *ASCII Encoding of the Name "Jane"*

## Numeric data

Numbers can be represented in a computer system by means of the corresponding characters. In the ASCII character set, the number 128 is represented by three bytes holding the decimal values 49, 50, and 56. You can confirm these codes in the ASCII table in Figure 3-3. Although numeric data is sometimes stored as characters, this representation of numbers is inefficient and awkward. Computers are binary machines and perform arithmetic operations only on binary numbers. This means that to multiply the number 128, encoded in ASCII digits, by the number 2, also in ASCII, the computer would first have to convert these text-like representations into binary. A more reasonable approach is to store numbers directly in binary. For example, the number 128 can be stored as the binary value

```
10000000
```

First note that in binary the number 128 is stored in one byte, while it requires three bytes if it is represented in ASCII characters. More importantly, binary arithmetic can be performed directly on the encoding without having to perform conversions.

Computer systems use straight binary representation for unsigned integer numbers. However, how would you represent negative and positive numbers in binary? One possible scheme is to devote a binary digit to represent the sign. By convention, a binary 0 represents a positive number, and a binary 1 represents a negative number. Usually the leftmost bit, called the high-order bit, is devoted to the sign. This arrangement is sometimes called a *sign-magnitude representation*. For example, the decimal numbers +93 and -93 are represented as follows:

```
01011101 = +93 decimal
11011101 = -93 decimal
```

Note that the leftmost bit is zero for +93 and it is 1 for -93. The remaining binary digits are the same in both numbers.

Sign-magnitude representation, although simple and straightforward, has its drawbacks. One of them is that there are two encoding for zero, one negative and one positive, as follows:

```
00000000 = positive zero
10000000 = negative zero
```

The representation for negative zero is usually unnecessary, since zero is neither positive nor negative. Furthermore, sign-magnitude representations make arithmetic complicated. To add two signed numbers you first have to determine if they have the same sign or different signs. If the sign is the same, then the numbers are added and given the common sign. If the numbers have different signs, then the smaller one is subtracted from the larger one and given the sign of the larger one. If either number is 0 or -0, then the result is the other element. If both numbers are -0, then the sum is 0.

Another type of signed binary encoding, called *radix-complement representation*, was developed to eliminate the negative zero and to simplify machine arithmetic. The radix of a number system is the same as its base. The radix of the decimal system is ten, and in this system the radix complement is also called the *ten's complement*. In binary, the base of the number system is two, and the radix-complement representation is called the two's complement.

The *two's complement* of a signed number is obtained by calculating the difference between the number and the next integer power of two that is greater than the number. Usually the machine hardware contains instructions that directly produce the two's complement. The great advantage of two's complement representations is that arithmetic addition and subtraction become a single operation, and that the arithmetic rules and manipulations are simpler and more effective.

Binary encoding of fractional numbers poses some additional problems. Since there is no way of representing a decimal point in binary, we must adopt some scheme to define where the decimal point is located. Several approaches are possible. In one of them, called a *fixed-point representation*, a previously determined number of binary digits are assigned for encoding the integer part, and another number of digits for the fractional part. Although the fixed-point approach was used in some of the earlier computers, it is wasteful and ineffective.

Another way of encoding fractional numbers is based on the same method used in scientific notation; it is also called *exponential form*. In scientific notation scheme, the number 310.25 is written as follows:

$3.1025 \times 10^2$

The value 310.25 is obtained by multiplying 3.1025 by 100. Numbers that are smaller than 1 can we written using a negative exponent, for example, the number .0004256 in scientific notation is

$4.256 \times 10^{-4}$

In order to avoid superscripts, computer technology uses the letter E for the exponent part. For example:

```
3.1025 E2
4.256 E-4
```

Because the decimal point *floats* according to the value of the exponent, these representations are called floating-point. For many years computers have used floating-point binary representations for encoding decimal numbers. Several computer manufacturers came up with their own schemes for representing decimal numbers in floating-point format. In 1985, the American National Standards Institute (ANSI) approved a binary floating-point standard based on the work of the Computer Society of the Institute for Electric and Electronic Engineers (IEEE). This standard, designated as ANSI-IEEE 754 is now generally followed. Java uses the ANSI-IEEE 754 formats for storing decimal numbers encoded in binary.

# Chapter 4

# Storing and Naming Data

## A Data-Processing Machine

A computer can be described as a machine that processes data. You can imagine a digital meat grinder into which raw data is fed. When you turn the grinder's handle, the raw data is converted into some form of consumable digital sausage. Using this same meat grinder image we can say that a program is a set of instructions that determine how the raw data is processed. Therefore, one of the main functions of a programming language, such as Java, is the classification, manipulation, and storage of computer data. In this chapter we look at how data is stored in a Java program and learn how to create and use different types of data.

## What is Computer Data?

Data is a general term that can be applied to many types of objects. It means an item of information.

---

### Incidentally...

Strictly speaking "data" is the plural of "datum" but, in practice, no one bothers making this distinction.

---

The following can be considered items of data:

```
3.1415
Minnesota
131 Calm Court
75
X
```

When we look at data we observe that it comes in two flavors: numbers and names. The main difference between numbers and names is that we can perform arithmetic on numbers, but not on names. Numbers belong to a type called numeric data, while names are *alphanumeric* or *character data*. You may have also noticed that some data items refer to individual objects and others are a collection of objects. For example, the data item "131 Calm Court" is a collection of three simpler items. Data types that encode individual objects are called *scalar* types, while those that represent collections of objects are called *structured* data types. Java provides means for storing and manipulating numeric and alphanumeric data objects of both scalar and structured types.

Once a data item is assigned to a particular type, its processing is done according to the rules for that particular type. In other words: you cannot do arithmetic on objects defined as a character type. By the same token, numeric data cannot be separated into its individual symbols. As a programmer you assign each data object to the data type that corresponds to its intended use. In doing this, you must not be confused by an object's appearance. For example, a telephone number, which is actually a collection of digits, is usually considered an alphanumeric data type. What would be the use of adding or subtracting telephone numbers?

## Identifiers

Before we get into the details of creating and using data we must take a brief look at the Java rules for naming program elements. Java *identifiers* are used to name data items, classes, and methods. Legal characters for identifiers are the letters and digits of the Unicode character set, as well as the symbols $ and _. The space is not a legal character in an identifier since Java uses the space to mark the end of names. Because Java is *case-sensitive*, the names aVar and Avar represent different identifiers. An identifier cannot start with a digit. The length of an identifier is virtually unlimited, although it is a good idea to keep identifiers to less than 30 characters. The following are legal identifiers in Java:

```
personalName
PI
y_121
$$128
user_address
The following identifiers are illegal:
1_value
User name
%%123
```

An identifier cannot be one of the special keywords used by the Java language. Appendix B lists the Java reserved words.

---

**Programmers note:**

---

One of the programmer's most important tasks is coming up with good identifiers. A good identifier is one that is descriptive and at the same time easy to type. For example, if a data item is to hold the age of an employee, a good name for this item may be employeeAge. Since spaces are illegal in identifiers, you can use capital letters or the underscore symbol to separate the individual words in a name. Cryptic or meaningless identifiers make the code difficult to understand and maintain. While identifiers that are too verbose or complicated are prone to typing errors.

---

## Creating and using variables and constants

To a programmer, a variable is a storage location that contains a data item of a specific type. The storage location is assigned a name so that it can be identified. The contents of a variable can be changed anywhere in the program. Therefore, a variable can be visualized as a labeled box, defined by the programmer, for storing a data object of a particular type. Figure 4-1 shows the data items listed previously.

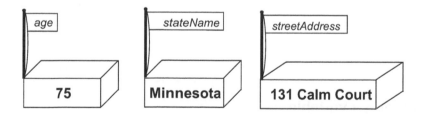

**Figure 4-1** *Variables as Labeled Boxes*

In the course of a program we can re-assign values to all our variables, as long as the new value is consistent with the original type. For example, we can replace the value of the numeric constant named "age" with another number, or the value of the variable named "stateName" with another name. *Constants*, on the other hand, represent values that do not change in the course of a program. For example, we can define a constant to store the value of Pi, which is the ratio between the diameter and the

circumference of a circle. Once defined, this value can be recalled any
time that it is needed.

## Java variable types

Java is a *strongly typed* language. This means that every variable must have
a declared type, and that the language strictly enforces type-checking.
Eight primitive data types are built into the Java language. Four of these
primitive types, called integer types, are used to store whole numbers. They
are named *byte, short, int,* and *long.* Two primitive types are used for storing decimal numbers. These types are named *float* and *double.* There is also
one character type, named *char,* and one boolean type, named *boolean.* Table 4-1 lists the Java primitive data types.

### Table 4-1
*Java Primitive Data Types*

|  | TYPE NAME | STORAGE SPACE | APPROXIMATE RANGE |
|---|---|---|---|
| INTEGRALS: | | | |
|  | int | 4 bytes | +/- 2 billion |
|  | short | 2 bytes | +/- 32,767 |
|  | long | 8 bytes | +/- 9.2 x 1018 |
|  | byte | 1 byte | -129 to 127 |
| FLOATING-POINT: | | | |
|  | float | 4 bytes | 7-8 digits |
|  | double | 8 bytes | 16-17 digits |
| CHARACTER TYPE: | | | |
|  | char | 2 bytes | 65,536 |
| BOOLEAN TYPE: | | | |
|  | boolean | | true and false |

## Declaring a variable

Before you can use a variable in a Java program you must first declare it by
specifying its type and assigning to it a name. The variable name must be a
legal Java identifier and the variable type must be one of the primitive data
types listed in Table 4-1. The purpose of the declaration statement is to inform the compiler of our intention of creating a variable of a specific type
and tagging it with a particular name. The result is that Java reserves a
memory space in which to store the data and associates it with the identifier that we assigned as a name. For example, the following declaration creates a variable of type int:

```
int age1;
```

You may also declare several variables of the same type by separating the variable names with commas, for example:

```
int age2, age3, age4;
```

At the time that a variable is declared, you can also assign to it a value. This is called the variable's *initialization*. The value assigned to the variable is preceded by the equal sign, for example:

```
float radius = 1.22;
```

In this statement we have created a numeric variable of Java's float type and named it radius. The variable was initially set to a value of 1.22.

You may also declare several variables while initializing some and not others, for example:

```
int valA = 1, val2, val3, val4 = 77;
```

In this case the commas separate the individual variables. However, these complicated variable declarations are not considered good programming style.

## Java strings

Programs frequently use groups of characters called *strings*. A Java string is a class, not a primitive type. The Java String class is part of the java.lang library that is directly accessible to any Java program. For this reason you can create objects of the Java String class as if they were variables of a primitive data type. Note that because String is a class it begins with an upper-case letter, while all the other primitive data types in Table 4-1 have names that start with a lower-case letter.

---

### Programmers note:

---

The Java String class is so often used in programming that we tend to think of it as another primitive data type. The fact that "String" starts with a capital "S" reminds us that it is a class.

---

A String object is used to represent a sequence of characters. In contrast with the primitive data types, once a string is created it cannot be changed. A String object is declared and initialized much like any of the primitive types. Double quotation marks are used to delimit the string; for example:

```
String uName = "Minnesota State University";
String ssn = "263-98-2233";
```

The Java String class contains several methods to manipulate and convert strings. These are discussed later in this book.

---

## Programmers note:

---

At the time it is declared a variable assumes certain specific attributes. One of these attributes is called the *scope*. A variable's scope is the part of a program over which it is recognized. The scope of a Java variable is determined by the closest set of roster symbols, { and }, that contain the variable. The variable can be used only in the part of the code that is located within these rosters. By strictly enforcing the variable scope rules, Java makes it difficult to misuse variables.

---

## Java constants

Java constants are variables defined with the *final* and *static* keywords. Java has strict rules for the declaration of constants. The language does not allow constants inside a particular method. Instead, constants must be defined at the class level. For this reason they are sometimes called *class constants*. If an application requires a local constant all it can do is define a variable and use it as if it were a constant. The following statement declares a constant:

```
static final double PI = 3.141592653589793;
```

Many programmers use all upper-case letters for constant names, as in the case of the constant PI listed above. This style makes it easy to identify variables and constants in the code listing.

# Classification of Java Data

In Table 4-1 we see that Java primitive data types are classified into three categories: numeric types, character types (also called alphanumeric data), and boolean types. Each of these data types serves a special purpose in a Java program. Before you can start serious Java programming you must first have a clear notion of the three categories of Java data and of the specific types in each one of them.

## Numeric data

Many Java programs must do number-crunching operations. Numeric data is used to perform mathematical operations and calculations.

---

### Programmers note:

---

In numeric data types the digit symbols represent quantities. In alphanumeric data types these same symbols are used as designators, as is
the case in a telephone or a social security number.

---

Numeric data can appear in Java code in the form of variables or con-
stants. In addition numeric data can be entered explicitly in an operation.
Explicit numeric data, called *literals*, are discussed later in this chapter.
The floating-point types are also called *reals*.

Each numeric data type corresponds to a category of numbers, for example, the integer data type allows representing whole numbers while the
floating-point data type allows representing fractional numbers. For each
data type, Java provides several *type specifiers* that further determine
the characteristic and range of representable values. These are listed in
Table 4-1.

## Character data

Character or alphanumeric data refers to items that serve as textual designators. The letters of the alphabet and other non-numeric symbols are often
used as designators. Number symbols are also valid in alphanumeric data.
This is the case of telephone numbers, street addresses, zip codes, social
security numbers, and many other designators.

In Java, alphanumeric data belongs either to the char data type or to
the String class. Data defined as char is treated by Java either as a 16-bit
unsigned integer, with values in the range 0 to 65535, or as a single
Unicode character. This means that the char data type can be used to represent unsigned integers in the range mentioned above, and that it supports basic arithmetic on these values. However, it is usually better to use
the numeric data types for this and leave the char type for alphanumeric
data.

The single quotation marks are used to declare a char data type. These
are sometimes called "tick" marks. For example:

```
char aLet = 'f';
```

Recall that String objects are declared using the double quotation
marks:

```
String aCity = "Mankato";
```

## Boolean data

The third data classification of the Java language is the *boolean*, represented by a single data type, also called boolean.

---
### Incidentally...
---

The boolean data type owns its name to the English logician George Boole who, in the nineteenth century, addressed the relations between mathematics and logic. Java is one of the languages that supports a boolean data type. Other languages, such as C and C++, use an integer data type to represent boolean data. In languages with no boolean data type, a value of 0 typically represents false and any other numeric value represents true.

---

A boolean variable can take only two values: true and false. In Java these values must be typed in lower-case letters. Typically, boolean variables represent program elements that indicate the truth or falseness of a statement or proposition. They are declared and initialized like numeric or alphanumeric types. For example:

```
boolean switchIsOn = true;
```

# Type Conversions

In Java programming, you will often encounter a situation in which one data type must be converted into another one. Suppose that you are developing a program that must calculate a ratio based on two integer values. Such would be the case if your program used variables to represent a control valve with a maximum flow and a series of flow-control settings, as follows:

```
int maximumFlow = 10;
int flowSetting = 5;
```

In this case, you could obtain the current gas flow ratio (0.5) by dividing the flow setting value (5) by the maximum valve flow value (10). The problem is that, in Java, integer arithmetic always produces integer values. Therefore, in Java integer arithmetic, the result of the operation 5 / 10 is 0.

The solution to this problem is to convert the two integer operands into floating-point types (float or double) in order to perform floating-point division. There are two forms of type conversions: *explicit* and *implicit*. In explicit conversions, code deliberately changes the data type of an operand by a process called *type casting*. Implicit conversions are performed automatically by the language.

## Implicit conversions

Java performs implicit conversions between numeric types only if no loss of precision or magnitude results from the conversion. In the case of unary conversions, operands of type byte and short are automatically converted to type int. All other types are preserved. In the case of binary conversions the rules are as follows:

1.  With integer types, if one of the operands is long, then the other one is converted to long. Otherwise, both operands are converted to int.

2.  Also in relation to integers, the expression is an int except if the value is too long for the int format. In this case the value is converted to a long.

3.  For operations on floating-point types, if one operand is a double, the other one is also converted to double and the result is of type double. Otherwise, both operands are converted to float and the result is a float type.

## Type-casting

Explicit conversions are performed by a process called *casting* or *type casting*. Type casting consists of preceding the operand with the desired type, enclosed in parentheses. Recall the case of the gas flow valve mentioned at the beginning of this section. Here we needed to convert two integer variables to a floating-point type. In this case the cast can be as follows:

```
int maximumFlow = 10;
int flowSetting = 5;
double flowRate;
. . .
flowRate = (double) maximumFlow / (double) flowSetting;
```

The variable flowRate now has the expected ratio of 0.5.

Java type casting must follow the following rules:

1.  Boolean variables cannot be cast into any other type.

2.  Any of the integer data types can be cast into any other type, except boolean. Casting into a smaller type can result in loss of data.

3.  Floating-point types can be cast into other float types or into integer types. These casts may result in loss of data.

4.  The char type can be cast into integer types. Since the char is 16-bits wide, casting into a byte type may result in loss of data or in garbled characters.

## Declaring literals

Java programs usually contain values expressed directly. These values are called *literal expressions*, or *literals*. You use a literal to initialize a variable or a constant. For example:

```
int age = 32;
String myU = "Minnesota State University";
```

In the declaration of literal values, Java assumes that floating-point literals are of type double. For this reason, the statement:

```
float aVal = 12.33;
```

generates an error. The reason for the error is that Java assumed that the value 12.33 is in double format, and there could be loss of precision when it is converted into the float type of the variable. The solution is to force the literal, in this case the value 12.33, into a float type, as follows:

```
float aVal = (float) 12.33;
```

Java also provides the following shorthand:

```
float aVal = 12.33f;
```

The small-case letter f following the literal value performs a type cast.

# Chapter 5

# Performing Input and Output

## Input and Output

So far you have learned about classification, storage, and initialization of data. These operations are internal to the program and, therefore, relatively independent from the machine's hardware. The designers of Java defined data types and data-manipulation instructions in a way that ensured that they could be implemented with relative ease, in any modern computer. This is not easy to achieve with data input and output operations. Input and output requires the intervention of hardware devices, such as the keyboard, the mouse, the video system, or the printer. This makes data input and output functions device-dependent and very difficult to define and implement in a language, such as Java, which aims at device-independence. The result is that input and output operations in Java are often considered difficult and complicated.

In this chapter, we describe a Java class named Keyin that we developed so as to simplify coding keyboard input operations. The elements of the Keyin class are explained in detail in Chapter 18. For the time being, you will use the class as a black box that contains methods for entering numbers, characters, and strings from the keyboard. Data output to the video display is supported by the Java libraries, although in a rather elaborate way.

## Data Input

There is no single instruction or library method in the Java language to perform keyboard input. This is also true of C and C++; however, C and C++ contain input functions that are part of their standard libraries. Not in Java, in which input takes place at the data stream level. This means that to input

45

an integer, a string, or a floating-point number, the programmer has to develop a rather complicated routine based on the methods and subclasses of the Java InputStream class, which is part of the java.io library. Alternatively, you could develop an input routine using the methods of the System class, which is part of the java.lang library, but it is also complicated and beyond your present understanding of the language.

Although the processing required for obtaining keyboard input is not difficult to implement, it is beyond our present level. On the other hand, even the simplest program requires some form of data input. It would be impossible to perform any kind of non-trivial programming in Java without means for obtaining keyboard data. For this reason we have developed a class to perform data input. The class, called Keyin, contains the following methods:

```
inChar() inputs a single keyboard character.
inString() inputs a string from the keyboard.
inInt() inputs an integer number.
inDouble() inputs a float in double format.
```

To use the methods inChar(), inString(), inInt(), and inDouble() you must have the Keyin class accessible to the code. The easiest way is to copy the file Keyin.class to your current development directory. This done, your program will be able to input characters, strings, integers, and floating-point numbers.

Each of the methods in the Keyin class displays a prompt message to inform the user of the input required. This message is passed as a parameter, as in the following code fragment:

```
int age1;
 . . .
age1 = inInt("Please enter your age" );
```

When the method inInt() executes, the prompt message "Please enter your age: " is displayed on the screen. Once the user enters a valid value and presses the <Enter> key the value is assigned to the variable age1. The methods inChar(), inString() and inDouble() are similar.

## On the Web

You may look at the code of the Keyin class by loading the file Keyin.java into your editor program. Keyin.java is found in the Chapter 18 folder at www.crcpress.com.

# Data Output

Data output in Java is easier to implement than data input. The out object, which is part of the System class, can be used to display program data directly. The System class is part of the java.lang library. The out object of the System class allows you to use the print() and println() methods of the PrintStream class, located in java.io. In the HelloJava program, developed in Chapter 2, we used the println() method to display a message on the screen. The following expression is part of the HelloJava.java program:

```
System.out.println("Hello World, this is Java");
```

The println() method automatically terminates the displayed line. The result is that the current text output marker, sometimes called the *cursor*, is moved to the next screen line automatically. The print() method, on the other hand, sends data to the video display at the current position of the text output marker, but does not index to the next screen line. For example, the statements:

```
System.out.print("value");
System.out.print("       number");
System.out.print("       code");
System.out.flush();
```

Produce the following output:

```
value       number       code
```

In this case, the flush() method, also of the PrintStream class, is used to terminate the line.

## Escape characters

The Java display methods, print() and println(), recognize special characters that serve to delimit and format the string or character to be displayed; also to display symbols that are used in the statement grammar. For example, the " symbol is used in print() and println() to mark the beginning and the end of the string to be displayed. If you were to include this symbol as a character, then the processing logic would be unable to correctly format the output. Suppose you wanted to display on the screen a message that contained a word inside quotation marks, for example:

```
She said her name was "Mary"
```

Since quotation marks are used to end the string to be displayed, the following statement would not execute correctly

```
System.out.println("She said her name was "Ellen"");
```

The processing logic would interpret that the second quotation mark symbol marks the end of the output string. But if the string ends in this symbol, then the rest of the statement is undecipherable and a compiler error is produced.

Other special characters are used to format output. For example, when the value 0x0a (decimal 10) is sent to the console the device moves the cursor to the next screen line. From the days of teletype machines and typewriters this is called a *linefeed*. By the same token, when the code 0x0d (decimal 13) is sent to the console the cursor is moved to the start of the line. This action is called a *carriage return*. The values that perform these special actions are called *control codes*.

Java uses the \ symbol as a special character. It serves to indicate that the character that follows is to be interpreted in a special way. The \ symbol is called the *escape character*. The escape character is used to display characters that are used in statement formatting and to execute control codes such as new line and carriage returns. Table 5-1 shows the Java Escape Characters.

**Table 5-1**

*Java Escape Characters*

| LITERAL | VALUE | ACTION |
|---------|-------|--------|
| \b | 0x08 | backspace |
| \t | 0x09 | horizontal tab |
| \n | 0x0a | new line |
| \f | 0x0c | form feed |
| \r | 0x0d | carriage return |
| \" |  | double quotation mark |
| \' |  | single quotation mark |
| \\ |  | backslash |

By using the escape character we can now reformat the previous statement, as follows:

```
System.out.println("She said her name was \"Mary\"");
```

The new line character (\n) is often used to end the current text line or to produce a blank line on the screen. The following code displays the words "Hello" and "World" separated by two blank lines.

```
System.out.print("Hello");    // First word
System.out.print("\n\n");     // Two blank lines
System.out.print("World");    // Second word
System.out.flush();
```

# A Sample Program

The following Java program demonstrates some of the programming elements and constructs discussed so far.

---

## On the Web

The source file for the program Area.java can be found in the Chapter 5 directory at www.crcpress.com.

---

```
//    File name: Area.java
//    Reference: Chapter 5
//
//    Java program to calculate the area of a circle
//    Topics:
//        1. Using numeric variables and constants
//        2. Obtaining keyboard input
//        3. Displaying program data
//        4. Performing simple numeric calculations
//
//    Requires:
//        1. Keyin class in the current directory

public class Area
{
   // Constant PI is defined at the class level
   static final double PI = 3.141592653589793;

   public static void main(String[] args)
     {
       // Local variables
       double radius, area;

       // Input radius from keyboard
       radius = Keyin.inDouble("Enter radius: ");

       // Perform calculations and display result
       area = PI * (radius * radius);
       System.out.println("The area is: " + area);
     }
}
```

# Chapter 6

# Introducing Arrays

## A New Data Type

In Chapter 4 you learned about Java's primitive data types and about the String class. The Java primitive data types serve to store a single alphanumeric or Boolean value. For example, you can use an int data type to store a whole number, or a float type to store a decimal number. But computer programs often need to store and manipulate data in groups of associated values. For example, a payroll program keeps track of the names, addresses, social security numbers, number of dependents, wages, and other items of information necessary for managing the company's employee database.

This is best accomplished by storing several data items, of the same type, in a single structure, called an *array*. For example, the payroll program can use an array to store the employee names, another one to store addresses, a third one for the employee's social security numbers, and so on. As you will see in this chapter, data placed in arrays is easy to save, retrieve, and process.

## Java Arrays

An array is an ordered list of data, all of the same type. A payroll program can use an array of Java Strings to store the last names of the employees and another one of int type to store the number of dependents. The glue that holds together the corresponding elements of several arrays is the order in which they appear. This relative position of the elements of an array is called the *index*. Figure 6-1 (on the next page) represents these arrays in a company with 10 employees.

|  | | Array "lastName" |
|  | | Array "dependents" |

| index | lastName | dependents |
|---|---|---|
| 0 | Whiteman | 0 |
| 1 | Jones | 2 |
| 2 | Lopez | 3 |
| 3 | Carlson | 1 |
| 4 | Ragavendra | 2 |
| 5 | Black | 5 |
| 6 | Smith | 4 |
| 7 | Kruger | 2 |
| 8 | Thompson | 1 |
| 9 | Stone | 1 |

**Figure 6-1** *Representation of Arrays*

An *array element* is an individual data value. Each element in an array can be considered as a stand-alone variable. In the array of Figure 6-1, Carlson is the fourth element of the array "lastName". Because the array index is zero-based, the fourth entry is located at index 3. The number of dependents for this employee is found at the same index, in the array named "dependents". In this case Carlson has one dependent. Note that to identify an array element you need to use the array name and the corresponding index.

## Creating an array

In Java there are three distinct operations with arrays:

1. The array declaration

2. The array creation or allocation

3. The array initialization or access

An array of type int is declared as follows:

```
int[] studentGrades;
```

The same array is actually created using the **new** operator

```
finalGrade = new int[14];
```

The declaration and the creation of an array can also be performed in a single statement:

```
int[] finalGrade = new int[14];
```

This statement creates an array named finalGrade, of type int, and allocates space for storing 14 elements. The first element is located at index number 0, and the last one at index number 13.

## Programmers note:

An array that allocates space for 14 elements does not have an element at index 14. The largest index in this case is 13. In programming arrays you must be careful not to attempt to access an element that does not exist.

You can now store information in the array finalGrade, as follows:

```
finalGrade[0] = 78;
finalGrade[1] = 88;
```

and so on. The last element in the array is accessed as follows:

```
finalGrade[13] = 55;
```

Java recognizes a special syntax in arrays in which the new operator is implicit. This allows declaring, creating, and initializing an array in a single statement; for example:

```
int nums[] = {0, 1, 1, 2, 3, 5, 8, 13, 21};
```

The resulting array contains nine elements. The first one is located at nums[0] and the last one at nums[8].

## Incidentally...

In contrast with its predecessor languages, C and C++, Java performs considerable checking on arrays. If you try to access a non-allocated array Java throws a NullPointerException. If you attempt to access an array element out of the array bounds, Java throws an ArrayIndex-OutOfBoundsException. Exceptions are discussed in Chapter 19.

A String array can be created and initialized as follows:

```
String[] studentNames = {"Jim", "Jane", "Harry", "Lucy"};
```

## The array brackets

For a beginning programmer it is confusing that in array declarations the brackets can be attached either to the array type or to the name. For example:

```
int[] Array1 = new int[12];        // Brackets on type
int Array1[] = new int[12];        // Brackets on name
```

You should pick whichever style you like best, and stick to it. It is not a good idea to mix both styles in the same program.

## Programmers note:

Java programmers usually prefer to place the brackets after the type.

## Accessing array elements

Array elements are accessed by means of the array name and the element's index. In a Java program that has created and initialized the following data:

```
int singleVal;
int scores[] = { 10, 12, 8, 13, 19 };
```

the array scores[] is of int type and contains five elements. The elements are located at index values 0 to 4. The value of scores[0] is 10, scores[1] = 12, and so on. You could now store the value located at array index 3 into the variable named singleVal, as follows:

```
singleVal = scores[3];
```

After this statement executes, the variable singleVal and the array element scores[3] both store the value 13. By the same token, you can use the array index to store data into an array. For example, if you want to change the value of the array element scores[4] to 25 you could code as follows:

```
scores[4] = 25;
```

You can also store a variable into an array element, as follows:

```
singleVal = 25;
scores[4] = singleVal;
```

## Programmers note:

Accessing arrays into primitive variables requires that the primitive variable be of the same type as the array. An element of an array of type int can be read into a variable of int type, and an element of an array of type double into a variable of type double. Attempting to access an array element into a variable of different type usually generates an error.

## The size of an array

The size of an array, also called the *array length*, is the number of elements it contains. The size of an array is defined when the array is created. Once an array is created, its length cannot be changed. However, arrays can be created using a variable or an expression to define the number of elements.

Suppose you wrote a program that used an array to store the names of the passengers in an airline flight, and that the airline operated airplanes with different seating capacities. One possible solution would be to allocate the array size for the largest aircraft. But this would waste storage space if the flight was to use a smaller airplane. A more reasonable option is to let the user of the program determine the size of the array at the time it is created. The program would question the user about the size of the aircraft and then allocate the number of elements in the array according to this value. For example:

```
int airPlaneSize;
airPlaneSize = inInt("Enter number of passengers: ");
String[] passenger = new String[airPlaneSize];
```

In this case the number of elements of the array passenger[] is determined by the value of the variable airPlaneSize, which is entered by the user. When the size of an array is determined as the program executes, we say that the array is allocated at runtime.

Programs often need to know the size of an array. For example, if you need to display the names of all the elements in the array passenger[], you would need to know how many elements were allocated when the array was created. Since arrays can be allocated at runtime, you are not able to determine the array size by inspecting the code. The Java length operator returns the number of elements allocated in an array. For example:

```
int passengerCount = passenger.length;
```

In this case the variable passengerCount is assigned the number of elements in the array passenger[]. The following program demonstrates the simultaneous declaration and initialization of arrays and the use of the length operator.

## On the Web

The source file for the program ArrayOps.java can be found in the Chapter 6 folder at www.crcpress.com.

```
//    File name: ArrayOps.java
//    Reference: Chapter 6
//
//    Java program to demonstrate arrays
//    Topics:
//       1. Simultaneous Array declaration and initialization
//       2. Use of the length operator
//
public class Arrays
{
    public static void main(String[] args)
    {
        int[] nums = {1, 1, 2, 3, 5, 8, 13, 21};
        char[] lets = {'t', 'h', 'i', 's', ' ', 'i', 's'};

        System.out.print("The value of nums[3] is " + nums[3]);
        System.out.print("\nThe value of lets[5] is " + lets[5]);

        System.out.flush();
    }
}
```

## Multi-dimensional arrays

A Java array can have more than one dimension. *Two-dimensional arrays* are often used to represent the entries in a table or other data that is organized in rows and columns. In the case of a two-dimensional array one index represents the table rows and another one the columns. A three-dimensional array can be used to represent a grid with breadth, width, and depth.

Suppose that you were to develop a program that keeps track of the pieces on a game of checkers. The standard checkerboard consists of eight columns by eight rows of cells into which the pieces can move. You could use the letter "r" to represent the red pieces and the letter "b" for the black pieces. Then the letter "R" would represent crowned red pieces and the letter "B" crowned black pieces. Figure 6-2 shows a possible position of the checker pieces of a game in progress.

Since the red and black pieces are identified by letters, the program could use a two-dimensional array of type char to represent the checkerboard. The array could be created as follows:

```
char[] checkerboard = new char[8][8];
```

Two-dimensional arrays in Java are in *row-major order*. This means that the first dimension represents the array rows and the second one the array columns. In the case of the checkerboard[] array we can store the piece located at row number 0, column number 2 as follows:

```
checkerboard[0][2] = 'b';
```

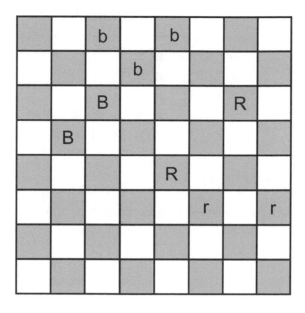

**Figure 6-2** *Black and Red Pieces on a Checkerboard*

Since the array index is zero-based the index value 0 represents the first row, and the index value 2 the third column. The other pieces can be stored in the checkerboard[] array, as follows:

```
checkerBoard[0][4] = 'b';
checkerBoard[1][3] = 'b';
checkerBoard[2][2] = 'B';
checkerBoard[3][1] = 'B';
checkerBoard[2][6] = 'R';
checkerBoard[4][4] = 'R';
checkerBoard[5][5] = 'r';
checkerBoard[5][7] = 'r';
```

A Java program could now use the checkerboard[] array to store the positions of all the pieces as the game progresses.

## Ragged arrays

Multidimensional arrays are actually faked by the Java language. Internally, a multidimensional array is implemented as a set of one-dimensional arrays. For this reason a two-dimensional array can be rectangular or ragged in shape, although rectangular ones are much more common. A ragged array can be pictured as in Figure 6-3.

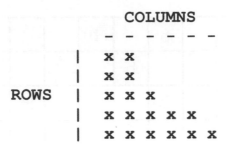

**Figure 6-3** *A Ragged Array*

To create a ragged array of 5 rows, with 2, 3, 4, 5, and 6 elements in each row you first allocate the five rows, as follows:

```
byte[][] raggedArray = new byte[5][];
```

Then, you allocate the elements in each row, as follows:

```
raggedArray[0] = new byte[2];
raggedArray[1] = new byte[3];
raggedArray[2] = new byte[4];
raggedArray[3] = new byte[5];
raggedArray[4] = new byte[6];
```

## Programmers note:

In Java, creating and manipulating ragged arrays is somewhat counter-intuitive. You have to be particularly careful in keeping track of the length of each element since attempting to access an array element that does not exist generates an error.

You have used the length operator to obtain the size of a one-dimensional array, but obtaining the size of a multidimensional array poses some new problems. The problem relates to the fact that, in Java, a multidimensional array can be a ragged array. For this reason, the size of a multidimensional array can be defined for the number of rows, but it is impossible to know the number of elements in each row.

To make things easier, the Java language assumes that if a multidimensional array is declared using constants, then it is rectangular. In this case it is possible to obtain the number allocated by means of the length operator, as follows:

```
// Declare array constants
int ROWS = 10;
int COLS = 5;
// Allocate rectangular array
byte[][] screenPix = new byte[ROWS][COLS];
// Obtain and store array dimensions
rowCount = screenPix.length;        // Number of rows
colCount = screenPix[COLS].length;  // Number of columns
totalSize = rowCount * colCount;    // Calculate total elements
```

The following expressions generate errors:

```
screenPix[ROWS].length
screenPix[ROWS][COLS].length
```

To obtain the size of a ragged array, you have to add the number of elements in each ragged row.

## Initializing multi-dimensional arrays

Like one-dimensional array, multidimensional arrays can be initialized when they are declared. For example:

```
byte[][] smallArray = {
                      {10, 11, 12, 13},
                      {20, 21, 22, 23},
                      {30, 31, 32, 33},
                      {40, 41, 42, 43}
                      };
```

Note that each array row is initialized separately; also that there must be a comma at the end of each row, except for the last one. A ragged array can also be initialized as it is declared, as follows:

```
byte[][] raggedSmall = {
                       {10, 11, 12, 13},
                       {20, 21, 22},
                       {30, 31},
                       {40}
                       };
```

The sample program named MultiArrays.java, listed here and in the book's CD ROM, demonstrates the creation and manipulation of multidimensional arrays.

---

## On the Web

---

The source file for the program MultiArray.java can be found in the Chapter 6 folder at www.crcpress.com.

```java
//    File name: MultiArray.java
//    Reference: Chapter 6
//
//    Java program to demonstrate multidimensional arrays
//    Topics:
//        1. Simultaneous declaration and initialization
//        2. Use of the length operator to obtain the size
//           of multidimensional arrays

public class MultiArray
{
    // Declare constants
    final static int ROWS = 10;
    final static int COLS = 5;

    public static void main(String[] args)
    {

    // Local variables
    int rowCount;
    int colCount;
    int totalSize;

    // Declare and allocate an array of bytes
    byte[][] screenPix = new byte[ROWS][COLS];

    // Obtain and store array dimensions
    rowCount = screenPix.length;
    colCount = screenPix[COLS].length;
    totalSize = rowCount * colCount;

    // To obtain the total number of elements of a
    // two-dimensional ragged array you need to get the size of
    // each array dimension separately

    // Display array dimensions
    System.out.println("Array row size:     " + rowCount);
    System.out.println("Array column size:  " + colCount);
    System.out.println("Total size:         " + totalSize);

    //*************************
    //        ragged arrays
    //*************************
    // First allocate the rows of an array
    byte[][] raggedArray = new byte[5][];

    // Now allocate the columns
    raggedArray[0] = new byte[2];
    raggedArray[1] = new byte[2];
    raggedArray[2] = new byte[4];
    raggedArray[3] = new byte[8];
    raggedArray[4] = new byte[3];

    // The resulting ragged array is as follows:
```

```
//   x   x
//   x   x
//   x   x   x   x
//   x   x   x   x   x   x   x   x
//   x   x   x

//***********************************
//     static array initialization
//***********************************
byte[][] smallArray = {
                        {10, 11, 12, 13},
                        {20, 21, 22, 23},
                        {30, 31, 32, 33},
                        {40, 41, 42, 43},
                      };

// Display the array element at row 2, column 3
System.out.println(smallArray[1][2]);  // Value is 21
}
}
```

# Chapter 7

# Java Operators

## The Action Element

An *expression* in a programming language consists of operators and operands. *Operators* are special symbols that indicate specific processing action. For example, to add two values in an expression, we use the familiar + sign, which is the addition operator in Java. Other operators are not as common as the + and - symbols. Such is the case with the && symbol which is one of the language's logical operators. In this chapter we start looking at the Java operators.

## Operators

Operators are the symbols and special characters used in a programming language to change the value of one or more program elements. The program elements that are changed by an operator are called the *operand*. We use the + symbol to perform the sum of two operands, as in the following example:

```
int val1 = 7;
int val2 = 3;
int val3 = val1 + val2;
```

---
### Programmers note:
---

The + symbol is also used in appending strings. When used in this manner it is called the *concatenation operator*. String concatenation is discussed later in this chapter.

---

In this case, the value of integer variable val3 (10) is found by adding the values of variables val1 and val2. The fundamental Java operators can be functionally classified as follows:

- simple assignment

- arithmetic

- concatenation

- increment and decrement

- logical

- bitwise

- compound assignment

In this chapter we discuss the assignment, arithmetic, concatenation, increment and decrement operators. The logical and bitwise operators are the topic of Chapter 8.

Java operators are classified according to the number of operands as follows:

- unary

- binary

- ternary

The one Java ternary operator (?:) is discussed in Chapter 9, in the context of decision constructs.

## Operator action

Java operators are used in expressions that produce program actions. For example, if $a$, $b$, and $c$ are variables, the expression

```
c = a + b;
```

uses the = and the + operators to assign to the variable c the value that results from adding the variables $a$ and **b**. The operators in this expression are the = (assignment) and + (addition) symbols.

Java operators must be used as elements of expressions; they are meaningless when used by themselves. In this sense the term

```
-a;
```

is a trivial expression that does not change the value of the variable. On the other hand, the expression

```
b = -b;
```

assigns a negative value to the variable *b*.

# The Assignment Operator

As you learn a programming language it is important to keep in mind that the language expressions are not usually valid mathematically. Consider the expression

```
a = a + 2;
```

Mathematically, it is absurd to state the value of the variable a is the same as the value that result from adding 2 to it. The reason for this apparent absurdity is that Java's = operator does not represent an equality. The = sign is used as a simple assignment operator. The result of the statement

```
b = b - 4;
```

is that the variable *b* is "assigned" the value that results from subtracting 4 from its own value. In other words, b "becomes" b - 4. It is important to note that this use of the = sign in Java is limited to assigning a value to a storage location referenced by a program element. For this reason a Java expression containing the = sign cannot be interpreted algebraically.

There are other differences between a Java expression and an algebraic equation. In elementary algebra we learn to solve an equation by isolating a variable on the left-hand side of the = sign, as follows:

```
2x = y
x = y/2
```

However, the Java statement line

```
2 * x = y;
```

generates an error. This is due to the fact that programming languages, Java included, are not designed to perform even the simplest algebraic manipulations.

## Incidentally...

Expressions in Java are usually not algebraically valid.

## The two sides of an assignment

If we look at a Java expression that uses the assignment operator, we note one part to the left of the = sign and another one to the right. In any programming language the part to the left of the = sign is called the *lvalues* (short for left value) and the one to the right is called the *rvalues* (short for right value). Therefore, an lvalue is an expression that can be used to the left of the = sign. In a Java assignment statement the lvalue must represent a single storage location. In other words, the element to the left of the = sign must be a variable. In this manner, if $x$ and $y$ are variables, the expression

```
x = 2 * y;
```

is a valid one. However, the expression

```
y + 2 = x;
```

is not valid since in this case the lvalue is not a single storage location but an expression in itself. By the same token, an expression without an rvalue is illegal in Java, for example:

```
y = ;
```

An assignment expression without an lvalue is also illegal, such as

```
= x;
```

## Arithmetic Operators

Java arithmetic operators are used to perform simple calculations. Some of the Java arithmetic operators coincide with the familiar mathematical symbols. Such is the case with the + and - operators which indicate addition and subtraction. But not all conventional mathematical symbols are available in a computer keyboard. Others are ambiguous or incompatible with the rules of the Java language. For example, the conventional symbol for division (÷) is not a standard keyboard character. Using the letter $x$ as a symbol for multiplication is impossible, since the language is unable to differentiate between the mathematical operator and the alphanumeric character. For these reasons Java uses the / symbol to indicate division and the * to indicate multiplication. Table 7-1 lists the Java arithmetic operators.

### Table 7-1
*Java Arithmetic Operators*

| OPERATOR | ACTION |
|:--------:|--------|
| + | addition |
| − | subtraction |
| * | multiplication |
| / | division |
| % | remainder |

## The remainder operator

One of the operators in Table 7-1 requires additional comment. The % operator gives the remainder of a division. The % symbol is also called the *modulus operator*. Its action is limited to integer operands. The following code fragment shows its use:

```
int val1 = 14;
int result = val1 % 3;
```

In this case, the value of the variable result is 2 since this is the remainder of dividing 14 by 3.

---

## Programmers note:

---

We prefer to call the % symbol the remainder operator since the word "modulus" is sometimes used in mathematics for the absolute value. In this sense the mathematical expression |-4| is said to be the modulus of -4, which is 4.

---

The remainder of a division finds many uses in mathematics and in programming. Operations based on the remainder are sometimes called "clock arithmetic." This is due to the fact that the conventional clock face is divided into 12 hours which repeat in cycles. We can say that the modulo of a clock is 12. The hour-of-day from the present time, after any number of hours, can be easily calculated by the remainder of dividing the number of hours by 12 and adding this value to the present time.

Suppose it is 4 o'clock and you want to calculate the hour-of-day after 27 hours have elapsed. The remainder of 27/12 is 3. The hour-of-day is then 4 + 3, which is 7 o'clock. In Java you can obtain the remainder with a single operator. The following code fragment shows the calculations in this example:

```
int thisHour = 4;
int hoursPassed = 27;
int hourOfDay = thisHour + (hoursPassed % 12);
```

Note that the expression

```
hoursPassed % 12
```

gives the remainder of 27/12, which is then added to the current hour to obtain the new hour-of-day.

---
**Incidentally...**
---

Modular arithmetic finds many computer uses. One of them is in calculating functions that have repeating values, called periodic functions. For example, the math unit of the Pentium microprocessor produces trigonometric functions in the range 0 to 45 degrees. Software must then use remainder calculations to scale the functions to any desired angle.

---

# Concatenation

In Java, the + operator, which is used for arithmetic addition, is also used to concatenate strings. The term "concatenation" comes from the Latin word "catena," which means chain. To concatenate strings is to chain them together. The following code fragment shows the action of this operator:

```
// Define strings
String str1 = "con";
String str2 = "ca";
String str3 = "ten";
String str4 = "ate";
// Form a new word using string concatenation
String result = str1 + str2 + str3 + str4;
// result = "concatenate"
```

The operation of the concatenation operator can be viewed as a form of string "addition." In Java, if a numeric value is added to a string the number is first converted into a string of digits and then concatenated to the string operand, as shown in the following code fragment:

```
String str1 = "Catch ";   // Define a string
int value = 22;           // Define an int
result = str5 + value;    // Concatenate string + int
                          // result = "Catch 22"
```

Note that concatenation requires that one of the operands be a string. If both operands are numeric values then arithmetic addition takes place.

# Increment and Decrement

Programs often have to keep count of the number of times an operation, or a series or operations, has taken place. In order to keep the tally count it is convenient to have a simple form of adding 1 to the value of a variable or subtracting 1 from the value of a variable. Java contains simple operators that allow this manipulation. These operators, which originated in the C language, are called the *increment* (++) and *decrement* (- -) operators. For example, the following expressions add or subtract 1 to the value of the operand.

```
x = x + 1;      // add 1 to the value of x
y = y - 1;      // subtract 1 from the value of y
```

The increment and decrement operators can be used to achieve the same result in a more compact way, as follows:

```
x++;            // add 1 to the value of x
y--;            // subtract 1 from the value of y
```

---

## Incidentally...

The name of the C++ programming language originated in the notion of a version of the C language that was extended and improved. In other words, C incremented, or C++.

---

The ++ and – – symbols can be placed before or after an expression. When the symbols are before the operand the operator is said to be in prefix form. When it follows the operand it is said to be in *postfix form*. For example:

```
z = ++x;   // Prefix form
z = x++;   // Postfix form
```

The prefix and postfix forms result in the same value in unary statements. For example, the variable $x$ is incremented by 1 in both of these statements:

```
x++;
++x;
```

However, when the increment or decrement operators are used in an assignment statement, the results are different if the operators are in prefix or in postfix form. In the first case (prefix form), the increment or decrement is first applied to the operand and the result assigned to the lvalue of the expression. In the postfix form, the operand is first assigned to the lvalue and then the increment or decrement is applied. The following code fragment shows both cases.

```
int x = 7;
int y;
y = ++x;            // y = 8, x = 8
y = x++;            // y = 7, x = 8
```

# Relational Operators

Computers can make simple decisions. For example, a computer program can take one path of action if two variables, *a* and **b**, are equal, another path if *a* is greater than *b*, and yet another one if *b* is greater than *a*. The Java relational operators evaluate if a simple relationship between operands is true or false. Table 7-2 lists the Java relational operators.

### Table 7-2
*Java Relational Operators*

| OPERATOR | ACTION |
|---|---|
| < | less than |
| > | greater than |
| <= | less than or equal to |
| >= | greater than or equal to |
| == | equal to |
| != | not equal to |

The == operator deserves special notice. This operator is used to determine if one operand is equal to the other one. It is unrelated to the assignment operator (=) which has already been discussed. In the following examples we set the value of a boolean variable according to a comparison between two numeric variables, $x$ and $y$.

```
boolean result;
int x = 4;
int y = 3;
result = x > y;      // Case 1 - result is true
result = x < y;      // Case 2 - result is false
result = x == 0;     // Case 3 - result is false
result = x != 0;     // Case 4 - result is true
result = x <= 4;     // Case 5 - result is true
```

Notice in case 3 the different action of the assignment and the relational operator. The assignment operator (=) is used in this expression to assign to the variable result the boolean true or false that results from comparing x to 0. The comparison is performed by means of the == operator. The result is false because the value of the variable x is 4. One common programming mistake is to use the assignment operator in place of the relational operator, or vice versa. This error is particularly dangerous because the resulting expression is often a legal one.

# Chapter 8

# Other Java Operators

## Logical Operations

The relational operators, described in the Chapter 7, are used to evaluate whether a condition relating two operands is true or false. However, by themselves, they serve only to test simple relationships. In programming, you often need to determine complex conditional expressions. For example, to determine if a user is a teenager you test whether the person is older than twelve years and younger than twenty years.

The *logical operators* allow combining two or more conditional statements into a single expression. As is the case with relational expressions, expressions that contain logical operators return true or false. Table 8-1 lists the Java logical operators.

**Table 8-1**

*Java Logical Operators*

| OPERATOR | ACTION |
|---|---|
| && | logical AND |
| \|\| | logical OR |
| ! | logical NOT |

For example, if $a = 6$, $b = 2$, and $c = 0$, the boolean variable result evaluates to either true or false, as follows:

```
boolean result;
int a = 6;
int b = 2;
int c = 0;
result = a > b && c == 0;    // Case 1 - result is true
result = a > b && c != 0;    // Case 2 - result is false
result = a == 0 || c == 0;   // Case 3 - result is true
```

71

```
result = a < b || c != 0;    // Case 4 - result is false
```

In case 1, the result evaluates to true because both relational elements in the statement are true. While case 4 evaluates to false because the OR connector requires that at least one of the relational elements be true and, in this case, both are false ($a > b$ and $c = 0$).

The logical NOT operator is used to invert the value of a boolean variable or to test for the opposite. For example:

```
boolean result;
boolean tf  = false;
result = (tf == !true);  // result is true
```

The preceding statement evaluates to true since !true is false and tf is false. The principal use of conditional expressions is in making program decisions, the topic of Chapter 9.

## Manipulating bits

You already know that computers store data in individual electronic cells that are in one of two states, sometimes callled ON and OFF. Also, that these two states are represented by the binary digits 1 and 0. In practical programming you often disregard this fact, and write code that deals with numbers, characters, boolean values, and strings. Storing a number in a variable of type double, or a name in a String object, does not usually require dealing with individual bits. However, there are times when the code needs to know the state of one or more data bits, or needs to change individual bits or groups of bits.

One of the reasons for manipulating individual bits or bit fields is simple economics. Suppose that you were writing an operating system program and needed to keep track of the input and output devices present in the machine. For example, your code may need to determine and store the following information:

- The number of printers (range 0 to 3).
- If there is a mouse installed (yes or no).
- The number of serial ports (range 0 to 7).
- If the Pentium CPU is equipped with MMX technology (yes or no).

One way to store this information would be in conventional variables. You could declare the following variable types:

```
int printers;
boolean mousePresent;
int serialPorts;
boolean hasMMX;
```

One objection to storing each value in an individual variable is the wasted space. When we devote an int variable for storing the number of printers connected to the system, we are wasting considerable storage space. An int variable consists of four memory bytes (refer to Table 4-1). This means that you can store over 2 million combinations in an int type. However, in this particular example the maximum number of printers is 3. You could use a variable of type byte or short but there would still be considerable waste. The same applies to all other data types previously listed.

A more economical option, memory wise, would be to devote to each item the minimum amount of storage necessary for encoding all possible states. In the case of the number of printers you could do this with just two bits. Two bits allow representing values from 0 to 3, which is sufficient for this data element. By the same token, a single bit would serve to record if a mouse is present or not. The convention in this case is that a binary 1 represents YES and a binary 0 represents NO. The number of serial ports (range 0 to 5) could be encoded in a three-bit field, while another single bit would record the presence or absence of MMX technology in the Pentium CPU. The total storage would be as follows:

- printers, 2 bits

- mouse present, 1 bit

- serial ports, 3 bits

- MMX present, 1 bit

## Incidentally...

The Multimedia Extension (MMX) is a modification of the architecture of the Pentium CPU used in the PC. The MMX provides an extended set of instructions that facilitate programming and enhance the performance of graphics, multimedia, and other high-performance applications.

The total storage required is seven bits. Figure 8-1 (on the next page) shows how the individual bits of a byte variable can be assigned to store this information.

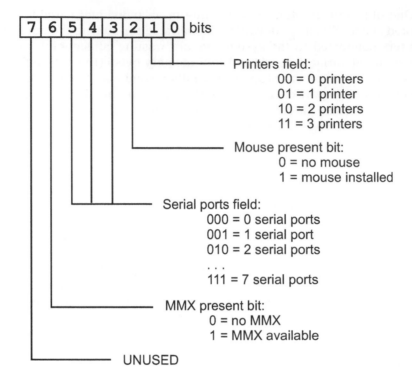

**Figure 8-1** *Bitmapped Data*

The operation of assigning individual bits and bit fields is called bitmapping. Another advantage of bitmapped data is that several items of information can be encoded in a single storage element. Since bitmapped data is more compact, it is easier to pass and retrieve information. For example, you could devote a byte variable to store the bitmapped data in Figure 8-1. The variable could be defined as follows:

```
byte systemDevices;
```

In order to manipulate bitmapped data you must be able to access individual bits and bit fields. This is the function of the Java bitwise operators.

In Table 8-2, the operators &, |, ^, and ~ perform bitwise functions on individual bits. The convention that a binary 1 corresponds to logical true, and a binary 0 to false, allows using binary numbers to show the results of a logical or bitwise operation. For example:

**Table 8-2**

*Java Bitwise Operators*

| OPERATOR | ACTION |
|----------|--------|
| & | bitwise AND |
| \| | bitwise OR |
| ^ | bitwise XOR |
| ~ | bitwise NOT |
| < | bitwise left-shift |
| > | bitwise right-shift |
| >> | bitwise unsigned right-shift |

```
1 AND 0 = 0
1 AND 1 = 1
1 OR 0 = 1
NOT 1 = 0
```

A table that lists all possible results of a bitwise or logical operation is called a *truth table*. Table 8-3 has the truth tables for AND, OR, XOR, and NOT. The tables are valid for both logical and the bitwise operations.

**Table 8-3**

*Logical Truth Tables*

| AND | | | OR | | | XOR | | | NOT | |
|-----|---|---|----|---|---|-----|---|---|-----|---|
| 0 | 0 | 0 | 0 | 0 | 0 | 0 | 0 | 0 | 0 | 1 |
| 0 | 1 | 0 | 0 | 1 | 1 | 0 | 1 | 1 | 1 | 0 |
| 1 | 0 | 0 | 1 | 0 | 1 | 1 | 0 | 1 | | |
| 1 | 1 | 1 | 1 | 1 | 1 | 1 | 1 | 0 | | |

When using logical and bitwise operators you must keep in mind that although they perform similar functions, the logical operators do not change the actual contents of the variables. The bitwise operators, on the other hand, manipulate bit data. Thus, the result of a bitwise operation is a variable with a value different from the previous one.

**Programmers note:**

It is customary to number the bits in an operand from right-to-left with the rightmost bit designated as bit number 0. Refer to Figure 3-2.

## The & operator

The & operator performs a boolean AND of the two operands. The rule for the AND operation is that a bit in the result is set only if the corresponding bits are set in both operands. This action is shown in Table 8-3.

The & operator is frequently used to clear one or more bits, or to preserve one or more bits in the operand. This action is consistent with the fact that ANDing with a zero-bit clears the result bit, and ANDing with a one-bit preserves the original value of the corresponding bit in the other operand. A specific bit pattern used to manipulate bits or bit fields is sometimes called a mask. An AND mask can be described as a filter that passes the operand bits that correspond to a 1-bit in the mask, and clears the operand bits that correspond to 0-bits. Figure 8-2 shows action of ANDing with a mask.

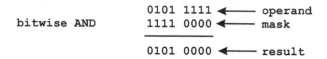

**Figure 8-2** *Action of the AND Mask*

The program named Bit7And listed below and contained in the book's CD ROM, allows the user to input a byte. The input value is then ANDed with a mask in which the high-order bit is set. The required mask corresponds to the decimal value 128, with the following bit pattern:

```
1 0 0 0 0 0 0 0
```

When ANDing the user's input with the mask 128 we can predict that the seven low-order bits of the result are zero. Recall that ANDing with a zero bit always produces zero. Also, that the value of the high-order bit of the result will be the same as the corresponding bit in the user's input.

In Figure 8-3, the high-order bit of the result can be either the value 0 or 1. Since the seven low-order bits are always zero, you can conclude that the result will be non-zero if bit 7 of the operand was 1. If the result is zero, then bit 7 of the operand was zero.

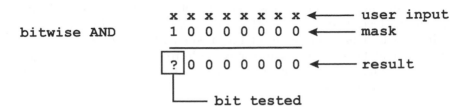

**Figure 8-3** *AND Testing a Single Bit*

## On the Web

The source file for the program Bit7And.java is found in the Chapter 8 folder at www.crcpress.com.

```
//    File name: Bit7And.java
//    Reference: Chapter 8
//
//    Java program to demonstrate the action of the bitwise
//    AND operator
//    Topics:
//       1. Using the bitwise AND to determine the state
//          of an operand bit
//    Requires:
//       1. Keyin class in the current directory

public class Bit7And
{
  public static void main(String[] args)
    {
       // Local variables
       int mask = 128;
       int userInput;
       int result = 0;

       // Processing
       userInput = Keyin.inInt("Enter value: ");
       result = userInput & mask;

       // If bit 7 was set in the user input, then
       // result = 128. Otherwise, result = 0
       System.out.println("result = " + result);
    }
}
```

## The | operator

The | operator performs the Boolean inclusive OR of two operands. The outcome is that a bit in the result is set if at least one of the corresponding bits in the operands is also set, as shown by the truth table in Table 8-3. A frequent use for the I operator is to selectively set bits in an operand. The action can be described by saying that ORing with a 1-bit always sets the result bit, whereas ORing with a 0-bit preserves the value of the corresponding bit in the other operand. For example, to make sure that bits 5 and 6 of an operand are set we can OR it with a mask in which these bits are 1. This is shown in Figure 8-4.

```
                          0101 0101 ◄─────── operand
       bitwise OR         1111 0000 ◄─────── mask
                          ─────────
                          1111 0101 ◄─────── result
```

**Figure 8-4** *Action of the OR mask*

Because bits 4, 5, 6, and 7 in the mask are set, the OR operation guarantees that these bits will be set in the result independently of whatever value they have in the first operand.

## The ^ operator

The ^ operator performs the Boolean exclusive OR (XOR) of the two operands. This action is described by stating that a bit in the result is set if the corresponding bits in the operands have opposite values. If the bits have the same value (1 or 0) the result bit is zero. The action of the XOR operation corresponds to the truth table of Table 8-3.

```
                          0101 0101 ◄─────── operand
       bitwise XOR        1111 0000 ◄─────── mask
                          ─────────
                          1010 0101 ◄─────── result
```

**Figure 8-5** *Action of the XOR mask*

It is interesting to note that XORing a value with itself always generates a zero result, since all bits will necessarily have the same value. On the other hand, XORing with a 1-bit inverts the value of the other operand, because 0 XOR 1 = 1 and 1 XOR 1 = 0 (see Table 8-3). By properly selecting an XOR mask the programmer can control which bits of the operand are inverted and which are preserved. To invert the two high-order bits of an operand you XOR with a mask in which these bits are set. If the remaining bits are clear in the mask, then the original value of these bits will be preserved in the result, as is shown in Figure 8-5.

## The ~ operator

The ~ operator inverts all bits of a single operand. In other words, it converts all 1-bits to 0 and all 0-bits to 1. This action corresponds to the boolean NOT function, as shown in Table 8-3. Figure 8-5 shows the result of a NOT operation.

```
bitwise NOT          0101 0011 ◀─────── operand

                     1010 1100 ◀─────── result
```

**Figure 8-6** *Action of the NOT Operator*

## The <, >, and >> operators

The Java shift left (<) and shift right (> and >>) operators are used to move operand bits to the right or to the left. All three operators require a value that specifies the number of bits to be shifted. The following expression shifts left, by 2 bit positions, all the bits in the variable bitPattern:

```
int bitPattern = 127;
bitPattern = bitPattern < 2;
```

The action of a left shift by a 1-bit position can be seen in Figure 8-7.

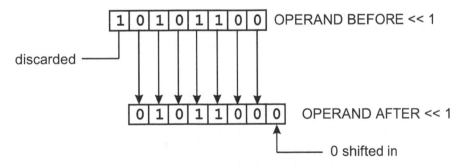

**Figure 8-7** *Action of the < Operator*

The operation of the left-shift, as shown in Figure 8-7, determines that the most significant bit is discarded. This could spell trouble when the operand is a signed number, since in signed representations the high-order bit encodes the sign of the number. Therefore, discarding the high-order bit can change the sign of the value. This would be true for all Java integer data types, except char, which is unsigned. In the example in Figure 8-7, the original number, which is negative (high-bit set), is changed into a positive value. You must take this into account when left-shifting signed quantities.

There are two right-shift operators in Java, > and >>. The simple right-shift operator (>) shifts the left operand by the number of bits contained in the right operand, for example:

```
int bitPattern = 127;
bitPattern = bitPattern > 1;
```

In the right shift, the low-order bit is discarded and the high-order bit is duplicated into all the bits that were abandoned by the shift. The result is extending the sign bit into the new operand. The action of a right shift by 1 bit position is shown in Figure 8-8.

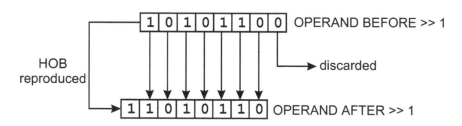

**Figure 8-8** *Action of the > Operator*

The unsigned right shift operator (>>) is similar to the right shift (>), except that in the >> the vacated positions on the left of the operand are filled with zeros. Figure 8-9 shows an unsigned right shift by 1 bit position.

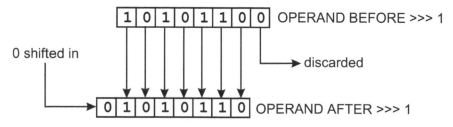

**Figure 8-9** *Action of the >> Operator*

## The compound assignment operators

Java contains several compound operators that were designed to make code more compact. The compound assignment operators consist of a combination of the simple assignment operator (=) with an arithmetic or bitwise operator. For example, to add 5 to the variable *y* we can code

```
y = y + 5;
```

Alternatively, we can combine the addition operator (+) with the simple assignment operator (=) as follows

```
y += 5;
```

In either case the final value of *y* is its initial value plus 5, but the latter form reduces the size of the program. Table 8-4 lists the compound assignment operators.

**Table 8-4**

*Java Compound Assignment Operators*

| OPERATOR | ACTION |
|----------|--------|
| += | addition assignment |
| -= | subtraction assignment |
| *= | multiplication assignment |
| /= | division assignment |
| %= | remainder assignment |
| &= | bitwise AND assignment |
| \|= | bitwise OR assignment |
| ^= | bitwise XOR assignment |
| <= | left shift assignment |
| >= | right shift assignment |
| >>= | compound right shift assignment |

**Programmers note:**

In compound assignments, the = sign always comes last.

Note that the compound assignment is not available for the NOT (~) bitwise unary operator or for the unary increment (++) or decrement (—) operators. The explanation is that unary (one element) statements do not require simple assignment; therefore, the compound assignment form is meaningless.

## Operator hierarchy

Programming languages have hierarchy rules that determine the order in which each element in an expression is evaluated. For example, the expression

```
int value = 8 + 4 / 2;
```

evaluates to 6 because the Java addition operator has higher precedence than the multiplication operator. In this case, the compiler first calculates 8 + 4 = 12 and then performs 12 / 2 = 6. If the division operation were performed first, then the variable value evaluates to 10. Table 8-5 lists the precedence of the Java operators.

**Table 8-5**

*Precedence of Java Operators*

| OPERATOR | PRECEDENCE LEVELS |
|---|---|
| . [] () | highest |
| + – ~ ! ++ — | |
| * / % | |
| < >  >> | |
| <  <=  > >  = > | |
| ==  != | |
| & | |
| ^ | |
| \| | |
| && | |
| \|\| | |
| ?: | |
| = | lowest |

## Associativity rules

In some cases an expression can contain several operators with the same precedence level. When operators have the same precedence, the order of evaluation is determined by the associativity rules of the language. Associativity can be left-to-right or right-to-left. In most programming languages, including Java, the basic rule of associativity for arithmetic operators is left-to-right. This is consistent with the way we read in English and the Western European languages.

In Java, the left-to-right associativity rule applies to all binary operators. However, unary operators, as well as the assignment operator (=), follow right-to-left associativity. Because of this variation in the associativity rules, you must exercise care in evaluating some expressions. Consider the following case:

```
int a = 0;
int b = 4;
a = b = 7;
```

If the expression $a = b = 7$ is evaluated left-to-right, then the resulting value of variable $a$ is 4, and the value of $b$ is 7. However, if it is evaluated right-to-left then the value of both variables is 7. Since the assignment operator has right-to-left associativity, the value of $b$ is 7 and the value of $a$ is also 7, in this case.

# *Chapter 9*

# Directing Program Flow

## Simple Decisions

The main difference between a computer and a calculating machine is that the computer can make simple decisions. Programs are able to process information logically because of this decision-making ability. The result of a program decision is to direct program execution in one direction or another one, that is, to change program flow. One of the most important tasks performed by the programmer is the implementation of the program's processing logic. This implementation is by means of the language's decision constructs. In this chapter you will learn how a Java program makes decisions.

## Java Decisions Constructs

To make a program decision requires several language elements. Suppose an application that must determine if the variable $a$ is larger than $b$. If this is the case, the program must take one course of action. If both variables are equal, or if $b$ is larger than $a$, then another course of action is necessary. As you can see, the program has to make a comparison, examine the results, and take the corresponding action in each case. All of this cannot be accomplished with a single operator or keyword, but requires one or more expressions contained in one or more statements. For this reason we talk about decision statements and decision constructs. In programming, a *construct* can be described as one or more expressions, contained in one or more statements, all of which perform a specific action.

Java contains several high-level decision operators and keywords that can be used in constructs which make possible selection between several processing options. The major decision-making mechanisms are called the if and the switch constructs. The conditional operator (?:), which is the only Java operator that contains three operands, is also used in decision-making constructs.

## The if construct

The Java if construct consists of three elements:

1. The if keyword

2. A test expression, called a conditional clause

3. One or more statements that execute if the test expression is true

The following program, named BeepIf, displays the message "BEEP-BEEP" if the user enters the number 1 or 2. Otherwise no message is displayed. The code uses an if construct to test if the typed keystroke matches the required numbers.

```
//    File name: BeepIf.java
//    Reference: Chapter 9
//
//    Java program to demonstrate simple decision
//    Topics:
//        1. Using the if construct
//
//    Requires:
//        1. Keyin class in the current directory

public class BeepIf
{

   public static void main(String[] args)
      {
         int userInput;

         userInput = Keyin.inInt("Enter 1 or 2 to beep: ");
         if(userInput == 1 || userInput == 2)
            System.out.println("BEEP-BEEP");
      }
}
```

The BeepIf program uses a simple form of the Java if construct. The compiler evaluates the expression in parentheses, following the if keyword, which in this case is

```
      if(userInput == 1 || userInput == 2)
```

The expression uses the logical OR operator (discussed in Chapter 8) to create a compound condition. The parenthetical expression evaluates to true if the variable userInput is equal to 1 or 2. If the expression evaluates to true, then the statement that follows is executed. If the expression evaluates to false, then the statement associated with the if clause is skipped.

## Statement blocks

The simple form of the if construct consists of a single statement that executes if the conditional expression is true. The BeepIf program, listed previously, uses a simple if construct. But your code will often need to perform more than one operation acording to the result of a decision. Java provides a simple way of grouping several statements so that they are treated as a unit. The grouping is performed by means of curly brace ({}) or roster symbols. The statements enclosed within the two rosters form a compound statement, also called a *statement block*.

You can use statement blocking to modify the BeepIf program so that more than one statement executes when the test condition evaluates to true. For example:

```
if(userInput == 1 || userInput == 2)
{
    System.out.println("BEEP-BEEP");
    System.out.println("The value entered is " + userInput);
}
```

The brace symbols ({ and }) are used to associate more than one statement with the related if. In this example, both println() statements execute if the conditional clause evaluates to true and both are skipped if it evaluates to false.

## The nested if

Several if statements can be nested in a single construct. The result is that the execution of a statement or statement group is conditioned, not to a single condition, but to two or more conditions. For example, we can modify the if construct in the BeepIf program so that the code provides additional processing for the case where the user input is the value 2, as follows:

```
if(userInput == 1 || userInput == 2)
    {
    System.out.println("BEEP-BEEP");
        if(userInput == 2)
        System.out.println("input was 2");
    }
```

In the above code fragment, the if statement that tests for a value of 2 in the user input is nested inside the if statement that tests for a user input of either 1 or 2. The inner if statement is never reached if the outer one evaluates to false. If the user enters the value 3, the first test evaluates to false and the second one never takes place. We have used indentation to indicate that the second if statement is subordinate to the first one. Although white space has no effect on the code, text line indentation does help visualize logical flow. Figure 9-1 is a flowchart of a nested if construct.

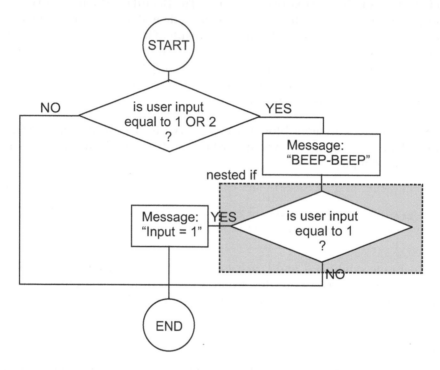

**Figure 9-1** *Flowchart of a Nested if Construct*

## The else construct

An if construct executes a statement, or a statement block, if the conditional clause evaluates to true, but no alternative action is taken if the expression is false. The if-else construct allows Java code to provide an alternative processing option for the case where the conditional clause is false.

---
**Programmers note:**
---

The else construct is sometimes called the if-else construct.

---

You can use the Java else construct to modify the BeepIf program so that a different message is displayed if the user inputs the numbers 1 or 2, or if the user enters a different value. The following code fragment shows the processing in this case:

```
if(userInput == 1 || userInput == 2)
     System.out.println("BEEP-BEEP");
else
     System.out.println("Input not 1 or 2");
```

It is customary to align the if and the else keywords in if-else constructs. This is another example of the use of white space to clarify program flow. As in the case of the if clause, the else clause can also contain a statement block delimited by rosters. A statement block is necessary if more than one statement is to execute on the else branch. Figure 9-2 is a flowchart of the preceding if-else construct.

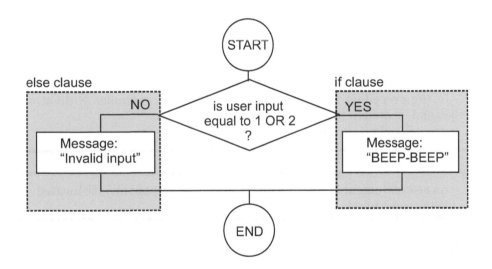

**Figure 9-2** *Flowchart of an If-Else Construct*

## The dangling else

The else statement is optional. Therefore, it is possible to have several nested if constructs, not all of which with a corresponding else clause. This case is sometimes called the "dangling else" problem. A dangling else statement can give rise to uncertainty about the pairing of the if and else clauses. In the following fragment there are two if statements and a single else clause.

```
if(a != 0 )
   if(a > 1)
     System.out.println("x is positive and non-zero");
   else
     System.out.println("x is zero or negative");
```

In the preceding code fragment, the path of execution is different if the else clause is paired with the inner if statement, or with the outer one. The general rule used by Java in solving the dangling else problem is that each else statement is paired with the closest if statement that does not have an else, and that is located in the same block. Indentation in the preceding code fragment helps you see that the else statement is linked to the inner if.

You can use rosters to force a different association between if and else statements, for example

```
if(a != 0 )
   {
     if(a > 1)
         System.out.println("x is positive and non-zero");
   }
else
   System.out.println("x must be zero");
```

In the preceding code fragment the closest if statement without an else, and located in the same block, is the statement

```
if(a != 0)
```

---

## Programmers note:

---

An else statement is paired with the closest if without an else located in the same block.

---

## Else-if clause

You have seen how the dangling else problem can cause unpredicted associations of an else clause with an if statement. The relationship between two consecutive if statements can also cause problems. The flowchart in Figure 9-1 shows the case of a cascaded if construct, in which a second if statement is conditioned to the first one being true. However, if the second if statement is not nested in the first one, then its evaluation is independent of the result of the first if. The following code shows this case.

```
if(userInput == 1 || userInput == 2)
     System.out.println("BEEP-BEEP");
if(userInput == 2)
     System.out.println("Input = 2");
```

In the preceding code fragment the second if statement is unrelated to the first one; therefore, the second statement is always evaluated.

The else-if construct allows subordinating the second if statement in case the first one evaluates to false. All you have to do is nest the second if within the else clause of the first one, for example:

```
int age;

   ...

if(age == 12)
   System.out.println("You are 12");
      else if(age == 13)
         System.out.println("You are 13");
            else if(age == 14)
               System.out.println("You are 14");
else
      System.out.println("You not 12, 13, or 14");
```

In the preceding code fragment, the last if println() statement executes only if all the preceding if statements have evaluated to false. If one of the if statements evaluates to true, then the rest of the construct is skipped. In some cases, several logical variations of the consecutive if statements may produce the desired results, while in other cases it may not. Flowcharting is an effective way of resolving doubts about program logic.

The else-if is a mere convenience. The same action results if the else and the if clause are separated. For example:

```
if(age == 12)
   System.out.println("You are 12");
      else
         if(age == 13)
            . . .
```

## The switch construct

It is a common programming technique to use the value of an integer variable to direct execution to one of several processing routines. You have probably seen programs in which the user selects among several processing options by entering a numeric value, as in the following example:

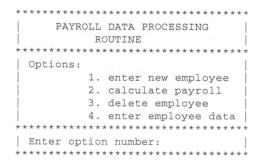

```
*************************************
|        PAYROLL DATA PROCESSING     |
|               ROUTINE              |
*************************************
| Options:                           |
|              1. enter new employee |
|              2. calculate payroll  |
|              3. delete employee    |
|              4. enter employee data|
*************************************
| Enter option number:              |
*************************************
```

When using this menu, the user enters an integer value for selecting the desired processing option in the payroll program. One way of implementing a menu selection is to use several consecutive if statements to test the value of the input variable. The Java switch construct provides an alternative mechanism for selecting among multiple options. The switch consists of the following elements:

1. The switch keyword

2. A controlling expression enclosed in parentheses. Must be of integer type.

3. One or more case statements followed by an integer or character constant, or an expression that evaluates to a constant. Each case statement terminates in a colon symbol.

4. An optional break statement at the end of each case block. When the break is encountered, all other case statements are skipped.

5. An optional default statement. The default case receives control if none of the other case statements have executed.

The switch construct provides a simple alternative to a complicated if, else-if, and else chain. The general form of the switch statement is as follows:

```
switch (expression)
{
    case value1:
       statement;
       statement;
       . . .
       [break;]
    case value2:
       statement;
       statement;
       . . .
       [break;]
       ...
    [default:]
       statement;
```

```
        statement;
        .  .  .
        [break;]
}
```

---
## Incidentally...
---

The preceding example uses a non-existent computer language, called *pseudocode*. Pseudocode shows the fundamental logic of a programming construct, without complying with the formal requirements of any particular programming language. There are no strict rules to pseudocode; the syntax is left to the programmer's imagination. The preceding pseudocode listing combines elements of the Java language with symbols that are not part of Java. For example, the ... characters (called ellipses) indicate that other program elements could follow at this point. The bracket symbols are used to signal optional components.

---

The controlling expression of a switch construct follows the switch keyword and is enclosed in parentheses. The expression, usually a variable, must evaluate to an integer type. It is possible to have a controlling expression with more than one variable, one that contains literal values, or to perform integer arithmetic within the controlling expression.

Each case statement marks a position in the code. If the case statement is true, execution continues at the code that follows the case keyword. The case keyword is followed by an integer or character constant, or an expression that evaluates to an integer or character constant. The case constant is enclosed in single quotation symbols (tic marks) if the control statement is a char type. The following code fragment shows a case construct in which the switch variable is of type char.

```
char charVar;
.  .  .
switch (charVar)
{
    case 'A':
        System.out.println("Input was A");
        break;
    case 'B':
        System.out.println("Input was B");
        break;
    .  .  .
}
```

The case constant does not require tic marks when the control statement evaluates to an int type. The following code fragment shows a case construct in which the switch variable is of type int.

```
int intVar;
. . .
switch (intVar)
{
   case 1:
       System.out.println("Input was 1");
       break;
   case 2:
       System.out.println("Input was 2");
       break;9
. . .
}
```

The break keyword is optional, but if it is not present at the end of a case block, then the following case or default blocks execute. In other words, execution in a switch construct continues until a break keyword or the end of the construct is encountered. When a break keyword is encountered, execution is immediately directed to the end of the switch construct. A break statement is not required on the last block (case or default statement), although the break is usually included to make the code easier to read.

The blocks of execution within a switch construct are enclosed in rosters; however, the case and the default keywords automatically block the statements that follow. Rosters are not necessary to indicate the first-level execution block within a case or default statement.

The following program shows the processing necessary for implementing menu selection using a Java switch construct.

## On the Web

The MenuDemo.java program is found in the Chapter 9 folder at www.crcpress.com.

```
//    File name: MenuDemo.java
//    Reference: Chapter 9
//
//    Java program to demonstrate menu selection
//    Topics:
//        1. Using the switch construct
//
//    Requires:
//        1. Keyin class in the current directory
```

```
public class MenuDemo
{

  public static void main(String[] args)
    {
      // Local variable
      int swValue;

      // Display menu graphics
      System.out.println("=============================");
      System.out.println("|    MENU SELECTION DEMO    |");
      System.out.println("=============================");
      System.out.println("| Options:                  |");
      System.out.println("|         1. Option 1       |");
      System.out.println("|         2. Option 2       |");
      System.out.println("|         3. Exit           |");
      System.out.println("=============================");
      swValue = Keyin.inInt(" Select option: ");

      // Switch construct
      switch(swValue)
      {
        case 1:
          System.out.println("Option 1 selected");
          break;
        case 2:
          System.out.println("Option 2 selected");
          break;
        case 3:
          System.out.println("Exit selected");
          break;
        default:
          System.out.println("Invalid selection");
          break;            // This break is not really necessary
      }
    }
}
```

# Conditional Expressions

Java expressions usually contain a single operand. There is one ternary operator that uses two operands. Java's ternary operator is also called the *conditional operator*. A conditional expression is used to substitute a simple if-else construct. The syntax of a conditional statement can be sketched as follows:

```
exp1 ? exp2 : exp3
```

In the above pseudocode exp1, exp2, and exp3 are Java expressions. First, exp1 is tested. If exp1 is true, then exp2 executes. If exp1 is false, then exp3 executes. Suppose you want to assign the value of the smaller of two integer variables (named *a* and *b*) to a third variable named min. You could code as follows using a conventional if-else construct:

```
int a, b, min;
. . .
if (a < b)
   min = a;
else
   min = b;
```

With the conditional operator the code can be shortened and simplified, as follows:

```
   min = (a < b) ? a : b;
```

In the above statement the conditional expression is formed by the elements to the right of the assignment operator (=). There are three elements in the rvalue:

1. The expression (*a* < *b*) which evaluates either to logical true or false.

2. The expression ? a determines the value assigned to the lvalue if the expression (*a* < *b*) is true.

3. The expression : b determines the value assigned to the lvalue if the expression (*a* < *b*) is false.

## Programmers note:

The *lvalue* is the element to the left of the equal sign in an assignment expression. The *rvalue* is the element to the right of the equal sign.

# Chapter 10

# Controlling Program Flow

## Repetition in Programs

Often computer programs must repeat the same task a number of times. Think of a payroll program that estimates wages and deductions by performing the same calculations for each employee in the company. If you were developing such a program, you could write code to perform salary calculations for each employee. If the company had 100 employees, you would end up with 100 different routines. Although this solution would work, it is cumbersome and awkward. A more reasonable approach is to write a single routine that performs the necessary calculations. The routine is executed for each employee by changing the data set. The result is more compact code that is much easier to develop and test.

Program repetitions usually take place by means of programming constructs called *loops*. In this chapter, we discuss the three Java loop constructs: the *for loop*, the *while loop*, and the *do-while loop*.

## Loops and iterations

Loops do not offer functionality that is not otherwise available in a programming language. Loops just save coding effort and make programs more logical and efficient. In many cases coding would be virtually impossible without loops. Imagine that you were developing a program that had to estimate the tax liability for each resident of the state of Minnesota. Without loops, you would have to spend the rest of your life writing the code.

In talking about loops it is convenient to have a word that represents one entire trip through the processing routine. We call this an *iteration*. To iterate means to do something repeatedly. Each transition through the statement or group of statements in the loop is an iteration. Thus, when

97

talking about a program loop that repeats a group of statements three times, we speak of the first, the second, and the third iteration.

---

## Programmers note:

---

The concept of program iteration is not limited to loop structures. The word "iteration" describes any form of repetitive processing, independently of the logical means by which it is performed.

---

## Elements of a program loop

A loop always involves three steps:

1. The initialization step is used to prime the loop variables to an initial state.

2. The processing step performs the processing. This is the portion of the code that is repeated during each iteration.

3. The testing step evaluates the variables or conditions that determine the continuation of the loop. If they are met, the loop continues. If not, the loop ends.

A loop structure can be used to calculate the factorial. The factorial is the product of all the whole numbers that are equal to or less than the number. For example, factorial 5 (written 5!) is

```
5! = 5 * 4 * 3 * 2 * 1 = 120
```

In coding a routine to calculate the factorial you can use one variable to hold the accumulated product and another one to hold the current factor. The first variable could be named facProd and the second one curFactor. The loop to calculate facProd can be as follows:

1. Initialize the variable facProd to the number whose factorial is to be calculated and the variable curFactor to this number minus 1. For example: to calculate 5! you make facProd = 5 and curFactor = 4.

2. During each iteration calculate the new value of facProd by making facProd = curFactor times facProd. Subtract one from curFactor.

3. If curFactor is greater than 1 repeat step 2, if not, terminate the loop.

Figure 10-1 is a flowchart of the logic used in the factorial calculation described above.

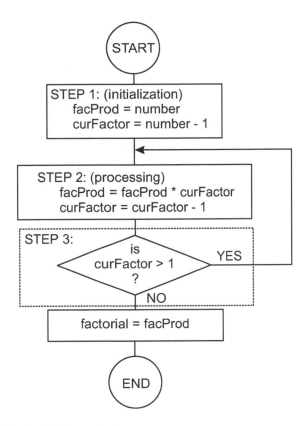

**Figure 10-1** *Factorial Flowchart*

---

### Programmers note:

---

In the factorial calculation we test for a factor greater than 1 to terminate the loop. This eliminates multiplying by 1, which is a trivial operation.

---

## For Loop

The for loop is the simplest iterative construct of Java. The for loop repeats
the execution of a program statement or statement block a fixed number of
times. A typical for loop consists of the following steps:

1.  An initialization step that assigns an initial value to the loop variable.

2.  One or more processing statements. It is in this step where the calculations
    take place and the loop variable is updated.

3.  A test expression that determines the termination of the loop.

The general form of the for loop instruction is shown in Figure 10-2.

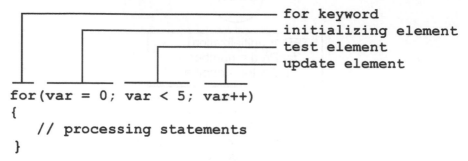

```
                                        ─── for keyword
                                        ─── initializing element
                                        ─── test element
                                        ─── update element

for (var = 0; var < 5; var++)
{
    // processing statements
}
```

**Figure 10-2** *Elements of the for Loop Construct*

We can use the for loop in the following code fragment for calculating the factorial according to the flowchart in Figure 10-1.

```
int number = 5;              // Factorial to be calculated
int facProd, curFactor;      // Local variables

// Initialization step
facProd = number;            // Initialize operational variable
for (curFactor = number - 1; curFactor > 1; curFactor--)
        facProd = curFactor * facProd;
// Done
System.out.println("Factorial is: ", + facProd);
```

Note that the expression

```
for(curFactor = number - 1; curFactor > 1; curFactor --)
```

contains the loop expression and that it includes elements from steps 1, 2, and 3. The first statement (curFactor = number - 1) sets the initial value of the loop variable. The second statement (curFactor > 1) contains the test condition and determines if the loop continues or if it ends. The third statement (curFactor --) diminishes the loop variable by 1 during each iteration.

Note that while the for loop expression does not end in a semicolon, it does contain semicolon symbols. In the case of the for loop, the semicolon symbol is used to separate the initialization, test, and update elements of the loop. This action of the semicolon symbol allows the use of multiple statements in each element of the loop expression, as in the following case:

```
unsigned int x;
unsigned int y;
for(x = 0, y = 5; x < 5; x++, y--)
    System.out.println("x is: " + x, " y is: " + y);
```

In the preceding code the semicolons serve to delimit the initialization, continuation, and update phases of the for loop. The initialization stage ($x = 0$, $y = 5$) sets the variables to their initial values. The continuation stage (x < 5) tests the condition during which the loop continues. The update stage ($x++$, $y--$) increments $x$ and decrements $y$ during each iteration. The comma operator is used to separate the components in each loop phase.

The middle phase in the for loop statement, called the test expression, is evaluated during each loop iteration. If this statement is false, then the loop terminates immediately. Otherwise, loop continues. For the loop to execute the first time the test expression must initially evaluate to true. Note that the test expression determines the condition under which the loop executes, rather than its termination. For example

```
for(x = 0; x == 5; x++)
    System.out.println(x);
```

The println() statement in the preceding loop does not execute because the test expression x == 5 is initially false. The following loop, on the other hand, executes endlessly because the terminating condition is assigned a new value during each iteration.

```
int x;
for (x = 0; x = 5; x++)
    System.out.println(x);
```

## Programmers note:

In the preceding loop the middle element should have been x = = 5. The statement $x = 5$ assigns a value to $x$ and always evaluates true. It is a very common mistake to use the assignment operator (=) in place of the comparison operator (= =).

It is also possible for the test element of a for loop to contain a complex logical expression. In this case, the entire expression is evaluated to determine if the condition is met. For example:

```
int x, y;
for(x = 0, y = 5; (x < 3 || y > 1); x++, y--)
```

The test expression

```
(x < 3 || y > 1)
```

evaluates to true if either x is less than 3 or if y is greater than 1. The values that determine the end of the loop are reached when the variable $x = 4$ or when the variable $y = 1$.

## Compound statement in loops

You have learned that the roster symbols ({ and }) are used in Java to group several statements into a single block. Statement blocks are used in loop constructs to make possible performing more than one processing operation. The following program, named Factorial.java, uses a statement block in a for loop to display the partial product during the factorial calculation.

## On the Web

The program Factorial.java is found in the Chapter 10 folder at www.crcpress.com.

```java
//    File name: Factorial.java
//    Reference: Chapter 10
//
//    Java program to demonstrate looping
//    Topics:
//        1. Using the for loop
//        2. Loop with multiple processing statements
//
//    Requires:
//        1. Keyin class in the current directory

public class Factorial
{

  public static void main(String[] args)
  {

      int number;
      int facProd;
      int curFactor;

      System.out.println("FACTORIAL CALCULATION PROGRAM");
      number = Keyin.inInt("Enter a positive integer: ");

      facProd = number;       // Initializing

      for(curFactor = number - 1; curFactor > 1; curFactor-)
      {
         facProd = curFactor * facProd;
           System.out.println("Partial product: " + facProd);
           System.out.println("Current factor:  " + curFactor);
      }

    // Display the factorial
    System.out.println("\n\nFactorial is: " + facProd);
  }
}
```

## While loop

The Java while loop repeats a statement or statement block "while" a certain condition evaluates to true. Like the for loop, the while loop requires initialization, processing, and testing steps. The difference is that in the for loop, the initialization and testing steps are part of the loop itself, but in the while loop these steps are located outside the loop body. The following program uses a while loop to display the ASCII characters in the range 0x10 to 0x20.

---

## On the Web

---

The program AsciiCodes.java is found in the Chapter 10 folder at www.crcpress.com.

---

```
//    File name: AsciiCodes.java
//    Reference: Chapter 10
//
//    Java program to demonstrate looping
//    Topics:
//        1. Using the while loop
//
//    Requires:
//        1. Keyin class in the current directory

public class AsciiCodes
{

   public static void main(String[] args)
   {

      char value = 0x10;

         while(value < 0x20)
         {
            System.out.println(value);
            value++;
         }
   }
}
```

In the program AsciiCodes.java, the initialization of the loop variable is performed outside the while construct. The loop variable is updated inside the loop. The only loop element contained in the loop expression is the test element. Figure 10-3 (on the next page) shows the elements of the while loop.

```
loopVar = 0;  ←──────────────  External initialization
while(loopVar != 10) ←─────── Loop continuation test
{
   // Processing statements
   loopVar++; ←─────────────── Loop variable update
}
```

**Figure 10-3** *Elements of the while Loop Construct*

---

## Programmers note:

---

The while loop evaluates the test expression before the loop statement block executes. For this reason the AsciiCodes program, listed previously, displays the values between 0x10 and 0x20, but not 0x20. This mode of operation is consistent with the meaning of the word while.

---

# Do-While Loop

A characteristic of the while loop is that if the test condition is initially false, the loop never executes. For example, the while loop in the following code fragment will not execute the statement body because the variable $x$ evaluates to 0 before the first iteration

```
int x = 0;
. . .
while (x != 0)
   System.out.println(x);
```

In the do-while loop, the test expression is evaluated after the loop executes. This ensures that the loop executes at least once, as in the following example:

```
int x = 0;
. . .
do
   System.out.println(x);
while (x != 0);
```

In the case of the do-while loop, the first iteration always takes place because the test is not performed until after the loop body executes. Figure 10-4 shows the elements of the do-while loop.

```
loopVar = 0;  ◄──────────────── External initialization
do  ◄───────────────────────── Start of loop
{
   // Processing statements
   loopVar++;  ◄─────────────── Loop variable update
}
while(loopVar != 10);  ◄─────── Loop continuation test
```

**Figure 10-4** *Elements of the do-while Loop Construct*

In many cases the processing performed by the do-while loop is identical to the one performed by the while loop.

---
## Programmers note:
---

The test expression in a do-while loop terminates in a semicolon symbol. Since a while statement does not contain a semicolon, it is a common mistake to omit it in the do-while loop.

---

# Chapter 11

# Programming with Loops

## Java Loop Constructs

Most programs contain many loops of different types. The programmer needs to be familiar with all types of loops and be able to select the most suitable one in each case. In this Chapter, you learn how to use the three loop constructs (for loop, while loop, and do-while loop) in practical programming situations.

## Selecting a Loop Construct

The for loop is a neat mechanism that contains the three required elements: initialization, test, and processing. This design makes the for loop suitable in situations in which you know the loop conditions in advance. For example, a routine to display the ASCII characters in the range 16 to 128 can be easily coded using a for loop, as follows:

```
for(char ascii = 16; ascii < 129; ascii ++)
    System.out.println(ascii);
```

### Programmers note:

In the preceding code fragment, the loop variable ascii is declared inside the for statement. The result is that ascii is a local variable whose scope is limited to the loop itself.

In contrast, the while loop repeats while a certain test condition is true. This makes the while loop useful in cases in which the terminating condition is initially unpredictable. For example, you may want a program to repeat a set of calculations until the user types a specific ending code. In this case you can use a while loop in which the processing continues until the special ending code is detected.

The do-while loop provides an alternative to the while loop in which the test condition is evaluated after the processing statements execute. This ensures that the do-while loop executes at least once.

Programs often contain several loop constructs. Often one loop is nested within another one. The program, named AsciiTable.java, listed below, displays the table of ASCII characters in the range 0x20 to 0x7F. The program uses four loops. The first two loops display the column heads for the table. The third loop is a while loop which takes care of the table's row heads and leading spaces. The fourth loop, nested in the third one, displays a row of 16 ASCII codes. The program's result is a labeled table of the ASCII character codes.

---

## On the Web

---

The program AsciiTable.java is found in the Chapter 11 folder at www.crcpress.com.

---

```
//    File name: AsciiTable.java
//    Reference: Chapter 11
//
//    Java program to demonstrate looping
//    Topics:
//       1. Using several loop constructs simultaneously
//       2. Nested loops
//
public class AsciiTable
{
  public static void main(String[] args)
  {
    // Local variables
    char hexLetter;             // For table header
    char ascCode = 0x20;        // First ASCII code
    // Counters for rows and columns
    int row = 2;
    int column;
    System.out.print("\n\n");
    System.out.print("                            ");
    System.out.println("ASCII CHARACTER TABLE");
    System.out.print("                            ");
    System.out.println("characters 0x20 to 0xff");
    System.out.print("\n    ");
    // Loops 1 and 2
    // Display column heads for numbers 0 to F hexadecimal
    for(hexLetter = '0'; hexLetter <= '9'; hexLetter ++)
       System.out.print("   " + hexLetter);
```

```
    for(hexLetter = 'A'; hexLetter <= 'F'; hexLetter ++)
        System.out.print("   " + hexLetter);
    // Blank line to separate table head from data
    System.out.println("\n");
    // Loop 3
    // While ASCII codes smaller than 0x80 display row head
    // and leading spaces
    // Loop 4 (nested in loop 3)
    // Display row of ASCII codes for columns 0 to 0x0F.
    // Add a new line at end of each row
    while (ascCode < 0x80)
    {
        System.out.print("   " + row);
            for (column = 0; column < 16; column ++)
              {
                System.out.print("    " + ascCode);
                ascCode ++;
              }
            System.out.print("\n\n");
        row ++;
    }
  }
}
```

Figure 11-1 is a screen snapshot showing the result of compiling and executing the AsciiTable program.

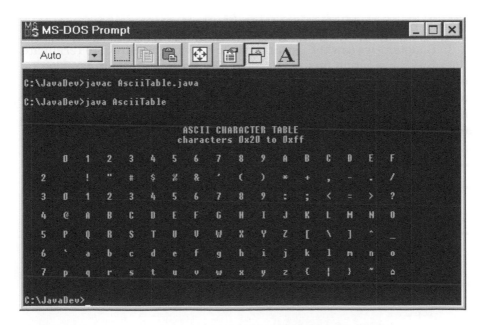

**Figure 11-1** *Screen Snapshot of the AsciiTable.java Program*

# Direct Flow Control

The loop statements discussed here and in Chapter 10, as well as the decision statements in Chapter 9, provide the programmer with ways of directing program execution. In loops and in the various flavors of the if statement, program execution flows according to the result of the test expression that evaluates to true or false. Because their action depends on the result of a logical expression, it is said that loops and decision statements indirectly change the flow of a program.

But occasionally you may need to change program execution immediately and without performing any test. Java contains instructions that abruptly change execution. These instructions are break, continue, and return. The return statement is associated with methods, therefore it is discussed in Chapter 12.

## Incidentally...

C and C++ contain an additional statement, named goto, that allows directing execution unconditionally to a specific destination. Although goto is a Java reserved word, the goto statement has not been implemented in the language.

## Using break in loops

In Chapter 9 we saw the use of break in a switch construct to terminate the processing action in a case block. The break statement can also be used in a for, while, or do-while loop. In the case of loops, the break statement directs execution to the line immediately after the currently executing level of the loop. When break is used in a nested loop, execution exits the loop level in which the statement is located. This is shown by the program named BreakDemo.java listed below.

## On the Web

The program BreakDemo.java is found in the Chapter 11 folder at www.crcpress.com.

```
//    File name: BreakDemo.java
//    Reference: Chapter 11
//
//    Java program to demonstrate direct flow control
//    Topics:
//        1. Action of the break statement
//
```

```
public class BreakDemo
{

  public static void main(String[] args)
    {
    int number = 1;
    char letter;

    while(number < 10 )
        {
        System.out.println("number is: " + number);
        number ++;
            for (letter = 'A'; letter < 'G'; letter ++)
            {
            System.out.println("  letter is: " + letter);
                if (letter == 'C')
                    break;
            }
        }
    }
}
```

There are two loops in the BreakDemo.java program. The first one is a while loop that displays the numbers 1 to 9. The second one, an inner loop, displays the capital letters A to F. An if statement tests for the letter C and executes a break in order to interrupt execution of the nested loop. Because the break statement acts on the current loop level only, the outer loop resumes counting numbers until the value 10 is reached.

---

## Programmers note:

---

The break keyword can only be used inside a switch construct or in a for, while, or do-while loop. An error results if the break keyword appears anywhere else in a Java program.

---

## The continue keyword

The break statement can be used with either a switch or a loop construct. The continue statement, on the other hand, works only in loops. The purpose of continue is to bypass all statements not yet executed in the loop and return immediately to the beginning of the loop.

The program named ContinueDemo.java contains a for loop designed to display the letters A to D. The continue statement in this loop serves to bypass the letter C, which is not displayed.

---
## On the Web
---

The program ContinueDemo.java is found in the Chapter 11 folder at
www.crcpress.com.

---

```
//    File name: ContinueDemo.java
//    Reference: Chapter 11
//
//    Java program to demonstrate direct flow control
//    Topics:
//       1. Action of the continue statement
//
public class ContinueDemo
{

   public static void main(String[] args)
      {
      char letter;
      for (letter = 'A'; letter < 'E'; letter ++)
         {
            if (letter == 'C')
               continue;
            System.out.println("  letter is " + letter);
         }
      }
}
```

## The labeled break

A break statement is used to exit the current level of a loop. Occasionally,
an application needs to immediately exit all levels in a loop; for example, if
an error is detected. One possible solution is to include an if statement in
the loop and add an additional terminating condition to the loop header.
But when dealing with several nesting levels these extra conditions can be
inconvenient and complicated.

The Java instruction that provides an immediate and unconditional
exit for any level of a nested loop is the labeled break. In this case, the
break statement is followed by the identifier of a program label. The label
itself is a place-marker ending in the colon symbol. The general form of
the labeled break is shown in Figure 11-2.

---
## Programmers note:
---

The label must precede the outermost loop level which you want to
exit.

---

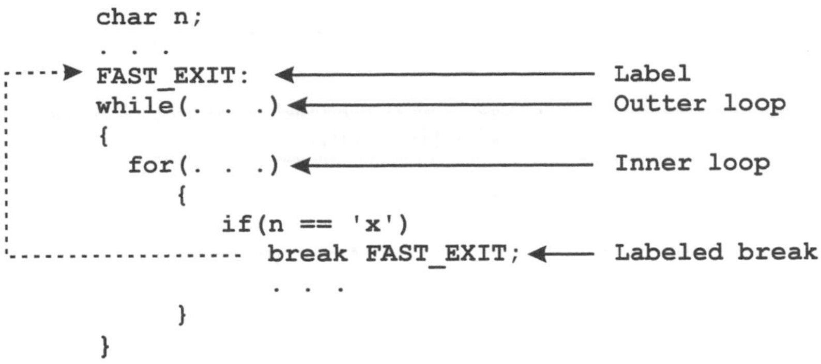

```
        char n;
        . . .
------> FAST_EXIT:    ◄————————————————  Label
        while(. . .) ◄————————————————  Outter loop
        {
          for(. . .) ◄————————————————  Inner loop
            {
               if(n == 'x')
               break FAST_EXIT; ◄———  Labeled break
               . . .
            }
        }
```

**Figure 11-2** *Action of a Labeled Break*

The following program shows the use of a labeled break to implement an error handler.

```java
//    File name: LabeledBreak.java
//    Reference: Chapter 11
//
//    Java program to demonstrate direct flow control
//    Topics:
//        1. Action of the labeled break statement
//        2. Use of a labeled break in an error handler
//
//    Requires:
//        1. Keyin class in the current directory

public class LabeledBreak
{

  public static void main(String[] args)
    {
    int number = 1;
    char letter;

    letter = Keyin.inChar("Enter any character, except C: " );

    FAST_EXIT:
    while(number < 10 )
        {
        System.out.println("number is: " + number);
        number ++;
          for (char ch = 'A'; ch < 'D'; ch++)
              {
                 System.out.println("  char is: " + ch);
                 if (letter == 'C' || letter == 'c')
                    break FAST_EXIT;
            }
        }
```

```
    if(letter == 'C' || letter == 'c')
       System.out.println("ERROR, invalid input");
   }
}
```

## On the Web

The program LabeledBreak.java is found in the Chapter 11 folder at www.crcpress.com.

# *Chapter 12*

# Program Building Blocks

## The Java Subprogram

It did not take long for programmers to discover that code often contained sections that performed identical operations. For example, a program that performed geometrical calculations had to calculate the area of a circle over and over again. Recoding the same routine wasted programming effort, made the program larger, and increased the possibility of error. The solution was to create subprograms within the main program. The subprogram would contain a processing routine that could be reused as often as necessary without having to recode it. An added advantage was that subprograms reduced code size and simplified testing and error correction. In this case, the subprogram to calculate the area of a circle would receive the radius parameter from the caller. The subroutine would then perform the required calculations and return the circle's area.

Java subprograms are called methods. Methods are the building block of a Java application. This chapter is about methods and how they work.

## Modules and Methods

Modern-day programming techniques are based on program *modules*. The program breaks the processing task into small units, called modules. The result is a program that is easier to manage and maintain. The processing engines within each module are called methods. In Java, a method is a subroutine designed to perform a specific and well-defined set of related processing operations. Each method has a single entry point and a single exit. A well conceived method rarely exceeds a few pages of code. It is better to divide processing into several simpler functions than to create a single more complex one.

## The Elements of a Method

A Java method is a collection of declarations and statements, grouped under a single structure, identified by a method name, and designed to perform a well-defined task. A Java method contains two clearly identifiable elements: the *declaration* and the *body*. The method is created and defined in its declaration statement, while the processing operations are contained in the method body. The following method, named getAverage(), adds all the elements in an array of int type and returns the average value.

```
public static int getAverage(int[] intArray)
{
    int sum = 0;             // Local variable

    // Calculate sum of all array elements
    for(int x = 0; x < intArray.length; x++)
        sum = sum + intArray[x];

    // Calculate and return average
    return sum / intArray.length;
}
```

## Incidentally...

It is popular among authors of computer books to follow the method name with parentheses, for example, main() or getAverage(). This seems reasonable since parenthesis are characteristic of Java methods. We follow this convention in this book.

## Declaration

The method declaration, also called the *method header*, is a single expression that states the method name and defines the type returned by the method and the parameters that it receives from the caller, if any. The method declaration can also contain other information, such as access specifiers and modifiers. These additional elements determine the method's visibility and its interaction with other program elements.

The method declaration can also contain exception-handling information. This topic is discussed in the context of Java exceptions, in Chapter 19. Figure 12-1 shows the principal elements in a method declaration.

## Programmers note:

The method declaration does not end with a semicolon symbol.

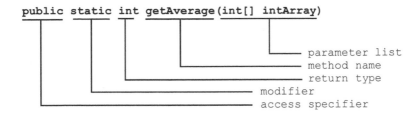

**Figure 12-1** *Elements of a Method Declaration*

## Access specifier

The method's *access specifier* is optional. The access specifier controls access to the method. The access specifiers are *public, protected,* and *private.* Public is the least restrictive one. Access specifiers for methods are discussed in the context of object-oriented programming in Chapter 14.

## Modifier

The *modifier* sets the properties for the method. The value for the modifier are *static, abstract, final, native,* and *synchronized.* Modifiers are related to the method's visibility and the method's attributes within the class structure.

You can also create methods that are unrelated to objects by using the static modifier. This is the case with the getAverage() method listed previously and with the main() method that you have been using in your programs.

## Return type

The *return type* is a required element in the method declaraction. The one exception is a special type of methods, called *constructors,* which are discussed in Chapter 15. All methods can return a single value to the caller. The return type identifies the data type of the returned value. Java methods can return any of the eight primitive data types ( int, long, short, byte, boolean, float, and double, and char) or more complex types, such as arrays and objects. Since a string is an object of the String class, a Java method can return a string object to the caller. When a method returns no value, its return type is declared to be void. If the method's return type is not void, it must return the type specified in the declaration.

The following method returns a type boolean:

```
public static boolean isOdd(int aValue)
{
```

```
    if(aValue % 2 != 0)
        return true;
    else
        return false;
}
```

## Method name

Every Java method must have a name, which must be a legal Java identifier. Most Java programmers start method names with a lower-case character, and then use upper-case letters for any other words in the name. This is the case in the methods getAverage() and isOdd () listed previously.

It is a matter of good programming style to select a method name that is consistent with the value returned by the method. The reason for this practice is that, in Java code, the method's name identifies the value returned. For example, you could name getAverage() a method that returns the average of the elements in a numeric array. While a method that returns true if the argument is an even number can be named isEven().

## Parameter list

The information passed to the method is defined by the method's parameter list. There is no limit to the number of elements that can be declared in the parameter list. The format for the parameters is as follows:

```
DataType VariableName, DataType VariableName, . . .
```

## Programmers note:

There is some confusion between the meaning of arguments and parameters in relation to methods. Arguments refer to the values passed to the method, while parameters are the values received by the method. Thus, we say that a method receives an int as a parameter, or that we call the method with an int argument.

A method that receives no arguments is declared with an empty parameter list, as follows:

```
public static void eraseAll()
```

# *Chapter 13*

# Using Methods

## The Method Call

You transfer control to a method by referencing the method's name in a program statement. The method call can appear at any point in the code from which the method is visible. Furthermore, a method can call itself. A method that calls itself is said to use *recursion.*

The following code shows a call to the method named getAverage(), discussed previously:

```
public static void main(String[] args)
{
  // Local variables
    int[] values = {1, 2, 3, 4, 5, 6, 7, 12};
    int average;

    // Call the method named getAverage()
    average = getAverage(values);

    // Display results
    System.out.println("Average is: " + average);
    . . .
```

The method call is contained in the statement:

```
    average = getAverage(values);
```

The call to getAverage() contains the name of the array passed as an argument. This argument becomes the only parameter in getAverage().

# Returning from a Method

A method concludes when it reaches the return keyword. At this point, execution returns to the caller at the statement that follows the call. A return statement can include an expression, optionally enclosed in parentheses, which represents the value returned to the caller. The method getAverage(), listed previously, has the following statement:

```
return sum / intArray.length;
```

The value returned by a method must always match the return type defined in its declaration. Parentheses can optionally be used to clarify the calculations of a returned value, as follows:

```
return (sum / intArray.length);
```

If the method's return type is void, then no value can follow the return statement. For example, a method with void return type concludes execution with the statement:

```
return;
```

If you do not code a statement, the method concludes at the line that precedes the closing roster. In this case, programmers say that the method "falls off the edge." A method can also return a constant to the caller, as in the following example:

```
public static double getPi()

{
    return 3.141592653589793;
}
```

In the preceding example, the method getPi() returns the constant PI to the calling routine.

---

## Programmers note:

---

A method without a return statement does not produce a compiler error. However, an explicit return is better, since it leaves no doubt about the programmer's intention.

---

The return statement can appear anywhere in the method body. A single method can contain several return statements. Each return statement can be associated with a different value. This is the case in the isOdd() method:

```
public static boolean isOdd(int aValue)
{
```

```
    if(aValue % 2 != 0)
        return true;
    else
        return false;
}
```

The following cases are possible in regards to a method's return:

1. The method can contain one or more explicit return statements. Each statement can be associated with a different value. For example:

   ```
   return (error_code);
   return((r + r) * PI);
   return 2 * radius;
   ```

2. A method can contain no return statement. In this case, execution concludes at the closing brace and the method is said to "fall of the edge." A non-void method that falls off the edge has an undefined return value.

3. A method can end with a simple return statement. This happens when the method concludes with the expression:

   ```
   return;
   ```

   In this case no specific value is returned to the caller. Void methods must use this style.

4. A method can return a constant, optionally enclosed in parentheses

   ```
   return 0;
   return (1);
   ```

# Arguments and Parameters

A method's declaration contains a list of the variables, enclosed in parentheses, whose values are passed by the caller. The method's call statement contains (also enclosed in parentheses) the value passed to the method as arguments. Suppose that you have coded a method named getArea() that calculates the area of a triangle from its height and base dimensions. Also assume that getArea() receives the height and base values as parameters, as follows:

```
double area;
double height = 12.7;
double base = 7.9;
. . .
// Calling the method
area = getArea(base, height);
. . .
// Method
public static double getArea(double b, double h)
{
```

```
    double result = (b * h) / 2;
    return result;
}
```

The method getArea() declares in its paramenter list two variables of type double, named *b* and *h*. While the method call references, in parentheses, the arguments base and height, whose values are passed to getArea().

---
### Programmers note:
---

The term "argument" relates to elements in the method's call, while the term "parameter" refers to the elements listed in the method's declaration. In other words, a value passed to a method is an argument from the viewpoint of the caller, and a parameter from the viewpoint of the method itself.

---

Data is passed to a method in the same order in which the arguments are listed in the call. The method's parameter list defines this order. In the case of the method getArea() previously listed, the first argument in the method's call, the variable base, becomes the parameter b declared in the method's header. While the second argument referenced in the call, the variable height, becomes the variable *h* in the method.

The value returned by a method is associated with its name. This explains why the variable contained in a method's return statement can be of local scope. Also notice that a method returns a single value to the caller.

## Methods and Global Variables

You have learned that the scope of a Java variable is the block in which it is declared. Since a method's body is defined within a block, a variable declared inside this block has *local scope*. Sometimes we say that method variables have *method scope*. For example:

```
public static double getArea(double b, double h)
{
    double result = (b * h) / 2;
    return result;
}
```

The scope of the variable result is the getArea() method. Data elements declared outside the methods of a class have *class (or global) scope*. The fact that methods can access global data provides a simple mechanism whereby a method can return more than one result to the caller.

The following program, named Circle.java, contains two global variables and a constant.

## On the Web

The source file for the program Circle.java can be found in the Chapter 12 folder at www.crcpress.com.

```
//    File name: Circle.java
//    Reference: Chapter 12
//    Java program to demonstrate global variables
//    and their use by methods
//    Topics:
//        1. Global variables
//        2. Variable visibility to methods
//        3. Method that returns several results in
//           global variables
//        4. Data is passed by reference to a method
//
//    Requires:
//        1. Keyin class in the current directory
public class Circle
{
    // Data elements defined at the class level
    static final double PI = 3.141592653589793;
    static double area;
    static double perimeter;

    //*********************************
    //          main() method
    //*********************************
    public static void main(String[] args)
        {
            // Local variables
            double radius;
            // Input radius from keyboard
            System.out.println("Caculating circle dimensions");
            radius = Keyin.inDouble("Enter radius: ");
            // Call method
            circleData(radius);
            // Display data stored globally
            System.out.println("Radius: " + radius);
            System.out.println("Area: " + area);
            System.out.println("Perimeter: " + perimeter);
        }

    //*****************************
    //      circleData() method
    //*****************************
    public static void circleData(double radius)
    {
        area = PI * (radius * radius);
```

```
    perimeter = PI * (2 * radius);
    radius = 0;                        // Fruitless effort!
    return;
  }
}
```

The method circleData() receives the radius of a circle as a parameter and calculates its area and circumference. The calculated values are stored in global variables; where they can be accessed by the caller.

---
## Programmers note:
---

The method circleData() of the program Circle.java, is defined with return type void. In this case the method returns nothing to the caller since the information is contained in global variables.

---

# Passing by Value and by Reference

Data is passed to methods in two different ways: *by value* and *by reference*. Data is said to be passed by value when the method receives a copy of the values in the caller's arguments. The result of passing by value is that the method has no access to the variables where the data is stored. On the other hand, when data is passed by reference, the method receives the addresses of the variables where the values are stored. In this case, the method can change the actual contents of the variables.

Java has simple rules that determine when data is passed by value or by reference. Primitive data types are always passed by reference to methods. In the program named Circle.java, listed previously, the method circleData() receives the radius of the circle as a parameter from the caller. The method attempts to change the value of this variable in the statement:

```
    radius = 0;                 // Fruitless effort!
```

In the comment to this line we said that this is a "fruitless effort." The reason is that the method circleData() has no access to the variable radius, which is local to the method main(). The first println statement in the caller's code shows that the value of the variable radius remains unchanged.

# Chapter 14

# Object-Oriented Programming

## Classes and Objects

A new approach to solving the software crisis, called *object-oriented programming* was introduced to program developers during the early 1980s. The idea behind object-orientation (often called OO) is to make programming more real. Instead of dealing with abstractions and concepts that only exist in the software world, OO programmers would model their products using objects. These objects belonged to "classes of objects" that contained the data structures and processing operations. The object-oriented approach proved to be a feasible alternative and is now a major force in the computing mainstream.

Java is an object-oriented programming language. It uses classes and objects, which are the fundamental elements of an OO system. Java also implements the three conceptual mechanisms associated with object-orientation: *data abstraction, inheritance,* and *dynamic binding.* You have already learned that every statement and every construct of a Java program must exist inside a class of objects. Because the Java libraries, which are defined as classes, in order to use and understand Java you must first grasp the fundamental notions of object-oriented programming. This chapter is about object orientation and about classes and objects.

## The Why and Wherefore of OO

The object-oriented approach dates back to the 1960s. The first notions of data abstraction are due to Kristen Nygaard and Ole-Johan Dahl from the Norwegian Computing Center. Simula, developed by Nygaard and Dahl, was a language intended for simulations and for use in a field of mathematics called *operations research*. Simula was described as a process-oriented language. A few years later a new version, Simula 67, was released.

Simula and Simula 67 never became popular programming languages. Their historical importance is the introduction of the notion of a *class*. In object-oriented systems, a class is a template that packages together data and processing routines. The class is a formal part of an OO language, not a concrete entity. The programmer creates instances of a class as they become necessary. The instances of a class are called *objects*.

The first description of a fully operational, object-oriented programming language was due to Alan Kay. Kay foresaw that desktop computers would have megabytes or memory and would be equipped with processors capable of executing millions of instructions per second. Since, in Kay's vision of the future, desktop machines would be used mostly by nonprogrammers, it was necessary that these computers be equipped with a powerful graphical interface.

An information processing system named Dynabook was a first effort in this direction. Dynabook was based on a virtual desktop on which some documents were visible and others were partially covered. The user would select documents, and move items around on the desktop using a touch-sensitive screen. The interface was similar to our present day windowing environments. The Flex programming language, loosely based on Simula 67,  performed the processing.

These ideas eventually evolved into the Smalltalk programming language, still considered one of the most powerful and refined object-oriented systems. The Smalltalk design team was led by Adele Goldberg. The Smalltalk language has become the standard to which other object-oriented languages are compared. In addition to Smalltalk, other notable object-oriented languages are Clos, Ada 95, C++, and Java.

## Object-Oriented Fundamentals

Not all object-oriented languages are created equal. Smalltalk, for example, implements object-orientation in a pure and strict form. In other OO languages, such as C++, object-orientation is an optional feature that can be turned on or off by the programmer. Object orientation in Java is not optional. In contrast with C++, all Java code must reside inside a class. Nevertheless, it is possible to write Java programs in which object-orientation is minimally visible. The programs developed so far in this book fall into this group.

---

### Incidentally...

Unlike automobiles and food blenders, software products don't wear out. As applications, programming languages, and operating systems become more refined and stable, customers have less reasons for investing in new versions and updates. For this reason, software companies are always in search of features that enhance their products in order to re-capture the interest of their customers. Object-oriented languages have been eagerly adopted by software vendors, not only because of their features, but also for purely commercial reasons.

---

## From Problem to Solution

A computer program is a machine-coded solution to a problem in the real-world. Programming projects usually start with the definition of a problem, or a problem-set. The resulting software product is a group of machine instructions that solve this problem. The art of programming facilitates the transit from the real-world problem-set to the machine-coded solution-set. In this wide sense programming consists of the analysis, design, coding, and testing of a software product.

Over the years many methods have been developed to facilitate the transition from a real world problem to a coded solution. Assemblers, high-level programming languages, CASE tools, software analysis and design schemes, formal specifications, and scientific methods of program testing are all efforts in this direction.

One of the first efforts at making programs easier to develop and more dependable was called *structured programming*. Structured programming techniques were based on fostering programs with a modular structure, clean flow, and a logical design. The results were faster development, more dependable execution, and easier maintenance. For many years the structured programming model was prevalent in the software industry.

But structured programming is a program development methodology. It does not deal with the real-world problem at the origin of every software project. We can say that structured programming focuses on the solution-set of a software project. But interpreting, defining, and modeling the problem-set is one of the major stumbling blocks of software development. The object-oriented approach focuses on this problem set. It uses mechanisms well known to science, such as features classification and inheritance. The object of the program corresponds to the objects of the real world.

The following are the most important claims of the object-oriented approach:

1. The OO model can be understood by clients and software users with no technical knowledge of programming or computers. For this reason, program analysis and design methods based on object-orientation facilitate communications with clients.

2. Real-world problems can be modeled in object-oriented terms. Structured programming does not address the problem set.

3. Object-oriented programming languages promote and facilitate code reuse. Reusing code increases programmer productivity.

4. Object-oriented programs are more resilient to change. This makes OO systems more able to accommodate the natural volatility of the problem-domain.

## Learning about Classes and Objects

Object-oriented programming is based on modeling the problem set using classes and objects. However, you must be careful not to equate an object in an OO language with an object in the real world. In OO terms, an object is an abstraction. It is not identical to an object in the physical sense. It is a conceptual entity related to the problem domain. You can think of an object, in object-oriented programming, as a hybrid that shares some characteristics of common objects with features of a computer construct. The best way to understand objects is to observe their properties:

1. An object belongs to a class. An object cannot exist without a class that defines it. You can visualize the class as a cookie cutter and the object as the cookie. More formally, an object is said to be an instance of a class.

2. A class is an encapsulation that includes data and its related processing operations.

3. Objects have attributes that serve to store and preserve the object's state. The attributes, which are the data element of the class, determine what is remembered about an object.

4. An object's methods are the only way of accessing its data or modifying its state. This is accomplished by sending a message to the object.

### The fundamental principles

Encapsulation and inheritance are the cornerstones of object orientation. Data abstraction, message passing, polymorphism, and dynamic binding are OO mechanisms based on encapsulation and inheritance. You must have a basic understanding of the fundamental principles before you start using object-orientation in your programs.

## Encapsulation

Encapsulation means that the elements of a class, data and methods, are packed in a single capsule. Encapsulation also relates to information hiding, since the data elements contained in the capsule are, in most cases, not accessible to code outside the class. Encapsulation hides the data. Before object-orientation came into existence, processing operations were based on routines and subprograms that shared global data or that received data passed by the caller. The object-oriented approach encapsulates data and methods in a single package, called the class, and hides the data so that it cannot be changed without following proper procedures.

A class consists of both data elements and processing elements. The data elements of a class are the attributes, and the processing operations are the methods. Attributes and methods are the class members: the attributes are called the *data members* and the methods are called the *member functions*.

---
### Incidentally...
---

A class is a structure visible to code, that is, it is a programming construct. End users of an object-oriented program do not see or access classes. Classes are for programmers. For this reason it is better to speak of the "clients" of a class than of the "users" of a class.

---

Encapsulation hides the implementation details and stresses the interface. In general, the interface is what the class exposes to its clients. In particular the class' interface are its methods and the protocols necessary to access these methods. The goal of encapsulation is to create a class abstraction. This abstraction forces the programmer to think conceptually.

In most cases, the data members of a class are invisible to the client. If a data member must be made accessible to the class' client, then the class provides a method that inspects the data element and returns its value. A class that exposes its data members is said to break encapsulation.

## Inheritance

Scientists who study the representation of knowledge were the first to observe the inheritance of properties. In this sense inheritance refers to the properties of a higher-level class being shared by its subclasses. Note that here we are using the common meaning of the word "class," not in the sense of a Java class structure. Using inheritance, knowledge is organized into hierarchies based on class relationships. Thus, we say that an individual inherits the properties of the class to which it belongs. For example, animals breathe, move, and reproduce. If the subclass bird belongs to the animal super-class, then we can deduce that the members of the bird class breathe, move, and reproduce since these properties are inherited from its base class. Scientific classifications are based on inheritance of properties. Figure 14-1 is an inheritance diagram for some classes of animals.

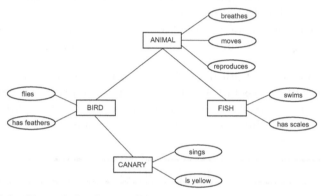

**Figure 14-1** *Class Inheritance Diagram*

Class inheritance is used in knowledge bases to ensure the highest levels of data abstraction. Suppose you are creating a knowledge base about birds. This knowledge base starts by defining the traits that are common to all birds. For example, all birds fly and have feathers. Then it defines the traits of the particular bird species. The canary is yellow and sings. The robin is red and migrates in the winter. The result is that the subclasses, canary and robin in this case, inherit the properties of their parent class, bird, which in turn, inherits the properties of its superclass, animal, and so on. The result is that the knowledge base is reduced, since common properties are asserted only once. Inheritance structures also serve to maintain the consistency of the knowledge base.

Object-orientated systems use inheritance so that subclasses acquire the public members of their parent classes. Here again, inheritance promotes the highest level of abstraction and simplifies the knowledge base. It allows the program designer to build a class hierarchy that goes from the most general to the most specific. Applying object-orientation to the class diagram in Figure 14-1, we can say that ANIMAL is the base class, and that BIRD, FISH, and CANARY are derived classes. A derived class incorporates all the features of its parent class, and may add some unique features of its own. Derived classes have access to all the public members of their base class. *Parent, child,* and *sibling* are terms sometimes used to express degrees of inheritance between classes. As in biological systems, sibling classes do not inherit from each other. Therefore, the properties of FISH (in Figure 14-1) are not inherited by its sibling class, BIRD. This rule is also applied in object-oriented class inheritance.

## Modeling with Classes

Software systems are complex, and object-oriented software development often results in complicated structures of related and unrelated classes and subclasses. In order to understand complex systems you can use a model that simplifies it. Architects create scale models of a building that can be shown to clients. An engineer draws a model of a mechanical component that is later used to manufacture the part. An aircraft designer creates a model of an airplane that can be tested in a wind tunnel. The more elaborate or complex a system the more useful the model.

In object-oriented software systems, classes and objects inherit properties from their parents and interact with their siblings. System designers work at a high level of abstraction and use models that show the interaction between the component elements. Several successful modeling tools have been developed over the years. The basic element of all these modeling tools is a notation for classes and objects and their relations. One of the most popular models is due to Coad and Yourdon. Booch, Jacobson, and Rumbaugh created the Unified Modeling Language (UML) that uses a notation similar to the one proposed by Coad and Yourdon. In either notations, Coad and Yourdon and UML, rectangular boxes are used to denote classes and several connectors represent class' associations and relationships. In this book we use the Coad and Yourdon notation, since it is the simplest one. At times, we introduce minor variations to the Coad and Yourdon model. Figure 14-2 shows the diagram of a class.

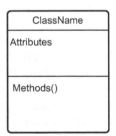

**Figure 14-2** *A Class Diagram*

Suppose you were creating a software system that had to keep track and model various dogs. You could start the design by creating a class named Dog. Each object of the Dog class would have certain specific attributes, such as a name, color, and weight. Also, the objects of the class Dog would have the ability to bark and jump. Using the class diagram we could model the class Dog as shown in Figure 14-3.

**Figure 14-3** *Modeling the Dog Class*

In modeling classes we note that there are two basic types of class associations. In one case, the subclass is "a kind-of" the parent class and in another case the sub-class is "a part-of" the parent. Suppose you used a class named Physician and a class named Surgeon to model a medical system. In this case you could say that a Surgeon is "a kind-of" a Physician. On the other hand, if you were modeling an automobile using a class named Engine and another class named Starter; in this case, the relationship between classes is that Starter is "a part- of" Engine.

The "kind-of" association is more properly named a generalization-specialization relationship (Gen/Spec for short). Part-of association is called a Whole/Part structure. In the Coad and Yourdon notation for class associations, the Gen/Spec relationship is shown using a semicircle to connect the subclasses to the parent class. The Whole/Part association is shown using a triangle to connect the subclasses to their parent. The notation can be seen in Figure 14-4.

Figure 14-4 shows a base class Physician that has the subclasses Surgeon and Pediatrician. In this case, the subclasses Surgeon and Pediatrician are specializations of the base class Physician. On the right-hand side of Figure 14-4 we have a class Automobile and the subclasses Chassis and Engine. Here the classes Engine and Chassis are parts of the whole, represented by the class Automobile. Therefore, the class association is a Whole/Part structure and the subclasses are "a part-of" the superclass.

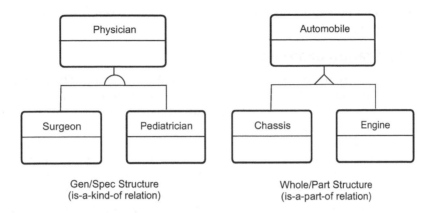

Figure 14-4 *Class Inheritance Notation*

# Polymorphism and Abstract Classes

In object-orientation it is possible to have a class that defines an interface to the system but contains no specific implementation. In other words, it is possible to create a class with dummy methods, that provide no actual processing. All these dummy methods do is define the interface to the class system. When a class contains no actual implementation we say that it is an *abstract class*. Methods that define the interface but contain no implementation are called *abstract methods*.

In Java programming an abstract class is one that has at least one abstract method. The purpose of abstract classes and abstract methods is to achieve greater generalization. The abstract class defines the protocol that must be followed to access the subclasses located lower in the hierarchy. The implementation is left to the lower-level classes. In this manner a dummy method (abstract method) is used as a template for the interface of a concrete method that shares the same name.

The idea of having several methods with the same name is called *polymorphism*. Literally, polymorphism means to have many forms. In object-oriented programming the term polymorphism is used in reference to a class or class system that contains two or more methods that share the same name. Polymorphism is used to implement class abstraction by having several methods with the same name (called polymorphic methods) located in different classes. Usually the method located in the highest class in the hierarchy is an abstract method. The abstract method defines the interface for all its polymorphic relatives, but provides no implementation. In the Coad and Yourdon notation, abstract classes are identified by a dashed rectangle.

## A classification example

Suppose you were to create a software system for a pet shop. The pet shop sold dogs, cats, and birds to the public and had to keep track of the inventory of these animals. An object-oriented approach to the problem could be based on creating an abstract base class called Pet. The notion of a pet class is an abstraction and the class Pet would be implemented as an abstract class. The concrete classes would be named PetDog, PetCat, and PetBird. The Pet class would define the interface for its subclasses. There would be a method called GetName() that returns the name of the individual pet animal. Another method called GetPrice() returns the sale price of the pet, and a method called GetLocation() returns the location in the pet shop where a specific animal can be found. To keep track of pet names, locations, and prices you would need three variables. The resulting system would appear as in Figure 14-5.

In relation to the class diagram in Figure 14-5, note the following:

- The association between the superclass Pet and the subclasses PetDog, PetCat, and PetBird is an is-a-kind-of relationship. The class structure is of type Gen/Spec. The sem-circular connector in the class diagram shows the Gen/Spec association.

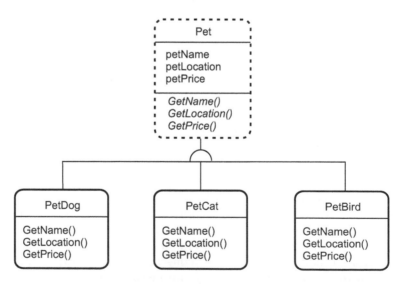

**Figure 14-5** *A Pet Store Class System*

- The class Pet is an abstract class. You can tell that it is an abstract class by the dashed rectangle.

- The methods GetName(), GetLocation(), and GetPrice() are the interface to the system. These methods are polymorphic in all the classes. In the abstract class Pet, the methods GetName(), GetLocation(), and GetPrice() are abstract methods. In a class diagram abstract methods are identified by typing the method names in italics.

- The attributes petName, petLocation, and petPrice are defined in the superclass only. It is not necessary to redefine the attributes in the subclasses.

# Chapter 15

# Object-Oriented Coding

## Working with Classes and Objects

It is now time to put to work your knowledge of object-orientation and your skills in Java programming. So far we have been dealing with small programs that contain a single class. Our programs have used static variables and methods. In fact, we have turned off object orientation and used Java as a semi-procedural language. But the advantages of Java are related to its object-oriented features. At this point you are ready to start developing true object-oriented programs and learning to use the OO features of Java.

## Thinking Objects

A Java program is a collection of classes. In a well-designed and well coded program, these classes interact with each other and provide a reasonable and reusable software environment. A class is a template: an object factory. The class defines the attributes and behavior of its objects. It is used to create objects. You must always keep in mind that the class is a programming construct. Although you define the data types and write methods in a class, the data the methods are contained by the object. In this sense we can say that the class is the cookie cutter, and the object is the cookie.

Because the functionality (methods) and the information (data) is in the object, not in the class, we sometimes say that the object *knows*. It knows the information contained in its data members, and it knows how to perform the operations in its method members. The object is a unit of data and processing. It is for these reasons that we talk about object-oriented programming, not class-oriented programming.

137

The art of object-orientation starts with learning how to think objects. Consider the following Java program:

## On the Web

The source file for the program VirtualDog.java can be found in the Chapter 15 folder at www.crcpress.com.

```java
//*****************************************************************
//    File name: VirtualDog.java
//    Reference: Chapter 15
//*****************************************************************
//
//    Java program to demonstrate a classes and objects
//    Topics:
//        1. Java application with multiple classes
//        2. Object instantiation
//
//    Note:
//        1. Only one class in a file can be public. The public
//           class must have the name of the Java source file.
//        2. The "this" operator refers to the current object.
//        3. Class variables are usually declared with private
//           accesibility in order to preserve encapsulation

//**********************************
//**********************************
//          CLASS Dog
//**********************************
//**********************************
class Dog
{
  // Class variables
  private int dogNum;      // Dog object number
  private String dogName;  // Dog object name

  //***********************
  //     setDogData()
  //***********************
  public void setDogData(int aNum, String aName)
  {
     this.dogNum = aNum;
     this.dogName = aName;
  }

  //***********************
  //     method bark()
  //***********************
  public void bark()
  {
     System.out.println("Arf!, Arf!");
  }
```

```
//***********************
//  method showDogData()
//***********************
public void showDogData()
{
    System.out.println("My name is " + this.dogName);
     System.out.println("I am dog number " + this.dogNum);
}
}


//***********************************
//***********************************
//         CLASS VirtualDog
//***********************************
//***********************************
public class VirtualDog
{
    public static void main(String[] args)
    {
        // Declare objects of class Dog
        Dog dog1 = new Dog();      // First object is named dog1
        Dog dog2 = new Dog();      // Second object is dog2

        // Assign names to Dog objects using setName() method
        dog1.setDogData(1, "Fido");       // dog1 name
        dog2.setDogData(2, "Maverik");    // dog2 name

        // Call methods of the class Dog using objects
        dog1.bark();                      // dog1 barks
        dog1.showDogData();               // dog1 says its name and
                                          // number
        dog2.showDogData();               // ... and so on
        dog2.bark();
    }
}
```

## Object instantiation

The program VirtualDog.java. listed previously, contains two classes. The class VirtualDog is called the *driving class*. Every Java program must contain a driving class. The method main() must be in the driving class. The other class in the program is Dog. Dog is a *helper class*. The class Dog contains two attributes, defined as follows:

```
// Class variables
    private int dogNum;     // Dog object number
    private String dogName; // Dog object name
```

Note that the object attributes are defined at the class level, that is, outside the methods. They are defined with the private qualifier so that they are not visible outside the class. Private attributes preserve encapsulation. When attributes are private, object data must be obtained through methods, not directly. This makes object data safe from unauthorized access. The class also contains the methods setDogData(), bark(), and showDogData().

In order to use a class you must first instantiate an object of the class. In the VirtualDog program, listed previously, the objects are instantiated as follows:

```
// Declare objects of class Dog
    Dog dog1 = new Dog();        // First object is named dog1
    Dog dog2 = new Dog();        // Second object is dog2
```

---

## Programmers note:

An object whose state can be changed externally breaks encapsulation.

---

Each object has:

1. A behavior (defined by its methods)
2. A state (determined by its fields)
3. An identity, which makes it different from all other objects of the same class

In most cases objects have different states, but two objects of the same class are unique and different, even if they have the same state. For example: a GasGauge object encodes the amount of gasoline in a tank. A truck with two tanks may have two GasGauge objects. These objects would be different, even if by chance both of them represented the same number of gallons of gas. In this case their state would be the same, but each object would still have its own identity.

## Field variables and method variables

In relation to their location in the class, Java variables can be of two types. *Field variables* are declared outside the methods, usually before any of the methods. Sometimes we just say "fields" to refer to field variables. The unique property of field variables is that they are accessible to all the methods in the class. Variables declared inside methods are called *local or method variables*. Local variables are visible inside the method that contains them and their lifetime is limited to duration of the method. For this reason local variables cannot be accessed by other methods, or by other classes. This explains why you cannot use access modifiers with local variables.

In the program VirtualDog.java, listed previously, the class Dog contains two data items: one is a variable of type int and another one is a string. Both are declared with the private access modifier in order to preserve encapsulation, as follows:

```
// Class variables
    private int dogNum;      // Dog object number
    private String dogName;  // Dog object name
```

The class Dog provides the method setDogData() that assigns a name and a number to each dog object created from the class. Another method, named showDogData(), returns the name and number of a dog object. Thus, data is encapsulated, since it is only accessible through methods in the Dog class. Client code cannot see or alter these variables. The class data is protected from unauthorized access.

## Object variables and class variables

*Object variables* are declared without the static keywords. The variables dogNum and dogName, listed previously, are object variables. Object variables are associated with the objects of the class. For every object instantiated from a class there is a copy of each of the object variables.

Another type of variable is declared with the static attribute. When a variable is of static type it is related to the class itself, not to the objects. Class variables are used in storing information that relates to all the objects of a class, and not to any object in particular. In the program VirtualDog, listed previously, you could have used a class variable to keep track of the number of dog objects instantiated. The use of class variables is discussed later in this chapter.

# Building Objects

A class is an object factory. To build an object the class uses a special method called a constructor. The constructor method is called whenever an object is created. The constructor has the same name as the class. You can write your own constructors for your classes; however, if you do not code a constructor, Java supplies one for you. The constructor created automatically by Java is sometimes called the default constructor. The only function performed by the default constructor is to set to a known state all object variables and class variables that were not initialized in their declarations. The various variable types are initialized as follows:

1. All numeric variables are set to 0

2. All strings are set to null

3.  All boolean variables are set to false

A unique characteristic of constructors is that they have no return type. Constructors can be public, private, or protected, but most constructors are public. A private constructor does not allow other classes to instantiate objects. Therefore, a class with a private constructor can only have static methods.

---
### Programmers note:
---

You use a private constructor when you want to prevent other classes from instantiating your class, but you still need access to the class' static methods.

---

## The default constructor

The constructor is called when an object of the class is created. For example, in the case of the VirtualDog.java program listed previously, the *default constructor* is called when the objects are created, as in the following statement:

```
// Declare objects of class Dog

   Dog myDog = new Dog();     // First object is named myDog
```

The default constructor creates the object and sets the field variables that were not initialized in their declaration to the default values mentioned previously. In the case of the sample program named VirtualDog.java, listed earlier, the default constructor sets the variable dogNum to zero, and the String dogName to null.

## Overloading the constructor

In general, the word *overloading* refers to using a program element for more than one purpose. For example, the Java + operator is overloaded since it is used to represent both addition and concatenation. When a Java class contains more than one constructor we say that the constructor is overloaded.

Overloaded constructors must follow the rule that each implementation of the constructor have a unique signature.

---

## Programmers note:

---

The signature of a method is its unique name and parameter list.

---

Since all constructors have the same name as the class, the constructors can only be identified by their unique parameter list. Overloaded constructors allow building objects in different ways. Java determines which constructor to use by looking at the object's parameters. Once you define a constructor, no matter its signature, the default constructor is not used in creating objects.

The following program, named PayrollDemo.java, shows the use of overloaded constructors.

---

## On the Web

---

The source file for the PayrollDemo.java program file can be found in the Chapter 15 folder at www.crcpress.com.

```
//******************************************************************
//    File name: PayrollDemo.java
//    Reference: Chapter 15
//******************************************************************
// Topics:
//      1. A class with object and class attributes
//         and object and class methods
//      2. Creating and using constructors
//      3. Polymorphism by overloaded constructors
//******************************************************************


//*********************************************
//*********************************************
//          Employee class
//*********************************************
//*********************************************
class Employee
{
    //*******************************
    //      attributes section
    //*******************************
    // field variables
    private String name = "no name";
    private String address;
    private String ssn = "xxx";
    private int dependants = 1;    // Default for dependants field
    private int empNum;

    // Class attribute (static qualifier)
    private static int empCounter = 0;
```

```
//*********************************
// methods section - constructors
//*********************************
// Fully parameterized constructor for Employee objects
public Employee(String n, String a, String s, int x)
{
    this.name = n;
    this.address = a;
    this.ssn = s;
    this.dependants = x;
    this.empNum = ++empCounter;
}

// Nonparameterized constructor assigns only an employee number
public Employee()
{
    this.empNum = ++empCounter;
}

// Partially parameterized constructor assigns name and
// consecutive employee number
public Employee(String n)
{
    this.name = n;
    this.empNum = ++empCounter;
}

//*********************************
// methods section - other methods
//*********************************
public void showData()
{
    System.out.print("number: " + this.empNum);
    System.out.print("\tname: " + this.name);
    System.out.print("\t\taddress: " + this.address);
    System.out.print("\n\t\tSSN: " + this.ssn);
    System.out.print("\t\tdependants: " + this.dependants +
                     "\n\n");
    System.out.flush();
}

// Class method is used to access a class variable without
// an object reference
public static void showTotal()
{
    System.out.println("Total employees: " + empCounter);
    System.out.println();
}
}
//*******************************************
//*******************************************
//                CLASS PayrollDemo
//*******************************************
//*******************************************
```

```
public class PayrollDemo
{
    public static void main(String[] args)
    {
    // First two objects of Employee class are created using
    // parameterized constructor
    Employee emp1 = new Employee("Jane", "131 Calm Street",
                                "263", 2);
    Employee emp2 = new Employee("Jim", "42 Curve Road", "2
                                6);

    // Third employee object is created with non-parameterized
    // constructor
    Employee emp3 = new Employee();

    // Fourth employee is created with partially parameterized
    // constructor
    Employee emp4 = new Employee("Mary");

    // Display data using an accessor method
    emp1.showData();
    emp2.showData();
    emp3.showData();
    emp4.showData();

    // Display total number of employees using a class method
    Employee.showTotal();
    }
}
```

The class Employee in the PayrollDemo.java program listed above contains three constructors, declared as follows:

```
public Employee(String n, String a, String s, int x)
public Employee()
public Employee(String n)
```

The first constructor has a four-parameter signature. Of these parameters three are strings and one is of type int. The second constructor is parameterless. This constructor overrides the default constructor. The third constructor receives a single parameter, of type string.

---
## Programmers note:
---

The three constructors can coexist in the same class because they have unique signatures.

---

The data elements for the class Employee are declared as follows:

// field variables

```
private String name = "no name";
private String address;
private String ssn = "xxx";
private int dependants = 1;    // Default for dependants field
private int empNum;

// Class attribute (static qualifier)
private static int empCounter = 0;
```

The class contains five fields and one class variable. The field variables are related to the objects of the class. The class variable named empCounter is used to keep track of the total number of objects created. Thus, the class-level variable allows the program to keep track of how many employees are in the payroll and assigns a consecutive number to each new employee. The class variable is associated with the class, not with objects. In this case the class variable keeps track of the consecutive number of the employee objects.

*Chapter 16*

# Using Inheritance

## Inheritance and Data Abstraction

In science, inheritance is a mechanism for organizing knowledge into hierarchies. In object-oriented computer languages, such as Java, inheritance is implemented by means of a class hierarchy in which one class, usually called the derived class, inherits the data members and the functionality of another one, usually called the base class or the superclass. In short, inheritance makes it possible for an object of a subclass to contain the attributes and properties of the superclass. This mechanism makes it easier to develop software by avoiding duplication and improving the organization of the knowledge base. It also makes programs more reliable and easier to extend and to repair. In this chapter we look at class inheritance in Java code and how inheritance promotes a higher level of abstraction.

## Java Inheritance

Inheritance makes it possible to reuse the data members and the processing capabilites of a class. From a programmer's view, the advantages of using class inheritance are that it fosters code reusability and simplifies coding. Java inheritance is achieved by making a class extend another class, for example:

```
class Bird extends Pet
{
   ...
}
```

In this case the subclass is Bird and the superclass is Pet. Bird inherits all the public members of the superclass Pet. But Bird is not limited to the attributes and methods of Pet, since it can have attributes and methods of its own.

Occasionally, you may want to provide clients with a class but you may also want to prevent this class from being extended by inheritance. This is accomplished by using the *final keyword* in the class declaration, as follows:

```
class final Gauge
{
  . . .
)
```

Now no other class can extend Gauge. Another option is to allow a class to be extended but to prevent one or more of its methods from being inherited by the subclasses. This is accomplished by using the final keyword in the method declaration. For example:

```
class Gauge
{
  . . .
public final SetGauge(int neddlePos)
{
```

If now a class extends Gauge, it does not inherit the method Set-Gauge(). However, since SetGauge() is a public method it can be accessible to other classes.

## Extending class functionality

Class inheritance is a powerful mechanism for extending class functionality. This said, you should note that inheritance is used only in cases in which the subclass "is a kind of" the superclass. In Chapter 14 we described this kind a class relationship as a Generalization/Specialization structure, and called it Gen/Spec for short. That is, the subclass is a special case of the superclass. Inheritance is not suitable when the subclass "is a part of" the superclass, which we call a Whole/Part structure.

---
### Programmers note:
---

The keyword super is used in a subclass to refer to a method of the superclass. The super keyword is often used to call constructors of the superclass.

---

Perhaps the principal feature of inheritance is that it allows reusing the data and functionality of a superclass while permitting the subclass to define its own data and methods. If there is an inheritance hierarchy between classes, and a method is called that is not implemented in the subclass, Java will search up the class hierarchy until a method is found in a superclass. A compiler error produced in the method is not found in any of the superclasses.

## Polymorphism

You saw, in Chapter 13, that it is possible to have methods with the same name as long as they have different parameter lists. We used this feature to implement several constructors in the same class. The compiler is able to determine which method is to be used by observing the signature.

The operation of connecting code to a particular method is called the *binding*. Binding can take place when the program compiles (called *static binding*) or when the program executes (called *dynamic binding*).

Polymorphism, on the other hand, means many forms. Two methods with the same name are polymorphic. Overloading generates static polymorphism, since the method to be used can be determined at compile time (static binding). Constructors with different signatures are overloaded, and are bound statically.

In inheritance, two or more methods with the same signature coexist in a class hierarchy. Note that in the case of inheritance it is possible for two methods with identical signatures to be located in the same class hierarchy. This is different from overloading, in which the methods with the same name must have different signatures.

When Java selects between two or more methods with the same signature, located in the same class inheritance structure, we say that the selection takes place by *overriding*. Overriding differs from overloading since in overriding the method linked to the object is dependent on the position of the method in the class hierarchy. Consider three classes named ClassA, ClassB, and ClassC and assume that there are two polymorphic methods named MethodA() and MethodB(). The class diagram is shown in Figure 16-1, on the next page.

In relation to Figure 16-1, several cases of polymorphism should be noted. First, when a call is made to MethodA() which of the two polymorphic implementations is used depends on the object making the call, as follows:

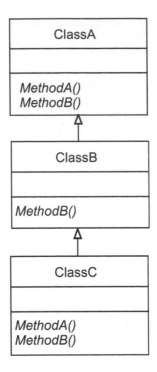

**Figure 16-1** *Polymorphism in Class Inheritance*

1. If the object making the call belongs to ClassA, then the implementation of MethodA() in ClassA is used. In this case inheritance is not applied since ClassA has no superclass and MethodA() is implemented within the class.

2. If an object of ClassB calls MethodA(), then the implementation in ClassA is used. The general rule is that Java searches up the inheritance hierarchy for the closest polymorphic method.

3. If an object of ClassC calls methodA() then MethodA() in ClassC is used. Here again, no inheritance is applied since the method is implemented in the object making the call.

## Modeling with inheritance

Let's start with a simple programming problem: suppose that you were required to write an application that calculates the payroll for the salaried employees of a company. In addition, the company occasionally employs part-time help which is paid by the hour. At the same time, much of the data and many of the calculations that relate to regular employees also apply to part-time employees. Since the part-time employees are a kind-of employee, we could conceivably model the system using class inheritance. In this case you could create a superclass called Employee, and a sub class named PartTimer. PartTimer would inherit all the methods of Employee and implement some of its own. The class diagram is shown in Figure 16-2.

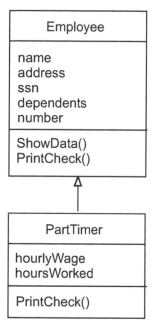

**Figure 16-2** *A Case of Class Inheritance*

In the diagram in Figure 16-2, assume that the method PrintCheck() in the class PartTimer has a different parameter list than PrintCheck() in the class Employee. This is consistent with a real-world situation in which the data required for a part-timer is typically different from the data for a salaried employee. The result of this inheritance scheme is that if an object of the PartTimer class calls the method ShowData(), then the method in Employee is used. However, if a PartTimer object calls the method PrintCheck() then its own implementation is used and not the one in the Employee class. The program named SimpleInherit.java, listed next, shows simple inheritance and method selection by overriding.

## On the Web

The source file for the program SimpleInherit.java can be found in the Chapter 16 folder at www.crcpress.com.

```java
//********************************************************************
//    File name: SimpleInherit.java
//    Reference: Chapter 16
//********************************************************************
// Topics:
//      1. Simple inheritance
//      2. Polymorphism by method overriding
//********************************************************************
//********************************************************************


//*******************************************
//*******************************************
//            Employee class
//*******************************************
//*******************************************
class Employee
{
  //********************************
  //       attributes section
  //********************************
  // Instance fields
  private String name;
  private String address;
  private String ssn;
  private int dependants;
  private int number;

  // Class attribute (note the static qualifier)
  private static int consecNum = 0;

  //********************************
  // methods section - constructors
  //********************************
  // Fully parameterized constructor for Employee objects
  public Employee(String n, String a, String s, int x)
  {
     this.name = n;
     this.address = a;
     this.ssn = s;
     this.dependants = x;
     this.number = ++consecNum; // class attribute is accessed
                                // from an object method
  }

  public void showData()
  {
      System.out.print("number: " + this.number);
     System.out.print("\tname: " + this.name);
     System.out.print("\t\taddress: " + this.address);
     System.out.print("\n\t\tSSN: " + this.ssn);
     System.out.print("\t\tdependants: " + this.dependants +
                      "\n\n");
     System.out.flush();
  }
```

```
    public void printCheck()
  {
     System.out.println("Printing check for regular employee");
  }
}
//*******************************************
//*******************************************
//        CLASS PartTimer
//*******************************************
//*******************************************
class PartTimer extends Employee
{
  //********************************
  //       attributes section
  //********************************
  private double hourlyWage;
  private int hoursWorked;

  //********************************
  //        methods section
  //********************************
  // Constructor
  public PartTimer(String n, String a, String s,
                   int x, double wage, int hours)
  {
    // Call the constructor in the superclass
    super(n, a, s, x);
    // Initialize specific fields
    this.hourlyWage = wage;
    this.hoursWorked = hours;
  }

  public void printCheck()
  {
     System.out.println("Printing check for part-timer");
  }
 }

//*******************************************
//*******************************************
//          Driving class
//*******************************************
//*******************************************
public class SimpleInherit
{

    public static void main(String[] args)
    {
    // First two objects of Employee class are created using the
    // parameterized constructor
    Employee emp1 = new Employee("Jane", "131 Calm Street",
                                 "263", 2);
    Employee emp2 = new Employee("Jim", "42 Curve Road",
```

```
                                    "261", 6);

        // Following object is of class PartTimer
        PartTimer emp3 =
            new PartTimer ("Jack", "11 Bumpy St.", "333",
                            8, 11.00, 40);

        // Display data using polymorphic methods
        emp1.showData();      // object of class Employee
        emp2.showData();      // object of class Employee
        emp3.showData();      // object of class PartTimer
        emp2.printCheck();    // check for object of Employee

         // An object of the subclass uses its own polymorphic method
        emp3.printCheck();

    }
}
```

Figure 16-3 is a screen snapshot of the SimpleInherit program.

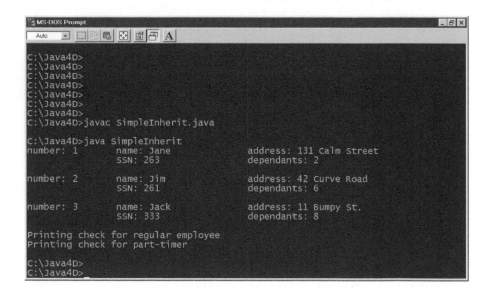

**Figure 16-3** *Screen Snapshot of the SimpleInherit Program*

Some interesting features of the program SimpleInherit.java should be noted:

- The class PartTimer contains a constructor that calls the constructor in the superclass, then proceeds to initialize the fields that are unique to the subclass. In this manner the superclass constructor is reused and supplemented.

- When a PartTimer object is built, the fields of the superclass are used for storing PartTimer data. This is possible even though the fields of Employee are defined with the private qualifier. However, the data defined in the Employee class remains encapsulated and is not directly visible to the class PartTimer. Thus, a PartTimer object can not access some of its own data, except by using the methods of the Employee class.

- The method printCheck() is polymorphic. In this example, since printCheck() has the same signature in the superclass and the subclass, method selection (binding) is based on the object making the call.

Note that this code provides only a stub for the printCheck() methods.

# Abstraction and Inheritance

In Java it is possible to have a method that performs no processing operations, such a method is called an *abstract method*. The reason for this apparent absurdity is that an abstract method serves to define the signature that must be used by all polymorphic methods in extended classes. Thus, an abstract method defines an interface in the base class, while leaving the implementation to the subclasses.

An abstract class is one that contains one or more abstract methods. You create an abstract class by including the abstract keyword in the class declaration statement. For example:

```
abstract class Dog
{
...
```

An abstract class cannot be instantiated but it can be extended, that it, you cannot create an object of an abstract class but other classes can inherit from it. Abstract classes can have concrete data and methods, which perform normally.

## Programming with abstract classes

Suppose that you were commissioned to develop a program for operating a pet shop which sells dogs, cats, and birds to the public. The owner needs to identify each animal that is available and keep track of its location and sale price. Specifically, the owner also wants to keep track of each dog and cat breed, and of the color of each bird. There is a plan to add other pet species at a future date, so the system should be easily expandable. After analyzing the software requirement you propose the following data elements:

1. Each pet is given a name, which is remembered in a string variable.

2. Each pet has a sale price, stored in a variable of type double.

3. A variable of type int keeps track of the location of each pet in the store. The pet store showroom is location 1, the backroom is location 2, and the store's basement is location 3.

4. There is also species-specific data that must be remembered: the breed of each dog, the breed of each cat, and the color of each bird.

Since a dog is a kind of a pet, and so is a cat and a bird, you can use inheritance to model the pet store system. A base class named Pet could be used to define the data elements that are common to all three pet species. Since the notion of a pet is an abstraction, the class Pet is defined as an abstract class. The Pet class also defines the interface for the methods that are implemented in the subclasses. The class diagram for the pet store is shown in Figure 16-4.

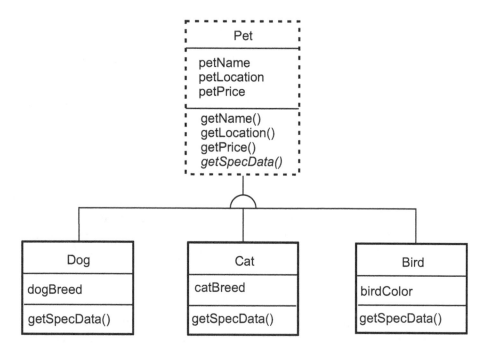

**Figure 16-4** *Class Diagram for the Pet Store System*

The implementation of the PetStore system is based on the class diagram in Figure 16-4. The class Pet holds variables for the name, location, and price of all pets in the store. It also contains three concrete methods to display the name, location, and price of each pet object. In order to preserve encapsulation, the accessor methods for the class-level attributes must be in the superclass. Recall that, with or without inheritance, private data is not visible outside the class.

In addition, the superclass Pet contains an abstract method named getSpecData(). The getSpecData() method is implemented in each of the subclasses. In the Dog class, getSpecData() displays the dogBreed. In the Cat class, getSpecData() displays the cat name. In the Bird class, getSpecData() displays the bird color. The following code listing is for the PetStore program.

## On the Web

The program PetStore is found in the Chapter 16 folder at www.crcpress.com.

```
//******************************************************************
//******************************************************************
// Program: PetStore
// Reference: Chapter 16
// Topics:
//      1. Using inheritance and abstract classes
//******************************************************************
//******************************************************************

//*********************************************
//*********************************************
//            CLASS Pet
//*********************************************
//*********************************************
abstract class Pet
{
    //******************************
    //      attributes section
    //******************************
    // Instance fields
       private String petName;
       private int petLocation;
         private double petPrice;

    //******************************
    //        methods section
    //******************************
    // Constructor.
    // Defines the initial pet state
```

```
   public Pet(String name, int location, double price)
   {
      this.petName = name;
      this.petLocation = location;
       this.petPrice = price;
   }

   // Concrete methods in the base class
   public void getName()
   {
      System.out.println ("Pet name: " + this.petName);
       return;
   }
   public void getLocation()
   {
      System.out.println("Pet location: " + this.petLocation);
       return;
   }
   public void getPrice()
   {
      System.out.println("Pet price: " + this.petPrice);
       return;
   }

   // Abstract method
   public abstract void getSpecData();
j}

//***********************************
//        concrete classes
//***********************************
class Dog extends Pet
{
   // Data specific for the Dog class
   String dogBreed;
   int dogAge;

   // Constructor for the Dog class uses the constructor
   // if the superclass
   public Dog(String name, int loc, double price, String race)
   {
   // Call the constructor in Pet
   super(name, loc, price);
   // Fill-in the dog-specific data
   this.dogBreed = race;
   }

   // Concrete methods in subclass
   public void getSpecData()
   {
     System.out.println("Dog race :" + this.dogBreed);
      return;
   }
}
```

```
class Cat extends Pet
{
  // Data specific for the Cat class
  String catBreed;

  public Cat(String name, int loc, double price, String race)
  {
  // Call the constructor in Pet
  super(name, loc, price);
  // Fill-in the cat-specific data
  this.catBreed = race;
  }

  // Concrete methods in subclass
  public void getSpecData()
  {
    System.out.println("Cat race: " + this.catBreed);
     return;
  }
}

class Bird extends Pet
{
  // Data specific for the Cat class
  String birdColor;

  public Bird(String name, int loc, double price, String color)
  {
  // Call the constructor in Pet
  super(name, loc, price);
  // Fill-in the cat-specific data
  this.birdColor = color;
  }

  // Concrete methods in subclass
  public void getSpecData()
  {
    System.out.println("Bird color: " + this.birdColor);
     return;
  }
}

//*****************************************
//*****************************************
//              Driving class
//*****************************************
//*****************************************
public class PetStore
{

    //****************************
    //          methods
    //****************************
```

```
public static void main(String[] args)
{

// Create two objects of class Dog
Dog dog1 = new Dog("Fido",2, 12.95,"Spaniel");
Dog dog2 = new Dog("Atila",3, 20.75,"Hound");

 // Create a Cat and a Bird object
 Cat cat1 = new Cat("Fifo", 3, 15.95, "Siamese");
 Bird bird1 = new Bird("Tweety", 1, 2.55, "Yellow");

 // Display pet data using superclass and subclass
 // methods
 dog1.getName();       // Method in superclass
 dog2.getName();       // Methods in superclass
 dog2.getLocation();
 dog2.getSpecData(); // Method in subclass
 bird1.getName();
 bird1.getSpecData();
 }
}
```

Do not assume that an abstract class should only have abstract methods. The general rule is to have as much functionality as possible in the superclass, whether or not it is an abstract class. Instance fields and non-abstract methods should all be in the superclass. Operations that cannot be implemented in the superclass are the only ones that should be in the subclasses. This approach is the one used in the PetStore program listed previously.

One of the advantages of using inheritance is greater code reusability. Suppose that the pet store owner decided to expand the store line to include pet lizards. In this case the functionality for keeping track of the name, location, and price of each pet lizard is already in place. The PetStore program could be easily modified by implementing a new class called Lizard, that extends Pet. Only the data and operations that are specific for each pet lizard would have to be implemented in the new class.

# Chapter 17

# Object Composition

## An Alternative to Inheritance

Class inheritance is a powerful mechanism for reusing code, minimizing data redundancy, and improving the organization of an object-oriented system. However, inheritance is not always suitable. You saw that inheritance is applied when classes are in a relationship in which the subclass "is a kind of" the superclass. But this is not always the case. Often we have class relationships in which the subclass is "a part of" the superclass. Attempting to apply inheritance in whole/part class relationships is an artificial and unnatural solution. Fortunately, there is a simple alternative to inheritance as a way of reusing class functionality, called *object composition*. In inheritance, the subclass extends the functionality of a superclass. In object composition a class reuses functionality simply by declaring and holding an object of the class it wants to reuse. In object composition, reusability is accomplished in a simpler manner.

## Inheritance Drawbacks

One of the problems with inheritance can be simply stated: *inheritance breaks encapsulation*. In the PetStore program, developed in Chapter 16, the subclasses Dog, Cat, and Bird use the constructor of the superclass Pet as well as some of its public methods. The data for the objects of the class Dog, Cat, and Bird is centralized in the superclass Pet and the processing operations are effectively reused in the superclass methods getName(), getLocation(), and getPrice(). But for this to happen, the subclasses must have knowledge of the structure of the superclass. A Dog object, a client object of the Pet class, needs to know that Pet remembers name, location, and price; even perhaps the type of variables where this data is stored. Although the dog object has no direct access to the private data members of the

161

superclass, it needs to know about this data. This knowledge of the subclass about the internals of the private members of the superclass breaks encapsulation.

A second possible problem with inheritance is that the subclasses sometimes loose control of their own data. In the case of the PetStore example developed in Chapter 16, the name, location, and price of a dog, cat, or bird object are stored in the superclass Pet. The subclasses must rely entirely on the methods of the superclass for accessing and changing this data. If the class Pet does not provide a method for changing a pet's name, then code would be unable to assign a new name to objects of Dog, Cat, and Bird. Since the pet name data is stored in the superclass, a change-of-name method cannot be simply implemented in a subclass. In summary, by using inheritance, the subclass loses some degree of control over its own objects.

# Reusing Class Functionality

Application designers and programmers of object-oriented systems sometimes become so entangled in the mechanisms of inheritance that they forget simple options. In Java, a class can reuse the public members of another class simply by instantiating an object of the class to be reused. When a class uses the methods of another one by means of an object we say that reusability is achieved through *object composition*.

Object composition is based on the following simple facts of the Java language:

1.  A class can access the public members of another class.

2.  A class can instantiate an object of another class.

3.  An object can be a member of a class.

In describing object composition we use the terms *client* and *host class*. The client class is the one that reuses the functionality and the host class is the one that contains the functionality to be reused.

## The new mind set

The inheritance model requires that we think of a class as being a kind-of another one. In object composition the relationship between classes is unimportant. All we need to know is that a host class is located within the scope of the client class and that the host contains public members that the client class wants to access.

The reuse mechanism is quite simple and straightforward, but designing systems based on object composition requires a new way of thinking. Suppose there is a system that contains a class named Rectangle, and that the Rectangle class contains a public method named area() that calculates the area of a rectangular figure. Now assume that you need to create a class named Window, and that the objects of Window are rectangular in shape. If an object of Window needed to calculate its area it could consider using the method area() in rectangle.

One possible approach is through inheritance; that is, you could make Window extend Rectangle. Since Rectangle is the superclass and Window the subclass, an object of Window can access the area() method in rectangle. The problem with this inheritance-based approach to class reuse is that it assumes that a Window "is a kind-of" a Rectangle. But if a Window object can also be circular or triangular in shape, then it is not accurate to say that a Window is a kind-of a Rectangle.

In reality, all you need to do is access the method area() in Rectangle, for which you do not need an inheritance relationship. The simple alternative is for Window to create an object of the Rectangle class and to use this object to access the method area(). Thus, we can say that Window "uses" Rectangle which, in this case, is a more accurate model of the class relationship and a simple approach to reusability.

## Thinking object composition

With this new model in mind you can rethink the PetStore program developed in Chapter 16. Let's restate the case:

You are commissioned to develop a program for operating a pet shop which sells dogs, cats, and birds to the public. The owner needs to identify each animal that is available and keep track of its location and sale price. Specifically, the owner also wants to keep track of each dog and cat breed and of the color of each bird. There is a plan to add other pet species at a future date, so the system should be easily expandable. After analyzing the software requirement you propose the following data elements:

1. Each pet is given a name, which is remembered in a string variable.

2. Each pet has a sale price, stored in a variable of type double.

3. A variable of type int keeps track of the location of each pet in the store.

4. There is also species-specific data that must be remembered: the breed of each dog, the breed of each cat, and the color of each bird.

Instead of thinking inheritance, we can consider the problem in simpler terms. First we note that there are operations that are the same for dogs, cats, and birds. To avoid duplication and wasted effort we create a class, called Pet, to handle these common operations. Second, the functions that are specific to dogs, cats, and birds are implemented in the respective classes. Third, the field data for the objects is located in the client classes. The result is that clients have total control over their objects and can expand their functionality as needed. The class diagram of Figure 16-4 is modified accordingly, as shown in Figure 17-1.

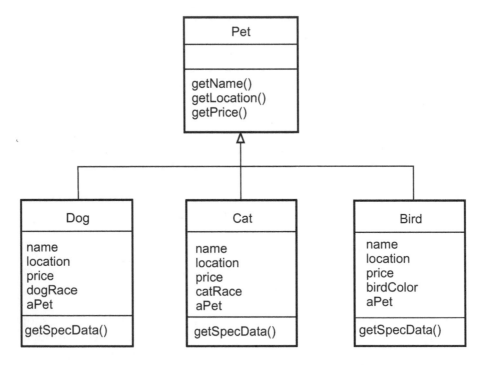

**Figure 17-1** *Alternative Class Diagram for the PetStore System*

Comparing the inheritance-based class diagram in Figure 16-4 with the one in Figure 17-1, you will notice the following differences:

• The arrow that connects the classes Dog, Cat, and Bird with the class Pet does not depict an inheritance relationship. The absence of the semicircle symbol indicates that the classes are not in a "is a kind-of" relationship.

• Since there is no inheritance, the class Pet is no longer an abstract class nor is the method getSpecData() defined in the class Pet.

- The field variables are now defined in the client classes Dog, Cat, and Bird. This does not mean that more data is stored by the code, since each object has its own state in either case.

- The client classes Dog, Cat, and Bird contain an object of the host class Pet. The object is named aPet in all the client classes.

The code must also be changed to reflect the new model. The program PetStore2, listed below, shows the new version. To save space we have implemented only the classes Pet and Dog in the PetStore2 program.

## On the Web

The source file for the program PetStore2.java can be found in the Chapter 17 folder at www.crcpress.com.

```java
//****************************************************************
//****************************************************************
// Program: PetStore2
// Reference: Chapter 17
// Topics:
//      1. Class reuse through object composition
//****************************************************************
//****************************************************************
//
//*******************************************
//*******************************************
//            CLASS Pet
//*******************************************
//*******************************************
class Pet
{
   // Concrete methods in the base class
   public void getName(String aName)
   {
      System.out.println ("Pet name: " + aName);
       return;
   }
   public void getLocation(int aLocation)
   {
      System.out.println("Pet location: " + aLocation);
       return;
   }
   public void getPrice(double aPrice)
   {
      System.out.println("Pet price: " + aPrice);
       return;
   }
}

//***********************************
```

```
//              CLASS Dog
//**********************************
class Dog
{
  // Data specific for the Dog class
  private String dogName;
  private int dogLocation;
  private double dogPrice;
  private String dogBreed;
  Pet aPet = new Pet();

  // Constructor for the Dog class
  public Dog(String name, int loc, double price, String race)
  {
  this.dogName = name;
  this.dogLocation = loc;
  this.dogPrice = price;
  this.dogBreed = race;
  }
  // Overloaded methods in the Dog class
  public void getName()
  {
     aPet.getName(this.dogName);
      return;
  }

  public void getLocation()
  {
     aPet.getLocation(this.dogLocation);
      return;
  }
  public void getPrice()
  {
     aPet.getPrice(this.dogPrice);
      return;
  }

  public void getSpecData()
  {
    System.out.println("Dog breed :" + this.dogBreed);
     return;
  }
}

//*******************************************
//*******************************************
//              Driving class
//*******************************************
//*******************************************
public class PetStore2
{

   //****************************
   //           methods
```

```
//*****************************
public static void main(String[] args)
{
// Create two objects of class Dog
Dog dog1 = new Dog("Fido",2, 12.95,"Spaniel");
Dog dog2 = new Dog("Atila",3, 20.75,"Hound");

// Display pet data using host class and client class
// methods
dog1.getName();      // Method in host class
dog2.getName();      // Method in host class
dog2.getLocation();
dog2.getSpecData(); // Method in client class
  }
}
```

## Aggregation

In the program PetStore2, listed previously, the class Dog is able to access the methods of the class Pet through an object of the class pet called aPet. The object is created in the following statement:

```
Pet aPet = new Pet();
```

In a sense the object aPet is a dummy object, since it serves merely to access methods in the host class. In cases like this we say that the relationship between the client and the host class is one of aggregation. In many of the other sample programs listed previously in this book, the driving class creates objects of other classes in order to access their methods. Aggregation is the simplest and most direct way of accessing the public members of another class.

The simplicity and directness of *aggregation associations* does not make it any less valuable. In many cases aggregation provides an alternative to class inheritance avoiding some of the pitfalls of the more complex model. Aggregation is often depicted in class diagrams by means of an arrow pointing from the client class to the host, as shown in Figure 17-2.

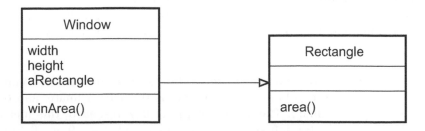

**Figure 17-2** *Modeling Aggregation*

# Objects as Parameters

In Chapter 12 you saw that any primitive variable can be passed as a argument to a method: an int, a double, a boolean, and so on. You also saw that a string, which is an object, can also be passed as an argument. The fact is that objects of any class can be passed as arguments. As in the case of primitive data types, the method that receives the object parameter can access it using an alias.

In the case of objects passed as parameters, there is only one copy of the object. This means that any change on the object by the method modifies this single copy and affects the original object. In other words, while primitive data types are always passed by value, objects are passed by reference.

---

## Incidentally...

---

Java classes are abstract data types and follow many of the rules of the primitive types that are part of the language. An object, which can be viewed as a variable of an abstract data type, is subject to similar rules as variables of primitive data types.

---

By the same token, a method can return an object. When the method that returns an object is declared, the declaration specifies the class of the object as a return type. Typically, the returned object is created in the method using the new operator. Methods that receive objects as parameters or that return objects are often of static type.

Consider the following case: a pixel (short for picture element) is the smallest addressable graphic unit on the video display. You can visualize a pixel as a small colored dot. The number of horizontal and vertical pixels that can be displayed determines the screen resolution. Thus, we speak of a video system with a resolution of 640-by-480 pixels when there are 640 individual dots in each screen row, and a total of 480 rows on the entire screen.

The screen location of a pixel is defined in terms of the screen column and row. Usually the column is designated as the $x$-coordinate, and the row is the $y$-coordinate. The screen mapping is zero-based; this means that the pixel at the top-left screen corner is located at $x = 0$, $y = 0$. Similarly, the pixel located at column 120 and row 62 is at coordinates $x = 120$, $y = 62$.

Suppose you were asked to write a Java class that defined the location of pixel objects and that this class is to have methods to display the location of a pixel and to calculate the mid-position between two pixels. One possible option in this case is that the method to calculate the mid-point between two pixels could receive pixel objects as parameters. The class can be coded as follows:

```
class Pixel
{
    // Pixel location attributes
    private int x;          // x coordinate
    private int y;          // y coordinate

    // Constructor
    public Pixel(int pixX, int pixY)
    {
        this.x = pixX;
        this.y = pixY;
    }

    // Method to calculate the mid point between two pixels
    public static Pixel midPix(Pixel p1, Pixel p2)
    {
    int midX = (p1.x/2) + (p2.x/2);
    int midY = (p1.y/2) + (p2.y/2);
    Pixel midOne = new Pixel(midX, midY);
    return midOne;
    }
    // Display the address of a pixel
    public void pixLocation()
    {
        System.out.print("Pixel x : " + this.x + "   ");
        System.out.print("Pixel y : " + this.y + "\n\n");
        System.out.flush();
    }
}
```

Note that the method midPixel() receives two pixel objects as parameters. midPixel() returns the result in a pixel object instantiated in the class. The objects passed as parameters are known under the aliases p1 and p2. The method uses the $x$ and $y$ coordinates of p1 and p2 to calculate the mid point. The program Pixels.java, listed below, demonstrates the processing of objects passed and returned to methods.

## On the Web

The source file for the program Pixels.java can be found in the Chapter 17 folder at www.crcpress.com.

```
//********************************************************
//********************************************************
// Program: Pixels
// Reference: Chapter 17
// Topics:
//      1. Objects passed as an arguments
//      2. Methods that return objects
//********************************************************
//********************************************************


//*******************************************
//              Pixel class
//*******************************************
class Pixel
{
   // Pixel location attributes
   private int x;          // x coordinate
   private int y;          // y coordinate

   // Constructor
   public Pixel(int pixX, int pixY)
   {
     this.x = pixX;
     this.y = pixY;
   }

   // Method to calculate the mid point between two pixels
   public static Pixel midPix(Pixel p1, Pixel p2)
   {
   int midX = (p1.x/2) + (p2.x/2);
   int midY = (p1.y/2) + (p2.y/2);
   Pixel midOne = new Pixel(midX, midY);
   return midOne;
   }

   // Display the address of a pixel
   public void pixLocation()
   {
     System.out.print("Pixel x : " + this.x + "   ");
     System.out.print("Pixel y : " + this.y + "\n\n");
     System.out.flush();
   }
}

//*******************************************
//*******************************************
//              Driving class
//*******************************************
//*******************************************
//
public class Pixels
{

    public static void main(String[] args)
```

```
    {
    // Create objects of the class Pixel
    Pixel pix1 = new Pixel(10, 50);
    Pixel pix2 = new Pixel(90, 200);

    // Since the method midPix is static, it is called with
    // a class reference
    Pixel pix3 = Pixel.midPix(pix1, pix2);

    // Display location of all three Pixel objects
    pix1.pixLocation();
    pix2.pixLocation();
    pix3.pixLocation();
    }
}
```

# Acquaintance Associations

We started this discussion considering the case of a class that contains an object of another class, which is called an aggregation relationship. However, in the program PixelOps.java, we see a class that receives as a parameter the object that it uses to access the methods of another one. Since in this case the object is not contained in the class, we speak of a case of object composition by *acquaintance*. In the acquaintance relationship the binding is looser than in object composition, since in the case of acquaintance the object may not be defined until runtime.

## Incidentally...

It is this looser binding that makes it possible to use acquaintance to implement dynamic binding.

Suppose an application has access to two methods to calculate areas. Both methods are named Area(). One Area() method, located in a class named Rectangle, calculates the area of a rectangular figure. Another Area() method is located in a class named Circle and calculates the area of a circular figure. Now suppose that we are coding a class named Window, which can be circular or rectangular in shape, and we wish to use the area-calculating methods in the classes Rectangle and Circle. One possible approach is to code two methods named WinArea() in the class Window. One method receives a Rectangle object as a parameter and the other one a Circle object. Since the WinArea() methods have different signatures they are not polymorphic. Which method is used depends on the object received as a parameter. The class diagram in Figure 17-3 shows the class structure in this example.

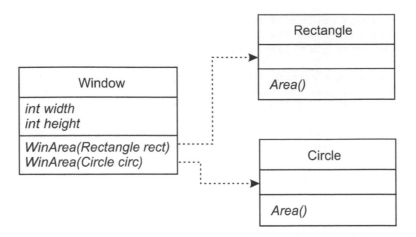

**Figure 17-3** *Acquaintance Association*

## Programmers note:

In order to distinguish object composition by aggregation and by acquaintance in a class diagram, we use a solid line to represent aggregation and a dashed line for acquaintance, as in Figure 17-3.

The following program, named Acquaintance.java, implements the class diagram in Figure 14-2.

## On the Web

The source file for the program Acquaintance.java can be found in the Chapter 17 folder at www.crcpress.com.

```
//************************************************************
//************************************************************
// Program: Acquaintance
// Reference: Chapter 17
// Topics:
//      1. The acquaintance relationship
//************************************************************
//************************************************************

//*****************************************
//            Rectangle class
//*****************************************
class Rectangle
{
  // Method Area()
```

```
  public double Area(int x, int y)
  {
    return (x * y);
  }
}

//*******************************************
//              Circle class
//*******************************************
class Circle
{
  // Method Area()
  public double Area(int x, int y)
  {
    return (3.1415 * (x * x));
  }
}

//*******************************************
//              Window class
//*******************************************
class Window
{
  // Attributes in Window class
  private int width;
  private int height;

  // Constructor for Window
  public Window(int w, int h)
  {
    this.width = w;
    this.height = h;
  }

  // First method WinArea()
  public void WinArea(Rectangle rect)
  {
    double thisArea;
    thisArea = rect.Area(this.width, this.height);
    System.out.println("Area of this Window is: " + thisArea);
  }

  // Second method WinArea()
  public void WinArea(Circle circ)
  {
    double thisArea;
    thisArea = circ.Area(this.width, this.height);
    System.out.println("Area of this Window is: " + thisArea);
  }
}

//*******************************************
//*******************************************
//              Driving class
```

```
//*******************************************
//*******************************************
public class Acquaintance
{

    public static void main(String[] args)
    {
    // Create objects of the class Window
    Window win1 = new Window(10, 20);
    Window win2 = new Window(20, 40);

    // Create objects passed as arguments
    Rectangle aRect = new Rectangle();
    Circle aCirc = new Circle();

    win1.WinArea(aRect);
    win2.WinArea(aCirc);
    }
}
```

# Combining Inheritance and Composition

An object is an instance of a class and a class is a collection of data and methods that work as a unit. The new operator is used in Java in order to create an object from a class. We have also seen that a class can be defined as an abstract data type. Since it is possible to create an array of any primitive data type, it is also possible to create an array of an ADT.

## Arrays of objects

When we create an array using a class, the result is an array of objects of the class. For example, if there is a class named Employee, we create an array of Employee objects the same way that we create an array of int.

```
int[] intArray = new int[14];
Employee[] empArray = new Employee[10];
```

After the array of type Employee has been created, we can store 10 objects of the class Employee in it. An interesting variation on arrays of objects is that we can store objects of a subclass in an array of a superclass. In this manner, if the class HourlyEmployee extends Employee, and emp4 is an object of the subclass, then we can code:

```
empArray[9] = emp4;
```

Note that the reverse is not true: an array of a subclass cannot store elements of its superclass, except by typecasting.

# Dynamic Binding

Arrays can store objects of different types, that is, of the base class and of any of its subclasses. This creates the possibility of defining an array of objects of a superclass and then filling the array at runtime with objects of any class in the inheritance hierarchy. Since the objects are created when the program runs, it is clear that the binding between the object and the method takes place at runtime, which is a case of true polymorphism.

The program named ObjectArray.java, listed below, uses the classes Employee and HourlyEmployee to demonstrate dynamic binding with an array of objects. During program execution the user selects an object of either class, which is then inserted in the object array. The binding is dynamic since the object is not known until the program runs.

## On the Web

The source file for the program ObjectArray.java can be found in the Chapter 17 folder at www.crcpress.com.

```
//*************************************************************
// Program: ObjectArray
// Reference: Chapter 17
// Topics:
//      1. Creating and using an array of objects
//      2. Creating an object at runtime
//      3. Demonstrates dynamic binding (runtime polymorphism)
//
//    Requires:
//        1. Keyin class in the current directory
//*************************************************************

//*****************************************
//*****************************************
//            Employee class
//*****************************************
//*****************************************
class Employee
{
    //*******************************
    //       attributes section
    //*******************************
    // Instance fields
    private String name;
    private String address;
    private String ssn;
    private int dependents;
    private int empNum;
    // Class attribute (note the static qualifier)
```

```
   private static int consecNum = 0;

   //********************************
   // methods section - constructors
   //********************************
   // Fully parameterized constructor for Employee objects
   public Employee(String n, String a, String s, int x)
   {
      this.name = n;
      this.address = a;
      this.ssn = s;
      this.dependents = x;
      this.empNum = ++consecNum; // class attribute is accessed
                                 // from an object method
   }

   public void showData()
   {
      System.out.print("number: " + this.empNum);
      System.out.print("\tname: " + this.name);
      System.out.print("\t\taddress: " + this.address);
      System.out.print("\n\t\tSSN: " + this.ssn);
      System.out.print("\t\tdependents: " + this.dependents +
                       "\n\n");
      System.out.flush();
   }
} // end of class Employee

class HourlyEmployee extends Employee
{
   //********************************
   //        attributes section
   //********************************
   private double hourlyWage;
   private int hoursWorked;

   //********************************
   //          methods section
   //********************************
   // Constructor
   public HourlyEmployee(String n, String a, String s, int x,
                         double wage, int hours)
   {
      // Call the constructor in the superclass
      super(n, a, s, x);
      // Initialize specific fields
      this.hourlyWage = wage;
      this.hoursWorked = hours;
   }

   public void showData()
   {
      super.showData();
      System.out.print("wage: " + this.hourlyWage);
```

```
      System.out.print("\thours: " + this.hoursWorked + "\n\n");

  }
} // End of class HourlyEmployee

//*********************************************
//*********************************************
//              Driving class
//*********************************************
//*********************************************
public class ObjectArray
{
    //*****************************
    //          data
    //*****************************
    // Define an array of type Employee with 4 elements
    static Employee[] empArray = new Employee[4];

    static int objType;      // Object type

    //*****************************
    //          methods
    //*****************************
    public static void main(String[] args)
    {
    // Create two objects of Employee class
    Employee emp1 = new Employee("Jane", "131 Calm Street",
                                  "263", 2);
    Employee emp2 = new Employee("Jim", "42 Curve Road",
                                  "261", 6);

    // Create an object of the class HourlyEmployee
    HourlyEmployee emp3 =
        new HourlyEmployee ("Jack", "11 Bumpy St.", "333",
                            8, 11.00, 40);

    // Fill the array of objects of type Employee with objects of
    // the superclass and the subclass.
    empArray[0] = emp1;
    empArray[1] = emp2;
    empArray[2] = emp3;    // This is an object of the subclass

    // The next object is entered from the keyboard.
    // The user first selects the object's class
     objType = Keyin.inInt("Type 0 for superclass or 1 for " +
                            "subclass: ");

     // Insert object in array according to user's input
    if(objType == 0)
        empArray[3] = new Employee("Lori", "222 Dumb Street",
                                    "333", 7);
    else
        empArray[3] = new HourlyEmployee ("Joe", "11 End St.",
                                           "999", 8, 11.00, 40);
```

```
   // Use runtime polymorphism with the showData() method
   empArray[0].showData();      // Object is of class Employee
   empArray[1].showData();      // So is this one
   empArray[2].showData();       // Object of subclass
   // The following object is either of the class HourlyEmployee
   // or of the class Employee, according to the user's input
   empArray[3].showData();
   }
}
```

# Chapter 18

# I/O Programming

## Java Input and Output

Compared to other programming languages, Java has little built-in support for input and output operations. This is not due to deficiencies in the language's design, or to omissions of implementation, but because Java is based on a different model. For example, C and C++ assume that the computer system interface consists of a text-based console and a keyboard with characters in a western European alphabet. Java, on the other hand, makes no assumption about input characters or devices and contains minimal support for a text-based console device and a command-line interface. The result of this design is that the application must provide its own input and output routines, often not a trivial task.

## Obtaining and Transmitting Data

The two limitations most often mentioned regarding Java input and output functions relate to the difficulty in obtaining alphanumeric data from the keyboard and in formatting output to the console device. So far you have been using the Keyin class to obtain keyboard input. In this session we explore Java input and develop the routines for obtaining alphanumeric data from the keyboard, including the Keyin class.

Keyboard processing functions that are common in other languages do not exist in Java. Most notably missing are functions to implement a live keyboard since there is no Java primitive to detect a single, raw keystroke. The same can be said about alphanumeric output formatting operations, also unavailable in Java.

179

## Character data

I/O usually relates to text, and text consists of characters. Since data is stored in computer memory as binary values, characters are represented by a conventional numeric encoding. In Chapter 3, you saw that the ASCII encoding the letter A is mapped to the number 65, the letter B to the number 66, the space to the number 32, and the digit 1 to the number 49 (see Figure 3-3).

Code must keep track of whether a stored value represents a binary number, a portion of a binary number, or an alphanumeric character. Some I/O devices are designed to assume that data always represents some specific character encoding. For example, when we send the value 66 to the console device, it knows to look up a bitmap for the letter B and displays it on the screen.

For many years computer technology assumed that character data consisted of the ten decimal digits, the upper- and lower-case letters of the English alphabet, and a few dozen additional symbols such as punctuation marks. Some systems later added a few other characters that were necessary in the western European languages and in mathematical expressions. However, these character sets do not allow representing characters in Arabic, Japanese, Chinese, Russian, Greek, and many other languages.

Java was conceived as a universal language. It supports dozens of character sets, including ASCII, ISO Latin-1, and Unicode.

The simplest and most limited Java character set is defined by the American Standard Code for Information Interchange, or ASCII, discussed in Chapters 3 and 4. This set contains 128 characters in the range 0 to 127. Some of these are control codes; for example, the value 10 is interpreted as a linefeed, the value 13 as a carriage return, and the value 8 as a tabulation code. The digits 0 to 9 are represented by the values 48 to 57. The upper-case letters A through Z of the English alphabet are encoded in the values 65 to 90. The lower-case letters are the values 97 to 122. The value 32 represents a space. The remaining values are used for symbols, such as !"#$%&'()*+,-./:;?{|} and ~.

---

## On the Web

---

The program AsciiSet.java, in Chapter 19 folder at www.crcpress.com, displays the characters in the ASCII set.

---

A second character set supported by Java is defined by the International Standards Institute Latin-1 standard, commonly referred to as ISO

Latin-1. This character set consists of a byte value in the range 0 to 255. The first 128 values are the same as those of the ASCII set. The remaining ones, in the range 128 to 255, are the characters needed to represent non-English languages, including French, Spanish, Italian, and German (in Roman script), typesetting symbols, some Greek letters often used in mathematics, mathematical symbols, copyright and trademark glyphs, common fractions, and others.

## On the Web

The program named LatinSet.java, in the Chapter 19 folder at www.crcpress.com, displays the ISO Latin-1 character set. Because DOS-based consoles do not support the first 32 character in ISO Latin-1, the first one displayed corresponds to the value 160.

The third and most comprehensive character set supported by Java is Unicode. Unicode characters are encoded in 16 bits, which allow values in the range 0 to 65,535. This is the same range as the Java char primitive data type. Unicode allows representing the characters of most modern languages, including Cyrillic, Greek, Arabic, Hebrew, Persian, Chinese, and Japanese. The first 256 characters of the Unicode character set coincide with the ISO Latin-1 set.

The fact that Unicode characters are encoded in two bytes may create problems when using stream-based read and write operations. Streams have traditionally assumed that alphanumeric data consists of single bytes. In order to read Unicode characters from the stream, the code reads a first byte, shifts all the bits 8 positions to the left, reads the second byte, then ANDs the low 8-bits of the second byte to the shifted bits of the first one. Alternatively, the same results are obtained by multiplying the first byte by 256 and adding the second one. One risk of reading 16-bit data, 8-bits at a time, is that code may lose step and combine the second byte of one character with the first byte of the next one.

Java readers and writers are designed for handling any of the supported character sets. If the host system is set for ASCII or ISO Latin-1, readers and writers operate one byte at a time. If the system is set for Unicode, then data is read from the stream two bytes at a time. Furthermore, streams are not intended for character-based data and do not support string operations. In this chapter we use readers and writers for performing file-based input and output.

# java.io Package

Input and output operations, I/O for short, are the subjects of the java.io library. This library is part of the Java application programming interface (API) which includes java.io, java.lang, java.math, java.net, java.text, and java.util. Note that, although most of the Java I/O support is in java.io, there are a few other I/O facilities located in the other packages.

Java I/O is divided into two general types: byte-based I/O and character-based I/O. The first type is handled by Java input and output streams and the second one by readers and writers. In either case, the general approach is to make an abstraction of the data source and of the destination. This makes possible using the same methods to read and write from a file, a text-based console, or a network connection. In other words, Java code need not be concerned with where the data is coming from or where it is going. Once the I/O stream has been defined, it is possible to automatically receive, send, format, filter, compress, and encrypt the data.

## Streams

The fundamental element of Java I/O is the *stream*. The stream concept is a metaphor for a stream of water. A data stream is defined as an ordered sequence of bytes of undetermined length. An input data stream moves bytes from some external source and an output data stream moves bytes to some external destination.

The java.io package contains two stream-based abstract classes named InputStream and OutputStream. Table 18-1 lists the subclasses.

**Table 18-1**

*Abstract Classes in java.io and Subclasses*

| INPUT STREAM | OUTPUT STREAM |
|---|---|
| ByteArrayInputStream | ByteArrayOutputStream |
| FileInputStream | FileOutputStream |
| FilterInputStream | FilterOutputStream |
| InputStream | OutputStream |
| ObjectInputStream | ObjectOutputStream |
| PipedInputStream | PipedOutputStream |
| SequenceInputStream | |
| StringBufferInputStream | |

Recall that streams are designed to operate on numeric data and that the stream's data unit is the byte. The byte is one of the Java integral data types. It is defined as an 8-bit number, in two's complement format, encoding a value in the range -128 to 127. The maximum positive value for a byte operand is 127. Therefore, the values 128 through 255 are not legal.

---
### Programmers note:
---

Two's complement representations are an encoding scheme for signed binary integers designed to facilitate machine arithmetic. The value of the two's complement is the difference between the number and the next integer power of two that is greater than the number. A simple way of calculating the two's complement of a binary number is negating all the digits and adding one to the result. An additional advantage of two's complement representations is that there is no encoding for negative zero.

---

One of the difficulties of Java stream operations is that the byte data type is not convenient. While many of the methods in the stream classes are documented to accept or return byte arguments, in reality, they operate on int data. The main reason is that there is no byte literals in Java, although the compiler sometimes makes automatic assignment conversions; for example:

```
byte val1 = 22;            // Valid assignment
byte val2 = 44;            // Valid assignment
however,
byte val3 = val1 + val2;   // Illegal. Requires type cast
byte val4 = 1 = 3;         // Illegal. Requires type cast
```

The small range of the byte data type explains why they are often converted to int in calculations. Later the calculated values are typecast back into the byte format. This means that although a stream is defined to operate on byte data, internal processing of numeric data by string-based classes is often done on int data types.

## Java InputStream class

The InputStream class, located in the java.io package, is the abstract class on which all input streams are based. The class contains several methods associated with input streams, including reading data from the stream, closing and flushing streams, and checking how many bytes of data are available. Table 18-2, on the following page, lists the methods of the InputStream class.

The method read() is designed to obtain byte data from the input stream. In Table 18-2 you can see read() is overloaded in three different implementations: read(), read(byte[] b), and read(byte[] b, int off, int len).

**Table 18-2**

*java.io.InputStream*

| RETURNS | NAME | DESCRIPTION |
|---|---|---|
| int | available() | Returns the number of bytes that can be read (or skipped over) from the current input stream without blocking. |
| void | close() | Closes this input stream. |
| void | mark(int readlimit) | Marks the current position in the input stream. |
| boolean | markSupported() | Tests if this input stream supports the mark and reset methods. |
| int | read() | Reads the next byte of data from the input stream. |
| int | read(byte[] b) | Reads a number of bytes from the input stream and stores them into the buffer array b. |
| int | read(byte[] b, int o, int l) | Reads up to l bytes of data from the input stream into an array b at offset o. |
| void | reset() | Repositions this stream to the position at the time the mark Method was last called. |
| long | skip(long n) | Skips over and discards n bytes of data from this input stream. |

The first implementation of read() has the following signature:

```
public abstract int read()
    throws IOException
```

This version reads the next byte of data from the input stream. The method waits until a byte of data is available or until the end of the stream is reached or an exception is raised. The value is returned as an int in the range 0 to 255. The value –1 is returned when the end of the stream is reached. Notice that this is an abstract method that cannot be instantiated.

The second implementation of read() has the following signature:

```
public int read(byte[] b)
    throws IOException
```

This version reads a number of bytes from the input stream and stores them in an array of type byte. The value returned is the number of bytes actually read. This method waits until input data is available, the end of file is detected, or an exception is raised. If the array passed to the method is null, a NullPointerException is raised. If the length of the array is zero, then no bytes are read and 0 is returned. If no byte is available because the stream is at the end of file, the value –1 is returned. The bytes read are stored in the array passed as an argument.

The third variation of read() has the following signature

```
public int read(byte[] b, int o, int l)
   throws IOException
```

The method reads up to one byte of data from the input stream. The data is stored at offset o, in the array b passed in the call. The method attempts to read length bytes, but a smaller number may be read, possibly zero. The return value, of type int, is the number of bytes actually read. This method waits until input data is available, end of file is detected, or an exception is raised.

## Java OutputStream class

The OutputStream class of java.io is the abstract class on which all output streams are based. The class contains several methods associated with output streams, including methods for writing data to the stream and for closing and flushing streams. The methods of the OutputStream class are shown in Table 18-3.

**Table 18-3**

*java.io.OutputStream*

| RETURNS | NAME | DESCRIPTION |
|---------|------|-------------|
| void | close() | Closes the current output stream. |
| void | flush() | Flushes this output stream. This forces any buffered output bytes to be written. |
| void | write(int b) | Writes the specified byte to the output stream. |
| void | write(byte[] b) | Writes b.length bytes from the specified byte array to this output stream. |
| void | write(byte[] b, int o, int l) | Writes l bytes from the specified byte array starting at offset o to this output stream. |

OutputStream is an abstract class. In Table 18-3 you can see that the method write() is overloaded in three different implementations. Two are concrete and one is abstract. The first implementation of write() has the following prototype:

```
public abstract void write(int b)
    throws IOException
```

The method writes the specified byte to the current output stream. The byte to be written is defined as the eight low-order bits of the argument b, which is of type int. The 24 high-order bits are ignored. Subclasses of OutputStream provide the implementation of this method. An IOException is raised if an I/O error occurs or if the output stream has been closed.

The second implementation has the following prototype:

```
public void write(byte[] b)
    throws IOException
```

This method writes b length bytes from the byte array passed as an argument to the current output stream. The method raises an IOException if an I/O error occurs.

The third implementation is prototyped as follows:

```
public void write(byte[] b, int o, int l),
    throws IOException
```

This method writes l number of bytes, from the byte array specified as an argument, starting at offset o, to the current output stream. This variation of the write() method of OutputStream calls the write() method on each of the bytes to be written. Subclasses override this method and provide a more efficient implementation. If the array passed as an argument is null, a NullPointerException is thrown. If o is negative, or l is negative, or o + l is greater than the length of the array b, then an IndexOutOfBoundsException is thrown. An IOException is raised if an I/O error occurs or if the output stream is closed.

## Standard Streams

Applications often use the keyboard as the input stream and the display system as an output stream. In this case it is said that the keyboard is the standard device for console input, and that the video display is the standard device for console output. In addition, an error stream is provided for directing error messages during debugging. The System class in the java.lang package contains three fields that relate to the standard streams, as follows:

```
public static final InputStream in;    // Standard input
```

```
public static final PrintStream out;   // Standard output
public static final PrintStream err;   // Standard error output
```

Note that PrintStream extends FileOutputStream, which extends OutputStream. PrintStream adds functionality by allowing the display of various data types. In addition, PrintStream contains the println() method, which we have often used in preceding chapters. This method adds a newline character (\n) at the end of the string or array and automatically flushes the stream.

The standard streams are always open and ready for use. This makes them convenient for Java console applications, such as the ones developed previously in this book.

## The Keyin Class

Thus far in this book we have used a class named Keyin to obtain console input for character and numeric types.

The Keyin class contains six static methods, as follows:

1. inString() allows the promptless input of a string. This method is used internally by the class to obtain the individual characters in an int or double variable.

2. InputFlush() ensures that there is no data available in the input stream. If data is found, the read() method is called to remove it. InputFlush() is called by the data input methods in the Keyin class.

3. inString(String prompt) is used to input a user string. The string passed as an argument is displayed as a prompt.

4. inInt(String prompt) allows the input of an int type value. The string passed as an argument is displayed as a prompt.

5. inChar(String prompt) allows the user to input a single value of type char. The string passed as an argument is displayed as a prompt.

6. inDouble(String prompt) allows the user to input a floating-point value and returns it as a value of type double. The string passed as an argument is displayed as a user prompt.

All methods of the Keyin class catch some of the exceptions raised by the read() method of the InputStream class. Exceptions are discussed in Chapter 19. The methods that input character data (inString and inChar) catch IOException. The methods that input numbers in int and float format catch the NumberFormatException.

## Flushing the input stream

The OutputStream class contains a method to flush the stream but there is no flush() method in InputStream. This means that, occasionally code may call the read() method and encounter unexpected characters that have not yet been removed from the stream. This is likely to happen when we attempt to remove a single character from the stream, as is the case when attempting to retrieve a single character. One of the methods of the Keyin class, called inputFlush(), addresses this potential problem by ensuring that there are no data bytes pending in the input stream.

The inputFlush() method uses the available() method of the InputStream class. This method returns the number of bytes that can be read without being blocked. The method returns zero if there is no data pending to be removed in the input stream. This can be interpreted to mean that the stream is clear and that the next call to the read() function will be blocked. The code for the InputFlush() method is as follows:

```
public static void inputFlush()
{
    int dummy;
    int bAvail;

    try
    {
    while((System.in.available()) != 0)
        dummy = System.in.read();
    }
    catch(java.io.IOException e)
    {
       System.out.println("Input error");
    }
}
```

The inputFlush() method contains a while loop that repeats while the input stream is not clear. In each iteration, the byte in the input stream is read into a variable named dummy and discarded. When the method returns, code can assume that the input stream contains no spurious data.

## Obtaining character data

Two methods of the Keyin class read character data. One reads and returns a string and the other one a char variable. The method named inChar() is used to input a single character.

```
public static char inChar(String prompt)
{
    int aChar = 0;
```

```
        InputFlush();
        printPrompt(prompt);

        try
           {
              aChar = System.in.read();
           }

        catch(java.io.IOException e)
           {
              System.out.println("Input error");
           }
        inputFlush();
        return (char) aChar;
}
```

Since there is no "raw mode" console input in Java, the method to read a single character waits until the user presses the key that terminates input, usually the one labeled <Enter> or <Return>. In fact, inChar() returns the first character typed but it cannot prevent the user from typing more than one character. For this reason the method calls inputFlush() before exiting. Also note that the input, which is of type int, is typecast into a type char in the return statement.

Capturing an input string requires a bit more processing. The method inString, listed here, performs the processing.

```
public static String inString()
{
    int aChar;
    String s = "";
    boolean finished = false;

    while(!finished)
       {
          try
          {
            aChar = System.in.read();
            if (aChar < 0 || (char)aChar == '\n')
              finished = true;
            else if ((char)aChar != '\r')
              s = s + (char) aChar;    // Append to string
          }

          catch(java.io.IOException e)
          {
            System.out.println("Input error");
            finished = true;
          }
       }
    return s;
}
```

The inString() method contains a while loop that terminates when the user presses the input terminator key or when read() returns -1. If the keystroke is not the <Return> key the input value is cast into a char type and appended to a local string variable. This string is returned to the caller when the method terminates.

An overloaded version of the inString() method flushes the input stream, displays the user prompt, and then calls inString() to obtain input.

## Obtaining numeric data

Obtaining numeric data from the keyboard consists of a two step process: first, we must retrieve the string of numeric characters typed by the user. Commonly this string will be in ASCII format. Second, convert the string of ASCII digits into the desired Java primitive. The first step is not difficult. We can use the inString() method, previously developed, in order to obtain the digit string. Parsing the string of digits into a binary value is another matter.

One possible approach would be to take on the conversion task directly. In the case of a decimal integer string we could isolate each string digit, proceeding left to right. Convert the ASCII value to binary by subtracting 0x30. Then multiply each digit by the power of ten that corresponds to its place value, and accumulate the total. The processing for an integer conversion is relatively straightforward and could be accomplished in a few lines of code. Much more complicated would be the conversion of a decimal number in floating-point format. In this case we would have to be familiar with the binary encoding defined in the ANSI-IEEE 754 Standard, which is adopted by Java. These formats were designed for computational efficiency; therefore they are not simple or intuitive.

Fortunately, the parsing of the strings into binary formats can be easily accomplished using methods provided in the java.lang library. In this processing we use the inString() method, developed in the preceding section, to input the string. The expression for obtaining the string and converting into an integer format is as follows:

```
int aValue = Integer.valueOf
            (inString().trim()).intValue();
```

In this case we use the trim() method to eliminate all spaces at either end of the string obtained by the inString() method. The intValue() method of the Integer class (located in java.lang) returns the integer value of the expression. Then the parsing into an int type is performed by the valueOf() method of the Integer class. A similar processing can be used for converting into other numeric types. For example, to convert into a double format we could use the following statement:

```
double aValue = Double.valueOf
                (inString().trim()).doubleValue();
```

The functions named inInt() and inDouble() in the Keyin class perform input of these two types.

## On the Web

The file Keyin.java is found in the Chapter 18 folder at www.crc-press.com.

# Chapter 19

# Handling Errors

## Program Errors

Errors seem to be in the nature of computer systems. The logical complexity of programs, as well as the mechanical diversity of the hardware, advises that we consider program errors as likely events. Ignoring the possibility of errors leads to a "hope for the best" attitude in programming that is both immature and dangerous. In this chapter we look at Java's extensive and powerful support for handling program errors.

## Error Types

Program errors can originate in hardware, in software, or in algorithmic or logical flaws. The possible solutions and the ideal error handling techniques differ in each case.

### Hardware and software errors

A program error can be hardware-related. For example, an application attempts to open a file that does not exist, send characters to a printer that is turned off, or communicate with a serial port that does not respond. Other error conditions are software-related. For example, code attempts to access an element that is beyond the bounds of the array or attempts to store a value that exceeds the capacity of a data format.

Hardware-related errors are usually detected and reported by the system. Software-related errors, on the other hand, must be detected by code. Other errors can be detected either by software, by hardware, or by both. For example, an application may inspect the divisor operand to make sure that a division by zero is not attempted. However, if a division

193

by zero does take place, the hardware in most computer systems produces an error response.

## Algorithmic errors

Another type of errors, sometimes called *algorithmic errors*, relate to flaws or intrinsic limitations of the real-world modeling performed by the computer. One example is the approximation that may take place when converting decimal numbers into binary format. Some decimal fractions have an exact binary representation, as is the case with the values 0.5, 0.25, 0.125, 0.0625, and so on. Other decimal fractions have no exact binary equivalent. In this case the computer uses the best binary approximation of the decimal fraction according to the machine's word length. This approximation entails a roundoff error that can propagate in the calculations and lead to incorrect results.

Numerical analysis is the discipline that deals with roundoff and truncation errors of various algorithms. In this case the programmer must be aware of the algorithms' error potential and use this knowledge to detect erroneous results or to avoid ill-conditioned data sets. It is algorithmic errors that are most often ignored by programmers.

# Exceptions

The term exception is used to denote hardware, software, and algorithmic errors. Thus, an exception can be broadly defined as any unusual event that may require special handling. Exception handling refers to the special processing operations that take place when an exception is detected. Raising an exception refers to the actions that generate the exception itself. The entire process can be described as follows:

1. A hardware, software, or algorithmic error takes place.

2. The error is detected and an exception is raised.

3. An exception handler provides the error response.

The detection of an error condition can originate in hardware or in software. However, the exception itself is a software process. The error handler can consist of many possible options, among them:

1. The error condition is ignored and the exception is cancelled.

2. The exception handler takes no specific action and passes the error condition along to another handler in the hierarchy.

3. The exception handler takes some action and passes the error condition along to another handler in the hierarchy for additional response.

4. The exception handler takes action and ends the exception response.

## Built-in exception handling

Programming languages differ widely in the level of built-in support for handling exceptions. Some languages provide no exception handling aid, while others contain sophisticated mechanisms to support error response and to ensure that all exceptions are adequately handled.

When languages like Java contain built-in exception handlers, there are various implementation issues and design issues that must be considered. For example:

1. Does the language's runtime environment provide default action for some or all exceptions?

2. Can user code raise exceptions?

3. Are hardware-detectable errors treated as exceptions?

4. Can the language's exception mechanism be temporarily or permanently disabled?

5. Where does execution continue after an exception response concludes?

PL/I was the first major language to provide exception handling. The PL/I exception handling facilities are powerful and flexible; however, most language designers consider them too complex. The most often-mentioned problem is that exceptions are bound dynamically to the handlers. A more reasonable model provides for statically bound exception handlers. The statically bound handlers were adopted in the Ada language, which also includes a mechanism for propagating unhandled exceptions to some other program unit.

## Java's approach

Java's approach to exceptions is based on the model proposed in the 1990 ANSI standardization committee for C++. This model, in turn, is based on the one used in the research language ML (Meta Language) developed at Bell Labs. The resulting approach to exception handling has been implemented in most modern versions of the C++ compiler, as well as in Java.

Java exception handling is based on three basic constructs, named *throw*, *try*, and *catch*. The throw keyword is used to raise or re-raise an exception. The try and catch blocks implement the exception handler. An additional optional block, named *finally*, is used within exception handlers to provide an alternate processing option.

According to their cause, Java exceptions can be classified into two types: implicit and explicit. *Implicit exceptions* take place when the program performs an illegal operation, for example, attempting a division by zero or accessing an element array whose index is out of range. Code cannot recover from this type of exception, although their cause can often be avoided. *Explicit exceptions* are generated by the application by means of a throw statement in order to handle some special condition. Implicit exceptions are called runtime exceptions in the Java literature while explicit exceptions are said to be user-defined. Runtime exceptions refer to the fact that implicit exceptions are thrown by the Java runtime library. In reality, all exceptions take place at runtime.

## Java exception classes

Java contains several classes that relate to exceptions. The class hierarchy is shown in Figure 19-1.

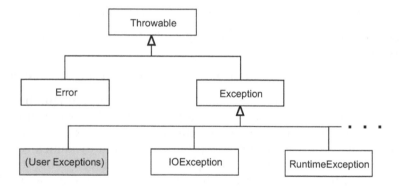

**Figure 19-1** *Java's Exception Class Hierarchy*

The Throwable class is at the top of the exception hierarchy. Throwable is extended by the classes named Error and Exception. The members of the Error class are system-level errors that are thrown by the Java virtual machine. System level errors are rare. Although it is possible for applications to catch these errors, the recommended approach is to let the system handle them. There is little an application can do if the system runs out of memory or encounters another terminal condition.

The most important part of the Java Throwable hierarchy is the one that goes through the Exception branch. There are currently 29 classes that extend Exception. In Figure 19-1, we have shown the two more notable ones: RuntimeException and IOException. Table 19-1 lists the classes that extend RuntimeException and IOException.

**Table 19-1**

*Subclasses of Exception*

| IO EXCEPTION | RUNTIME EXCEPTION |
|---|---|
| ChangedCharSetException | ArithmeticException |
| CharConversionException | ArrayStoreException |
| EOFException | CannotRedoException |
| FileNotFoundException | CannotUndoException |
| InterruptedIOException | ClassCastException |
| MalformedURLException | CMMException |
| ObjectStreamException | CurrentModificationException |
| ProtocolException | EmptyStackException |
| RemoteException | IllegalArgumentException |
| SocketException | IllegalStateException |
| SyncFailedException | ImaginingOpException |
| UnknownHostException | IndexOutOfBoundsException |
| UnknownServiceException | MissingResourceException |
| UnsupportedEncodingException | NegativeArraySizeException |
| UTFDataFormatException | NoSuchElementException |
| ZipException | NullPointerException |
| | ProfileDataException |
| | ProviderException |
| | RasterFormatException |
| | SecurityException |
| | SystemException |
| | UnsupportedOperationException |

In addition, application code can extend the Java Exception class in order to provide its own exception conditions. This possibility is shown by the class in a gray rectangle in Figure 19-1. Providing your own exception handlers is discussed later in this chapter.

## Advertising exceptions

Java specifications state that exceptions that derive from the class Error or from the class RuntimeException are classified as unchecked exceptions. All other exceptions are checked. Unchecked exceptions are either beyond program control, as those related to the Error class, or relate to conditions that are beyond program action, as is the case with an array index out of bounds. Code must deal with checked exceptions.

A Java method informs the user that it could generate an exception by declaring it in the method header. For example, a method named WriteToFile() that could produce an exception named NameError would be declared as follows:

```
public void WriteTo File()
   throws NameErrorException
```

In this case the throws keyword is used to advertise the exceptions raised by the method. The general rule is that a method must declare all checked exceptions that it throws, but not the unchecked exceptions. This means that all Java exceptions that are part of the Error and RuntimeException classes need not be advertised.

# Exceptions Programming

The rationale behind the exception handling mechanism of Java is based on two assumptions:

1. The compiler should ensure that all error conditions are adequately handled by code.

2. It is better to handle errors separately from the program's main task.

The exception-handling strategy of a Java application should consider the following issues:

1. Possible additional response to system errors. Code should not intercept the system handler but may provide some additional diagnostics. For example, upon detecting a system-level terminal error caused by a memory shortage, an application may post a message warning the user of possible loss of data.

2. Designing or modifying application code in order to avoid exceptions generated in the classes IOException and RuntimeException. For example, making sure that a division-by-zero error is not produced by previously examining the divisor operand.

3. Handling exceptions generated by non-terminal conditions in Java built-in classes. For example, providing code to recover from a file-not-found error.

4. Providing application-defined exception handlers for local error conditions. For example, a user-developed method that finds the average value in an integer array generates an exception if the user passes a null array as the argument.

5. Deciding what part of the code should handle an exception. This means determining if a particular exception should be handled within the method that detects it, or if it should be propagated down the program's method hierarchy to be addressed by another handler.

The first one of these listed issues requires no additional discussion. The remaining four are examined later in this section.

## Java exception processing

Processing exception conditions in Java code consists of three basic operations:

1. Raising user-defined exceptions by means of a throw clause. This usually requires extending the Java Exception class in order to provide the exception response.

2. Handling exceptions, either system generated (implicit) or user-defined (explicit). Exception handling is based on coding the corresponding try, catch, and finally clauses.

3. Propagating exceptions into the application's method hierarchy. This is accomplished by means of a throws clause.

Note that the throw keyword is used to raise an exception and the throws keyword to propagate it. It is unfortunate that the designers of the Java language were unable to find more adequate mnemonics for two functions that produce so different results. In this book, we try to reduce the confusion by referring to the action of the throw keyword as raising an exception and that of the throws keyword as throwing an exception.

## Raising exceptions

Code can use its own exception classes in order to accommodate specific error conditions. This can be accomplished by defining subclasses of Exception, or more commonly, by extending Java's Exception class. The Java Exception class contains two constructors, defined as follows:

```
Exception()
Exception(String s)
```

The easiest way to create an exception handler is to extend the Java Exception class and to call its parameterized constructor. For example, the following method provides an exception handler for a division by zero error; the following class extends the Java Exception class and provides a simple handler for a division by zero error:

```
class DivByZeroException extends Exception
{
    // Parameterized constructor
    public DivByZeroException(String message)
    {
      super(message);
    }
}
```

The method that intends to use the handler in the DivByZeroException must declare that it throws a DivByZeroException. This done, a throw clause gains access to the exception handler code, as shown in the following code fragment:

```
public class DivByZeroDemo
{
    public static void main(String[] args)
      throws DivByZeroException      // Declaring exception
    {
       int dividend = 100;
       int divisor, result;

       divisor = Keyin.inInt("Enter divisor: ");
       if(divisor != 0)
         {
            result = dividend / divisor;
            System.out.println("result = " + result);
         }
       else
          throw new DivByZeroException("Invalid divisor");
    }
}
```

Notice that the throws clause is used in the signature of the main() method to declare that the method raises a DivByZeroException. Because DivByZeroException is a checked exception, not advertising it results in a compiler error.

## Handling exceptions

Code can handle exceptions raised in other methods, whether these are local methods or part of the Java libraries. For example, if you try opening a non-existing file the FileNotFoundException class of IOException(see Table 19-1) will raise an exception. Your code can be designed to intercept Java's error response mechanism for this error and provide alternate processing. One of the possible advantages of intercepting the error response chain is the prevention of a terminal error that terminates execution. Exception handlers can also refer to extrinsic extension.

Three Java keywords are used in coding exception handlers: try, catch, and finally. The try block contains the processing operations. Its execution continues until an exception is raised. The catch block contains the actions to take place if an exception is raised. The catch block is skipped if no exception is raised in the try block. The finally block, which is optional, executes whether or not an exception is thrown. The finally statement is often used in deallocating local resources. The following code fragment shows an exception handler designed to intercept a system's division by zero error.

The following program, named CatchDBZ, intercepts the Java ArtihmeticException error response in the case of a division by zero. Note that because ArithmeticException is unchecked it does not have to be advertised in the header of the main() method.

## On the Web

The source file for the program CatchDBZ.java can be found in the Chapter 19 folder at www.crcpress.com.

```
//****************************************************************
//****************************************************************
// Program: CatchDBZ
// Reference: Chapter 19
// Topics:
//      1. Catching Java's ArithmeticException error in a
//         division by zero
// Requires:
//      1. Keyin class in the current directory
//****************************************************************
//****************************************************************

public class CatchDBZ
{
    public static void main(String[] args)
    {
        int dividend = 100;
        int divisor, result;

    while(true)
    {
        divisor = Keyin.inInt("Enter divisor (100 to end): ");

        if(divisor == 100)
            break;

        try
        {
            result = dividend / divisor;  // May raise exception
            System.out.println("result = " + result);
        }
        catch(ArithmeticException msgText)
        {
            System.out.println("Error is : " + msgText);
        }
    }
  }
}
```

The CatchDBZ.java program, listed previously, allows the user to enter the divisor of an integer division operation. A special value of 100 is used to terminate execution. The main() method's signature contains a throws clause for Java's ArithmeticException class. The try clause performs the division operation. If an ArithmeticException error is produced, then execution continues in the catch clause; it displays a message followed by the string returned by the ArithmeticException handler. In this case the program recovers and prompts the user for another divisor.

## Throwing exceptions

The basic rule of Java's error handling mechanism is that an exception must either be handled by the method in which it is raised, or passed along the call chain for another method to handle. In this case we say that the exception has propagated along the call hierarchy. This principle has been described by saying that a Java method must either handle or declare all exceptions.

The declaration of an exception refers to the throws clause that is part of the method's signature. What this means is that code can refuse to handle a possible exception raised by the method being called. For example, suppose a call chain consists of methodA(), which calls methodB(), which calls methodC(). Furthermore, suppose that methodC() can raise Exception1. In this case methodC() can either handle Exception1 or pass it along the call chain so that it is handled by methodB(). Here again, if methodB() does not handle the exception, Java will continue looking up the call chain for a handler, in this case, in methodA(). Finally, if no handler is found within the application's code, Java will then generate the exception and terminate execution.

The following program, named Handler.java, demonstrates exception propagation and handling:

## On the Web

The source file for the program Handler.java can be found in the Chapter 19 folder at www.crcpress.com.

```
//***************************************************************
//***************************************************************
// Program: Handler
// Reference: Chapter 19
// Topics:
//      1. Propagating exceptions along the call chain

// Requires:
//      1. Keyin class in the current directory
//***************************************************************
```

```
//*****************************************************************
public class Handler
{
    public static void main(String[] args)
    {
        int dividend = 100;
        int divisor, result;

        divisor = Keyin.inInt("Enter divisor: ");
        try
        {
            result = PreDivide(dividend, divisor);
            System.out.println("result = " + result);
        }
        catch(DivisionException msgText)
        {
            System.out.println("In main(): " + msgText);
        }
    }
    static int PreDivide(int numerator, int denominator)
    throws DivisionException
    {
        int quotient;
        quotient = Divide(numerator, denominator);
        return quotient;
    }

    static int Divide(int x, int y)
    throws DivisionException
    {
        int value = 0;
        if(y == 0)
            throw new DivisionException("Illegal Division");
        else
            value  = x / y;
            return value;
    }
}
//*****************************
//   Exception handler class
//*****************************
class DivisionException extends Exception
{
    // Parameterized constructor
    public DivisionException(String message)
    {
        super(message);
    }
}
```

The program Handler.java, listed previously, contains two classes. The driving class (Handler) includes the methods main(), PreDivide(), and Divide(). The class DivisionException extends Exception and provides a handler for a division by zero error.

The division by zero error is raised in the method Divide() but it is not handled in that method. Note that Divide(), which does not contain a try block, throws the DivisionException in the method's signature. Neither does the PreDivide() method handle the exception. Here again, the exception is passed along the call chain by the throws clause in the method's signature. The main() method, on the other hand, handles the exception that was raised in the Divide() method. For this reason main() contains a try block with the corresponding catch clause. The exception handling chain, in this case, ends in main().

# *Part II*

## Java Programming for Engineers

# Chapter 20

# Computer Number Systems

## The Hindu-Arabic Numerals

By the year 800 A.D. the Arabs were using a ten-symbol positional system of numbers which included the special symbol for 0. This system (later called the Hindu-Arabic or Arabic numerals) was introduced into Europe during the 8th century, probably through Spain. Pope Sylvester II, who had studied the Arabic numbers in Spain, was the first European scholar to support them. The Latin title of the first book on the subject of "Indian numbers" is *Liber Algorismi de Numero Indorum*. The author is the Arab mathematician al-Khowarizmi. The Hindu-Arabic numerals have been adopted by practically all the nations and cultures of the world.

In spite of its advantages, the Arabic number system originally confronted considerable debate and controversy. Some scholars of the time considered that Roman numerals were easier to learn and more convenient for operations on the abacus. The supporters of the Roman numeral system, called *abacists*, engaged in intellectual combat with the *algorist*, who were in favor of the Arabic numerals. Abacists and algorists debated about the advantages of their systems for several centuries, with the Catholic church often siding with the abacists. Because of their origin the Hindu-Arabic numerals were sometimes called *heathen numbers*.

Perhaps the most significant feature of the Arabic numbers is the presence of a symbol (0), which by itself represents no quantity, but which can be combined with other symbols to form larger numbers. This use of the digit 0 results in a system in which the value of each digit depends on its position in a digit string. For example,

```
   1 = one
  10 = ten
 100 = hundred
1000 = thousand
```

In Arabic numbers the almost-magical symbol 0 does not correspond to any unit-amount, but is used as a place-holder in a multi-column scheme. All modern number systems, including decimal, hexadecimal, and binary, are positional. The digits in the decimal number 2497 have the following positional weights:

```
      2000  ——-  2 thousand units
       400  ——-  4 hundred units
+       90  ——-  9 ten units
         7  ——-  7 units
      ————
      2497
```

or also

$$2 * 10^3 + 4 * 10^2 + 9 * 10^1 + 7 * 10^0 = 2497$$

(Recall that $10^1 = 10$ and $10^0 = 1$)

# Computer Number Systems

The computers built in the United States during the early 1940s operated on decimal numbers. However, in 1946 von Neumann, Burks, and Goldstine published a seminal paper titled *Preliminary Discussion of the Logical Design of an Electronic Computing Instrument*. In it they state:

> *"In a discussion of the arithmetic organs of a computing machine one is naturally led to a consideration of the number system to be adopted. In spite of the long-standing tradition of building digital machines in the decimal system, we must feel strongly in favor of the binary system for our device."*

In this paper the authors also consider the possibility of a computing device that uses binary-coded decimal numbers, called BCD. The idea is discarded in favor of a pure binary encoding with the argument that binary numbers are more compact. Later in this chapter you will see that BCD numbers are sometimes used today. Nevertheless, the von Neumann computer model is essentially a binary machine.

## Radix or base

In any positional number system the weight of each column is determined by the total number of symbols in the set, including zero. This is called the *base* or *radix* of the system. The base of the decimal system is 10, the base of the binary system is 2, and the base of the hexadecimal system is 16.

In radix-positional terms a decimal number can be expressed as a sum-of-digits expressed by the formula

$$\sum d_i \times 10^i \quad \text{for } 0 \leq d_i \leq 9 \; (d_i \text{ an integer})$$

The summation formula for a binary radix, positional representation is as follows

$$\sum b_i \times 2^i \quad \text{for } b_i = 0 \text{ or } 1$$

where $d_i$ and $b_i$ are the $i^{th}$ decimal and binary digits, respectively, as ordered from right to left, starting at the 0 position.

# Types of Numbers

By the adoption of special representations for different types of numbers the usefulness of a positional number system can be extended beyond the simple counting function.

## Whole numbers

The digits of a number system, called the positive integers or *natural numbers*, are an ordered set of symbols. The notion of an ordered set means that the numerical symbols are assigned a predetermined sequence. A positional system of numbers also requires a special digit, named zero. The special symbol 0, by itself, represents nothing. However, 0 assumes a cardinal function when it is combined with other digits, for instance, 10 or 30. The *whole numbers* are the set of natural numbers, including the number zero.

## Signed numbers

A number system can also be used to represent direction. We generally use the + and - signs to represent opposite numerical directions. The typical illustration for a set of signed numbers is as follows

```
-9 -8 -7 -6 -5 -4 -3 -2 -1  0 +1 +2 +3 +4 +5 +6 +7 +8 +9
negative numbers  <-       zero       -> positive numbers
```

The number zero, which separates the positive and the negative numbers, has no sign of its own. Although in some binary encodings, which are discussed later in this book, we end up with a negative and a positive zero.

## Rational and irrational numbers

A number system can also be used to represent parts of a whole. For example, when a carpenter cuts one board into two boards of equal length we can represent the result with the fraction 1/2. The verbalization of this operation states that the fraction 1/2 indicates one of the two parts which constitute an object. *Rational numbers* are those expressed as a ratio of two integers, for instance, 1/2, 2/3, 7/248. Note that this use of the word *rational* is related to the mathematical concept of a ratio, not to reason.

The denominator of a rational number expresses the number of potential parts. In this sense 2/5 indicates two of five possible parts. There is no reason why the number 1 cannot be used to indicate the number of potential parts, for example 2/1, 128/1. In this case the ratio $x/1$ indicates x elements of an undivided part. Therefore, it follows that $x/1 = x$. The implication is that the set of rational numbers includes the integers, since an integer can be expressed as a ratio by using a unit denominator.

But not all non-integer numbers can be written as an exact ratio of two integers. The discovery of the first *irrational number* is usually associated with the investigation of a right triangle by the Greek mathematician Pythagoras (approximately 600 BC).

The Pythagorean theorem states that in any right triangle the square of the longest side (hypotenuse) is equal to the sum of the squares of the other two sides.

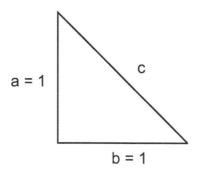

For this triangle, the Pythagorean theorem states that

$$a^2 + b^2 = c^2$$
$$2 = c^2$$
$$c = \sqrt{2}$$

Therefore, the length of the hypotenuse in a right triangle with unit sides is a number that, when multiplied by itself, gives 2. This number (approximately 1.414213562) cannot be expressed as the exact ratio of two integers. Other irrational numbers are $\sqrt{3}$, $\sqrt{5}$, as well as the mathematical constants $\pi$ and e.

## Real and complex numbers

The set of numbers that includes the natural numbers, the whole numbers, and the rational and irrational numbers is called the *real numbers*. Most common mathematical problems are solved using real numbers. However, during the investigation of squares and roots we notice the following:

```
+2  *  +2  =  4
-2  *  -2  =  4
```

Since the square of a positive number is positive and the square of a negative number is also positive, there can be no real number whose square is negative. Therefore, the value of $\sqrt{-2}$ does not exist in the real number system. But mathematicians of the 18th century extended the number system to include operations with roots of negative numbers. They defined the *imaginary unit* as

$$i^2 = -1$$
$$i = \sqrt{-1}$$

Numbers that consist of a real part and an imaginary part are called *complex numbers*. Some of the uses of complex numbers are in finding the solution of a quadratic equation, in vector analysis, graphics, and in solving many engineering, scientific, and mathematical problems.

## Storage of Numerical Data

The von Neumann definition requires that the computing machine be capable of storing and retrieving numerical data. In practice, numerical data items are stored in standard formats, designed to minimize space and optimize processing efficiency. Historically, numeric data was stored in structures devised according to the architecture of a specific machine, or the preferences of the designers. It was not until 1985 that the Institute of Electrical and Electronics Engineers (IEEE) and the American National Standards Institute (ANSI) formally approved mathematical standards for digital computers.

Since electronic technology is based on bi-stable components, the binary number system has been almost universally adopted for computer data. Data stored in processor registers, in magnetic media, in optical devices, or in punched tape, is encoded in binary. The programmer and the machine operator often ignore the physical characteristics of the storage medium, since a binary number can be represented by holes in a strip of paper tape, by magnetic charges on a mylar-coated disk, by voltage levels in an integrated circuit memory cell, or by the depth of minute craters on the surface of the CD.

## Computer word size

In electronic devices states are represented by a binary digit. Circuit designers group several individual cells to form a unit of storage that holds several bits. In a particular machine the basic unit of data storage is called the *word size*. Table 20-1 lists the word size of some historical computer systems.

### Table 20-1
*Computer Word Size in Historical Systems*

| COMPUTER FAMILY | WORD SIZE |
|---|:---:|
| TRS 80 Microcomputers (Z80 processor) <br> Apple Microcomputers (6502 processor) | 8 bits |
| Original PC and other microcomputers <br> equipped with Intel 8086, 8088 or 80286 CPU <br> DEC PDP 11 | 16 bits |
| PS/2 line and other PCs equipped with <br> the Intel 80386, 486, or Pentium <br> IBM 360/370 series <br> IBM 303X, 308X series <br> DEC VAX 11 <br> Prime computers | 32 bits |
| DEC 10 <br> UNIVAC <br> Honeywell | 36 bits |
| CDC 6000 <br> CDC 7000 <br> CDC CYBER series | 60 bits |

In most computers the smallest unit of individually addressable storage is 8 bits (one byte). Individual bits are not directly addressable and must be manipulated as part of larger units of data storage.

The machine's word size determines the units of data storage, the machine instruction size, and the units of memory addressing. PCs equipped with the Intel 8086, 8088, or 80286 CPU have 16-bit wide registers, transfer data in 8 and 16-bit units to memory and ports, and address memory using a 16-bit base (segment register) and 16-bit pointers (offset register). Since the data registers in these CPUs are 16-bits wide, the largest value that can be held in a register is 11111111 11111111 binary, or 65,535 decimal. PCs that use the Intel 80386, 486, and Pentium CPU have 32-bit internal registers and a flat address space that is 32-bits wide. In these machines the word size is 32 bits. For compatibility reasons some operating systems and application code use the 80386, 486, and Pentium microprocessors in a mode compatible with their 16-bit predecessors.

# Representing Integers

The integers are the set of whole numbers, which can be positive or negative. Integer digits are located one storage unit apart and do not have a decimal point. The computer storage of unsigned integers is a straightforward binary encoding. Since the smallest addressable unit of storage in the PC is one byte, the CPU logic pads with leading zeros numbers that are smaller than one byte. Figure 2.1 is a representation of an integer number stored electronically in a computer cell.

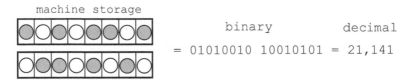

**Figure 20-1** *Representation of an Unsigned Integer*

### Sign-magnitude integers

Representing signed numbers requires a special convention in order to differentiate positive from negative magnitudes. The most generally accepted scheme is to devote one bit to represent the sign. A common signed number storage format sets the high-order bit to indicate negative magnitudes and clears it to indicate positive magnitudes and zero. In this scheme the decimal numbers 93 and -93 are represented as follows:

```
01011101 binary = 93 decimal
11011101 binary = -93 decimal
|
|------------ sign bit
```

Note that the left-most digit is set for a negative number and clear for a positive one. This way of designating negative numbers, called a *sign-magnitude* representation, corresponds to the conventional way in which we write signed numbers longhand. That is, we precede the number by its sign. Sign-magnitude representation has the following characteristics:

1. The absolute value of positive and negative numbers is the same.

2. Positive from negative numbers can be distinguished by examining the high-order bit. If this bit is 1, then the number is negative. Otherwise, the number is positive.

3. There are two possible representations for zero, one negative (10000000B) and one positive (00000000B).

One limitation of the sign-magnitude representation is that the logic required to perform addition is different from that for subtraction. While this is not insurmountable, there are other numeric representations (discussed later in this chapter) in which addition and subtraction are a single operation. Another limitation of straight sign-magnitude representations is the presence of negative zero. The negative zero reduces the numerical range of the representation and is unnecessary for most practical purposes.

The limitations of the sign-magnitude format can be seen in the complicated rules required for the addition of signed numbers. Assuming two signed operands, x and y, the following rules must be observed for performing addition:

1. If $x$ and $y$ have the same sign, they are added directly and the result is given the common sign of the addends.

2. If the absolute value of $x$ is larger than or equal to the absolute value of $y$, then $y$ is subtracted from $x$ and the result is given the sign of $x$.

3. If the absolute value of $y$ is larger than the absolute value of $x$, then $x$ is subtracted from $y$ and the result is given the sign of $y$.

4. If both $x$ and $y$ are –0, then the sum is 0.

The rules for subtracting numbers in sign-magnitude form are even more complicated.

## Radix-complement integers

Arithmetic complements arise during subtraction. In general, the radix complement of a number is defined as the difference between the number and the next integer power of the base that is larger than the number. In decimal numbers the radix complement is called the *ten's complement*. In the binary system the radix complement is the *two's complement*. For example, the radix complement of the decimal number 89 (ten's complement), is calculated as follows:

```
     100  = higher power of 10
 -    89
     ----
      11  = ten's complement of 89
```

The use of radix complements to simplify machine subtraction can best be seen in an example. Suppose the operation to be performed is $x = a - b$ with the following values:

```
     a = 602
     b = 353

                602
              - 353
              -----
     x =        249
```

Notice that in the process of performing longhand subtraction you had to perform two borrow operations. Now consider that the radix complement (ten's complement) of 353 is

```
     1000 - 353 = 647
```

Using complements, we can reformulate subtraction as the addition of the ten's complement of the subtrahend, as follows

```
                602
            +   647
              -----
              1249
              |_____ discarded digit
```

The result is adjusted by discarding the digit that *overflows* the magnitude of the operands.

In longhand decimal arithmetic there is no advantage in replacing subtraction with ten's complement addition, since the additional labor required for calculating the ten's complement cancels out any other possible benefit.

In binary arithmetic the use of radix complements entails significant computational advantages, principally because a binary machine can calculate complements very rapidly. For example, the two's complement of a binary number is obtained in the same manner as the ten's complement of a decimal number, that is, by subtracting the number from an integer power of the base that is larger than the number. In this manner the two's complement of the binary number 101 is:

```
    1000B  =  2³ =  8 decimal (higher power of 2)
  -  101B  =        5 decimal
     ----       ---------
     011B  =        3 decimal
```

By the same token, the two's complement of 10110B is calculated

```
  100000B  =  2⁵ = 32 decimal (higher power of 2)
  - 10110B  =       22 decimal
   -------       ----------
   01010B         10 decimal
```

You can perform the binary subtraction of 11111B minus 10110B by finding the two's complement of the subtrahend, adding the two operands, and discarding any overflow digit, as follows:

```
            11111B  =  31 decimal
          + 01010B  =  10 decimal (two's complement of 22)
            -------
           101001B
  discard_____|
            01001B  =   9 decimal (31 minus 22 = 9)
```

## Diminished-radix integers

In addition to the radix complements (ten's complement in the decimal system and two's complement in the binary system), there is a *diminished radix representation* that is often useful. This encoding, sometimes called the *radix-minus-one* form, is created by subtracting the number from an integer power of the base minus 1. In the decimal system, the diminished radix representation is called the *nine's complement*. In the binary system it is called the *one's complement*. The nine's complement of the decimal number 76 is calculated as follows:

```
    100  = next highest integer power of 10
     99  = 100 minus 1
  -  76
    ----
     23  = nine's complement of 89
```

The one's complement of a binary number is obtained by subtracting the number from an integer power of the base that is larger than the number, minus one. For example, the one's complement of the binary number 101 (5 decimal) can be calculated as follows:

```
1000B  =  2³ = 8 decimal

 111B  =  1000B minus 1 =   7 decimal
-101B                       5 decimal
-----                       --------
 010B  =                    2 decimal
```

Note that the one's complement can also be obtained by changing every 1 binary digit to a 0 and every 0 binary digit to a 1. In the above example, 010B is the one's complement of 101B. In this context the 0 binary digit is often said to be the complement of the 1 binary digit, and vice versa.

An interesting side effect is that the two's complement can be derived by adding one to the one's complement of a number. Therefore, instead of calculating

```
 100000B
- 10110B
 -------
 01010B
```

we can find the two's complement of 10110B as follows

```
 10110B  = number
 01001B  = change 0 to 1 and 1 to 0 (one's complement)
+    1B    then add 1
--------
 01010B  = two's complement
```

A third way of calculating the two's complement is subtracting the operand from zero and discarding the overflow.

One advantage of numeric complements is that the high-order bit can be used to detect the sign of the number. Another advantage is that there is no representation for negative 0.

## Representing Fractional Numbers

In a positional number system the weight of each integer digit can be determined by the formula:

$$P = d \times B^C$$

where $d$ is the digit, $B$ is the base or radix, and $C$ is the zero-based column number, starting from right to left. In this manner, the value of a multi-digit positive integer to $n$ digits can be expressed as a sum of the digit values:

$$d_n B^n + d_{n-1} B^{n-1} + d_{n-2} B^{n-2} + .... + d_0 B^0$$

where $d_i$ $(i = 0,...,n)$ is the value of the digit and $B$ is the base or radix of the number system. This representation can be extended to represent fractional values. Recalling that

$$x^{-n} = \frac{1}{x^n}$$

we can extend the sequence to the right of the radix point, as follows:

$$. + d_{n-1} B^{-1} + d_{n-2} B^{-2} ....$$

In the decimal system, the value of each digit to the right of the decimal point is calculated as 1/10, 1/100, 1/1000, and so on. The value of each successive digit of a binary fraction is the reciprocal of a power of 2, hence the sequence: 1/2, 1/4, 1/8, 1/16, etc. Figure 20-2 shows the positional weight of the integer and the fractional digits in a binary number.

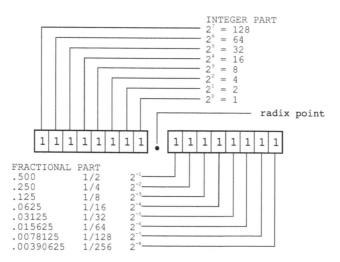

**Figure 20-2** *Positional Weights in a Binary Fraction*

The positional weight of the binary digits can be used to convert a binary number to its decimal equivalent. A similar method can be used to convert the fractional part of a binary number to a decimal fraction, as follows

```
                                    .1 0 1 0 1
                                     |   |   |
          .500    _____|   |   |
          .125    _____|   |
          .03125  _____|
          ------
          .65625
```

## Fixed-point representations

The encoding and storage of real numbers in binary form presents several difficulties. The first one is related to the position of the radix point. Since there are only two symbols in the binary set, and both are used to represent the numerical value of the number, there is no other symbol available for representing the radix point. The decimal number 58.125 can be represented by using one element to encode the integer part, and another one for the fractional part, for example:

```
          58 = 111010B
        .125 = .001B
```

In longhand decimals, you can write 58.125, but in computers it is impossible to explicitly encode a binary fraction. One possible scheme for representing binary fractions is to assume that the radix point is located at a fixed position. Figure 20-3 shows one possible convention for storing a real number in a fixed point binary format.

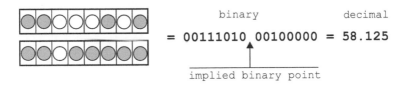

```
              binary                decimal
      = 00111010 00100000 = 58.125
                     ↑
        _____
        implied binary point
```

**Figure 20-3** *Binary Fixed-Point Representation*

Figure 20-3 assumes that the binary point is positioned between the eighth and the ninth digit of the encoding. A fixed point representation assumes that there are a certain number of digits to the left and right of the decimal point, which is the greatest limitation of the fixed point formats. Suppose you wanted to store the value 312.250. This number can be represented in binary as follows:

```
312 = 100111000
.250 = .01
```

The total number of binary digits required for the binary encoding is 11. The number can be physically stored in a 16-digit structure (as the one in Figure 20-3) with five cells to spare. However, since this fixed point format assigns eight cells to represent the integer part of the number, 312.250 cannot be encoded because the integer part (312) requires nine binary digits.

## Floating-point representations

Floating-point representations, on the other hand, do not use a fixed position for the radix point. The idea of separately encoding the position of the radix point originated in what is usually called *scientific notation*. In conventional scientific notation a number is written as a base greater than or equal to 1 and smaller than 10, multiplied by a power of 10. For example, the value 310.25 in scientific notation is written:

$$3.1025 \times 10^2$$

A number in scientific notation has a real part and an exponent part. Using the terminology of logarithms these two parts are sometimes called the *mantissa* and the *characteristic*. The following simplification of scientific notation is used in computers:

```
3.1025 E2
```

Here the multiplication symbol and the base are implicit. The letter E, which signals the start of the exponent part of the representation, accounts for the name *exponential form*. Numbers smaller than 1 can be represented in scientific notation or in exponential form by using negative powers. For example, the number .0004256 can be written:

$$4.256 \times 10^{-4}$$

or as

```
4.256 E-4
```

This notation is called a *floating-point* to indicate that the radix point floats according to the value of the exponent. Floating-point representations provide a more efficient use of computer storage.

## Standardized floating-point formats

Both the significand and the exponent of a floating-point number can be stored either as an integer, in sign magnitude, or in radix complement form. At the same time, the number of bits assigned to each field can vary according to the range and the precision required. For example, the computers of the CDC 6000, 7000, and CYBER series used a 96-digit significand with an 11-digit exponent, while the PDP 11 series used 55-digit significands and 8-digit exponents.

Historical variations, incompatibilities, and inconsistencies in floating-point formats created a need to standardize. In March and July 1985, the Computer Society of the Institute of Electric and Electronic Engineers (IEEE) and the American National Standards Institute (ANSI) approved a standard for binary floating-point arithmetic (ANSI/IEEE Standard 754-1985). This standard established four formats for encoding binary floating-point numbers. Table 20-2 summarizes the characteristics of these formats.

**Table 20-2**

*ANSI/IEEE Floating Point Formats*

| PARAMETER | SINGLE | SINGLE EXTENDED | DOUBLE | DOUBLE EXTENDED |
|---|---|---|---|---|
| total bits | 32 | 43 | 64 | 79 |
| significand bits | 24 | 32 | 53 | 64 |
| maximum exponent | +127 | +1023 | +1023 | +16383 |
| minimum exponent | -126 | +1022 | −1022 | +16382 |
| exponent width | 8 | 11 | 11 | 15 |
| exponent bias | +127 | --- | +1023 | --- |

# Binary-Coded Decimals (BCD)

Binary floating-point encodings are usually considered the most efficient format for storing numerical data in a digital computer. Other representations are also used in computer work. *Binary-coded decimal* (BCD) is a representation of decimal digits in binary form. There are two common ways of storing BCD digits. One is known as the *packed* BCD format and the other one as *unpacked.* In the unpacked format, one BCD digit is represented in one byte of memory storage. In packed form two BCD digits are encoded per byte of storage. The unpacked BCD format does not use the four high-order bits of each byte, which is wasted storage space. On the other hand, the unpacked format facilitates conversions and arithmetic operations on some machines. Figure 20-4 (on the following page) shows the memory storage of a packed and unpacked BCD number.

## Floating-point BCD

Binary-coded decimal representations and BCD arithmetic have not been explicitly described in a formal standard. Each machine, programming language, or application, stores and manipulates BCD numbers in unique and often incompatible ways.

UNPACKED  BCD                                    PACKED  BCD

| | | |
|---|---|---|
| 0 0 0 0 | 0 0 1 0 | 2 |
| 0 0 0 0 | 0 0 1 1 | 3 |
| 0 0 0 0 | 0 1 1 1 | 7 |
| 0 0 0 0 | 1 0 0 1 | 9 |

| | | |
|---|---|---|
| 0 0 1 0 | 0 0 1 1 | 23 |
| 0 1 1 1 | 1 0 0 1 | 79 |

**Figure 20-4** *Packed and Unpacked BCD*

The advantage of BCD representations is that the precision of the calculations is not limited by a pre-defined encoding. A programmer can develop a BCD format for representing any number of digits, to any decimal precision. The main disadvantage of BCD mathematics is their much slower speed of execution and the greater difficulty in developing mathematical software.

The *java.math* library uses BCD and provides simple arithmetic to unlimited precision. The java.math library is discussed in Chapter 21.

# Chapter 21

# Fixed-Precision Numeric Data

## Java Numeric Data Types

Java numeric data types can be classified into two groups: the language's fixed-precision primitive data types, and the arbitrary- or variable-precision numeric types implemented in the java.math library. Variable-precision numeric types are the subject of Chapter 22.

## Primitive Data Types

In Chapter 4 you saw the standard numeric data types supported by Java. These include four integer types (int, short, long, and byte) and two floating-point types (float and double). Table 21-1 shows the formatting of Java's primitive numeric data types.

**Table 21-1**

*Java Fixed-precision Numeric Types*

| TYPE | BITS | MAXIMUM | MINIMUM | DESCRIPTION |
|------|------|---------|---------|-------------|
| Int | 32 | 2,147,483,648 | -2,147,483,648 | Signed integer |
| Short | 16 | 32,767 | -32,768 | Signed integer |
| Long | 64 | 9.2233...E17 | -9.2233...E17 | Signed integer |
| Byte | 8 | 128 | -127 | Signed integer |
| Float | 32 | 3.40282...E38 | 1.40129...E-45 | IEEE single |
| Double | 64 | 1.79769...E308 | 4.94065...E-324 | IEEE double |

Java primitive numeric data types correspond to IEEE 754 Standard for Binary Floating-Point Arithmetic. Understanding computer arithmetic in general, and Java arithmetic in particular, requires some knowledge of the Standard.

# IEEE 754 Standard

Originally, the computer implementation of floating-point mathematics was based on proprietary data formats and processing routines developed by each manufacturer. The results were unreliable and often erroneous, including a Cray supercomputer that was unable to perform exact divisions by 2, a Honeywell computer in which the precision guard bits would disappear unexpectedly, and several cases in which multiplication by 1.0 could cause an overflow.

The first suggestion of a computer mathematics standard was an article entitled *A Proposed Standard for Binary Floating-Point Arithmetic*, published in the SIGNUM Newsletter of the Association for Computing Machinery (ACM) in October, 1979. This was followed by an article by Jerome T. Coonen, titled *An Implementation Guide to a Proposed Standard for Floating-Point Arithmetic*. This one appeared in *Computer* Magazine, January, 1980. Draft 8.0 of the proposed standard was published in the March 1981 edition of *Computer*. The standard was approved by the IEEE Standards Board on March 21, 1985, and by the American National Standards Institute in July, 1985. The standard was reaffirmed on December 6, 1990. A more general standard was published in 1987, under the designation of *IEEE Standard 854 for Radix-Independent Floating-Point Arithmetic*.

The Foreword to IEEE 754 states that the intent of the standard is to promote the portability of numeric software, to provide a uniform environment for programs, and to encourage the development of better, safer, and more sophisticated mathematical code. Among the specific refinements of IEEE 754 are the diagnosis of anomalies at execution time, the improved handling of exception conditions, and the implementation of interval arithmetic. In addition, the standard provides for standard elementary functions, very high precision calculations, and the use of algebraic symbolism in numerical operations.

A system in compliance with the IEEE 754 Standard can be implemented in hardware, in software, or in both. However, conformance to the standard is not determined by the internal properties of a system, but by the user's perception. In other words, if a hardware product requires additional software to comply with the provisions of the standard, it cannot state that it conforms. The standard includes the following topics and operations:

1. Floating-point numeric formats

2. The arithmetic operations of addition, subtraction, multiplication, division, square root, remainder, and compare

3. Conversions between integer and floating-point, between the various floating-point formats, and between decimal strings and floating-point formats

4. Handling of errors and exceptions

The following topics are specifically excluded from the standard:

1. Decimal and integer formats

2. Interpretation of the sign and the significand fields in non-numeric encodings (called NaNs)

3. Binary to decimal and decimal to binary conversion of numbers encoded in the Standard's extended formats

## Numeric data encoding

IEEE 754 defines four floating-point encodings divided into two groups. The first group is called the basic group and the second one is the extended group. The basic formats are specified in detail by the standard; for the extended formats, the standard lists only the minimum requirements. Both groups have a single and a double precision encoding. Table 21-2 shows the requirements for the four formats.

**Table 21-2**

*Numeric Data Encodings in IEEE 754*

|  | SINGLE | | DOUBLE | |
|---|---|---|---|---|
|  | BASIC | EXTENDED | BASIC | EXTENDED |
| significand bits | 24 | 32 | 53 | 64 |
| maximum exponent | +127 | +1023 | +1023 | +16383 |
| minimum exponent | −126 | +1022 | -1022 | −16382 |
| exponent bias | +127 | ------ | +1023 | ------ |
| exponent bits | 8 | 11 | 11 | 15 |
| total bits | 32 | 43 | 64 | 79 |

Each binary encoding in the IEEE 754 contains three elements or fields:

1. The first field is the most significant bit and is used to encode the sign of the number. A 1-bit represents a negative number and a 0 bit a positive number.

2. The second field is used for encoding the exponent of the number in biased form. The biased encoding makes it unnecessary to store the exponent sign. An exponent smaller that the bias is in the negative range. An exponent larger than the bias is in the positive range. The exponent is zero if it is equal to the bias.

3. The third field is called the significand, or the fraction field. In IEEE formats, this field has an implied 1-bit to the left of an also implied binary point. However, the standard validates encodings in the extended format in which the significand's leading bit is explicitly represented.

Figure 21-1 shows the bit structure and fields in the single and double format of the IEEE 754 Standard.

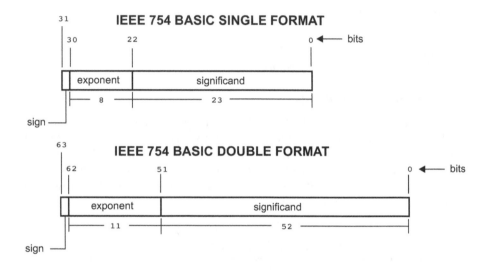

**Figure 21-1** *IEEE 754 Single and Double Format*

IEEE 754 leaves considerable freedom of implementation in the extended formats. These formats are defined as having a minimum number of parameters and an unspecified exponent bias, as shown in Table 21-2. The standard states that the developer may encode values redundantly, and reserve bit strings for purposes not described. The standard requires that all implementations support the single format and recommends that at least one extended format be implemented for the widest basic format used. This means that an implementation that supports the single basic formats, should also have an extended single encoding. By the same token, an implementation that supports the basic double format should also have an extended double. The intention of this recommendation is that the extended formats be used for storing intermediate results with more precision than the format used for the result. This scheme serves to improve computational accuracy.

# Rounding

Rounding (or rounding-off) is the process of adjusting a numerical value so that it fits in a particular format. In general, the purpose of rounding operations is to reduce the error that arises from the loss of one or more digits. For example, the number 27,445.89 can be reduced to an integer value by truncating it to 27,445 or by rounding to 27,446. In this case the rounded value is a more accurate representation of the original number than the one obtained by chopping off the last two digits.

IEEE 754 requires that implementations provide the following rounding modes:

1. *Round to Nearest.* This should be the default rounding mode. In this mode the result is the nearest representable value. The standard also describes how rounding is to take place when the result is equally near two representable values. This case, sometimes called the halfway case, occurs when rounding decimal numbers in which the last non-zero digit is 5.

   For example, with the number 128.500 the arbitrary rounding rule often taught in high-school is to round up. This value would be rounded to the integer 129. An alternative rounding mode is called *round to nearest even*. In rounding the value 20,000.50 to an integer value there are two equally near options: 20,001 and 20,000. In the rounding to the nearest even mode the number 20,000 is preferred since it is an even number. Binary representations can be easily rounded to the nearest even result by selecting the value in which the least significant bit is zero. Note that this method is also valid with binary coded decimals.

2. *Round to positive infinity.* In this rounding mode the result is rounded to the next highest representable value. This rounding mode is sometimes called rounding up.

3. *Round to negative infinity.* In this rounding mode the result is rounded to the next lowest representable value. This rounding mode is sometimes called rounding down.

4. *Truncate.* According to the definition at the beginning of this section, truncation is not considered a rounding mode. Truncation, also called chopping or chopping-off, consists in discarding the non-representable portion and disregarding its value. The chop-off operation is sometimes used in generating an integer result from a fractional operand.

# Interval arithmetic

The possibility of selecting rounding to positive infinity or negative infinity (round-up and round-down) allows the use of a technique known as *interval arithmetic.* Interval arithmetic is based on executing a series of calculations twice: once rounding up and once rounding down. This allows the determination of the upper and lower bounds of the error. Using interval arithmetic, it is possible, in many cases, to certify that the correct result is a value not larger than the result obtained while rounding up, and no smaller than the result obtained while rounding down. This places the exact result within a certain boundary.

Although IEEE 754 does not specifically mention interval arithmetic, it does require directed rounding modes. Interval arithmetic can be a powerful numerical tool, although there are exceptional cases in which these results are not valid. Not all mathematical calculations can be subject to interval analysis. The fundamental rules are as follows:

1. The operation must consist of multiple steps.

2. At least one intermediate result in the calculations must be subject to rounding.

3. The value zero should not be in the error range, that is, both results must have the same sign. The subsequent possibility of division by zero or by a very small number introduces other potential problems that are not evident in interval arithmetic.

4. The calculations should not be, in themselves, a method for approximating results. Compounded approximations render invalid intervals.

## Treatment of infinity

The concept of infinity arises in relation to the range of a system of real numbers. One approach, called a *projective closure*, describes infinity as an unsigned representation for very small or very large numbers. When projective infinity is adopted, the symbol $\infty$ is used to represent a number that is either too small or too large to be encoded in the system.

An alternative approach, called *affine closure*, recognizes the difference between values that exceed the number system by being too large ($+\infty$) or too small ($-\infty$) to be represented. Figure 21-2 graphically represents the projective and the affine methods for the closure of a number system.

According to the standard, infinity must be interpreted in the affine sense. That is, any representable finite number $x$ shall be located

$$-\infty \quad (\mathrm{x}) \quad +\infty$$

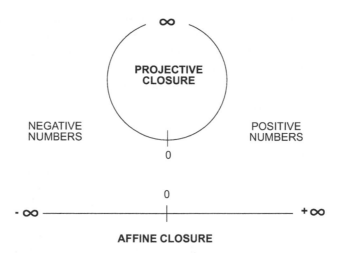

**Figure 21-2** *IEEE 754 Representations of Infinity*

The standard also provides that arithmetic operations with one or more infinity operands must be exact. Nevertheless, certain operations on infinity are considered invalid and generate the corresponding exception, specifically:

1. Addition (or subtraction) of infinities with opposite signs, for instance, $(-\infty)$ + ( $+\infty$ ).

2. Multiplication of 0 times $\infty$.

3. Division of $\infty$ by $\infty$.

4. Remainder operations in the form $x$ REM $y$, when $x = \infty$.

5. When infinity is created by the overflow of a finite operand.

The practical consequence of the affine treatment of infinities is that when infinity forms part of an arithmetic operation the results are algebraically valid.

Note in Table 21-2 that in the basic encoding of the single format the exponent (bias 127) is in the range +127 to −126. This leaves unrepresented the exponent values 0H and FFH. Also, in the encoding of the double format, the exponent values 0H and 7FFH are unrepresented. These values are intentionally left unused by the standard so that they are available for encoding un-normalized numbers, infinity, and non-numeric values that represent invalid operations.

In the single and double formats infinity is represented with an exponent of all one bits, and a significand of all zeros in the fractional portion.

In other words, in encodings that use an implicit 1-bit in the significand, the significand for an infinity appears as all zeros. On the other hand, in encodings with an explicit 1-bit, infinity is represented as 100...00. In IEEE 754 affine treatment of infinity is achieved by setting the number's sign bit for negative infinity and clearing it for positive infinity.

## Not a number (NaN)

IEEE 754 requires that a number that exceeds the capacity of the destination format due to overflow or underflow, including the representable denormals, be replaced with the special encoding for infinity. Thereafter infinity arithmetic generates exact and valid results on these operands and no exception is signaled, except for the special conditions already mentioned.

On the other hand, certain operations generate results that are absurd, unrepresentable, or mathematically undefined; for example, attempts to perform division by zero, to multiply $0 * \infty$, and to calculate the square root of a negative number. In these cases the standard provides a special encoding to represent results that are classified as Not a Number (NaN). The general pattern is an exponent of all 1-bits (as in the encoding for infinity) and a non-zero fractional portion of the significand. Note that the NaN encoding is easily differentiated from the infinity encoding because infinity requires all zeros in the fractional portion of the significand. Since these are the only requirements of the standard for a NaN encoding, implementations are free to use variations of the non-zero significand to represent different types of NaNs.

## Signaling and quiet NaNs

IEEE 754 requires the support of two different types of NaNs: *signaling NaNs* and *quiet NaNs*. The difference between them is that when a signaling NaN appears as an operand in an arithmetic calculation it forces the generation of an error exception. Quiet NaNs, on the other hand, will silently propagate signaling no error.

In the standard, signaling NaN and quiet NaN encodings are left to the implementor's discretion. The standard does mention that signaling NaNs are typically used in representing uninitialized variables, complex infinity encodings, or other particular enhancements of the implementation. The signaling mechanism provides a way of detecting an attempt to use NaNs as numeric operands. It is left to the implementation to decide whether the simple copying of a signaling NaN generates an error.

According to IEEE 754, signaling NaNs are not to be propagated by the system. If the result of an operation is a NaN it should be represented as a quiet NaN, even if both operands are signaling NaNs. Since the only requirement of the NaN encoding is that the exponent be formed with all one-bits and that the significand be non-zero, there is an abundant number of possible NaN combinations, even in the smaller formats. For example, in the single format which uses a 23-bit significand, there are over eight million possible encodings for positive NaNs, and as many for negative NaNs. How these encodings are assigned to the various signaling and non-signaling NaNs is also left to the implementation.

# Exceptions

IEEE 754 requires the identification and signaling of five different error conditions:

1. Invalid operation

2. Division by zero

3. Overflow

4. Underflow

5. Inexact result

The signaling of an exception condition is performed by setting a flag, executing a trap routine, or both. The default response is to bypass the trap routine. The trap (which is different for each exception condition) transfers control to the user's error handler. The implementation must provide a different error flag for each exception.

## Invalid operation exception

According to IEEE 754 the following conditions generate an invalid operation exception:

1. An operation on a signaling NaN

2. Addition or subtraction operations in which one or both operands are infinities

3. Multiplication of 0 times $\infty$

4. Division of 0/0 or $\infty/\infty$

5. Remainder operation, in the form $x$ REM $y$, in which $x = 0$ or $y = \infty$

6. The square root of a negative number

7. Conversion operations from binary floating-point formats into integer or decimal formats that produce a result that cannot be faithfully represented

8. Comparison operations in which one or both operands are NaNs.

## Division by zero exception

This exception occurs when the divisor is zero and the dividend is non-zero. According to the standard the result is encoded as infinity. Note that the operation 0/0, which generates an invalid exception, is not considered a division by zero.

## Overflow exception

Table 21-2 shows the exponent encodings in the IEEE 754 basic single format, which ranges from -126 to +127. Since this exponent is bias 127, the maximum absolute exponent is the decimal value 254 (11111110B) and the minimum absolute exponent is the decimal value 1 (00000001B). The exponent encodings of 0 (00000000B) and 255 (11111111B) are not used in representing real numbers in the basic single format. An analysis of the valid exponents in the other formats confirms that the exponent digit value of 00...00B and of 11...11B are also not part of the legal range assigned for the representation of real numbers.

This approach is based on the fact that any computer representation of real numbers is necessarily limited to a certain range. Numbers approach the limits of this range as they become very large or very small. The *overflow* condition takes place whenever a real number exceeds the representable range by becoming too large. In the standard's basic and extended formats the maximum representable values have an exponent in the form 11...10B and a significand of 11..11B. With positive real numbers, adding the smallest possible value to this encoding generates a number that exceeds the representable range (overflow).

The standard requires that when an overflow condition is detected, an exception be signaled and a special encoding be entered as a result of the operation. There are four possible variations of the actual results, depending on the selected rounding mode, as follows:

1. If round to nearest is selected, the result of an overflow is encoded as an infinity with the sign of the intermediate result.

2. If the truncate mode is selected, the result of an overflow is represented with the format's encoding for the largest representable number.

3. If round to negative infinity is selected, the result of a positive overflow is represented with the format's encoding for the largest representable value and a negative overflow with the encoding for $-\infty$.

4. If round to positive infinity is selected, the result of a negative overflow is represented with the format's encoding for the smallest representable value, and a positive overflow with the encoding for $+\infty$.

Note that overflow is always *abrupt* (also called a *sudden overflow*). Because of the limitations in the representation of real numbers there are no provisions for gradual overflow. The result of the overflow of a positive number results in $+\infty$ or in the larger representable positive real, while the overflow of a negative number results in $-\infty$ or in the smallest representable negative real. Which action is taken depends on the selected rounding mode.

## Underflow exception

Overflow conditions take place as the absolute value of a number becomes very large. Underflow, on the other hand, takes place as the absolute value of a number becomes very small, in other words, as its value approximates zero. One method of handling numbers that approximate zero is to make them equal zero. This operation, sometimes called *flush to zero*, has been frequently used as a simple solution to the problem of underflow. But this *sudden underflow* presents some peculiar problems.For example, in the equation

$$(x-y)+y = x$$

if $y$ is a sufficiently large number, then the portion $(x - y)$ could suddenly underflow to zero.

According to the provisions of IEEE 754, overflow conditions are handled by abruptly converting the result to an infinity, or to the largest representable real. Which method is adopted depends on the rounding mode in effect. In order to avoid the dangers of sudden underflow, the standard requires using a special un-normalized representation of real numbers, called *denormals*.

To understand *gradual underflow* you must recall that a floating-point representation is said to be normalized when the first digit of the significand is non-zero. Normalization is designed to preserve the maximum number of significand digits and the precision of the stored value. You can deduce that the smallest representable number in either format is encoded with an exponent pattern of 00...01B and a significand of 00...00B. Gradual underflow is based on the use of a special encoding for real numbers (the so-called denormals) which are characterized by an exponent in the form 00...00B and a denormalized significand. This representation, easily identified by an exponent containing all zero bits, allows representing numbers smaller than the smallest one that could be encoded using a normalized significand. Gradual underflow is made possible at the expense of precision. As the significand becomes denormalized, the number of its significant digits diminishes.

IEEE 754 requires the use of denormalized representations as well as the gradual underflow of very small numbers. The standard describes two correlated events that can contribute to underflow. One is the creation of a representable number which is yet so small that it may generate an error exception. An example is the overflow condition that could result from dividing by a very small operand. The second event is the loss of accuracy that results from representing very small numbers by denormalizing the significand.

## Inexact result exception

The inexact results can occur from many arithmetic operations performed on valid operands. For example, the division operations 1/3, 1/7 and 1/9 cannot be exactly represented in binary form. This exception, sometimes called the *precision exception*, is designed as a warning that the rounded result of the previous operation cannot be exactly represented. In most computational situations this is the most frequent exception, and also the error condition that is most often ignored.

# IEEE 754 in Java

Java floating-point arithmetic is a partial implementation of IEEE 754. The support includes overflow and underflow and the representation of invalid expressions as a NaN. However, Java arithmetic does not detect, trap, or signal IEEE 754 exceptions such as invalid operation, division by zero, overflow, underflow, or inexact result.

Java's only rounding mode is rounding to the nearest even. This means that inexact results are rounded to the nearest representable value. In case of there being two equally distant values, Java uses the one with a zero least-significant bit (even number). This rounding mode corresponds to the default rounding in IEEE 754, called *round-to-nearest or even*. The fact that Java does not provide user-selectable rounding modes determines that interval arithmetic is not possible. The class Math in the java.lang library does provide several truncation methods for casting floating-point values into integers. These methods, named ceil(), floor(), rint(), and round(), are described later in this section.

Java does provide the programmer with some methods that relate to IEEE 754 data types and special forms. These methods are located in the classes Double and Float of the java.lang library. These methods are described in the following sections.

# java.lang Class Double

This class contains several methods for converting and manipulating data defined in IEEE 754 double format as well as methods for creating constants and special types.

The following constants are defined in the class:

## MAX_VALUE

This constant returns the largest magnitude that can be held in a variable of type double. The constant is defined as:

```
public final static double MAX_VALUE;
```

The largest value is the same for positive or negative numbers. MAX_VALUE returns:

$$1.79769313486231570e+308$$

## MIN_VALUE

This constant returns the smallest magnitude that can be held in a variable of type double. The constant is defined as:

```
public final static double MIN_VALUE;
```

The smallest value is the same for positive or negative numbers. MIN_VALUE returns:

$$4.94065645841246544e-324$$

## NaN

This constant returns an IEEE 754 Not-a-Number in double format. The constant is defined as follows:

```
public final static double NaN;
```

The value returned as a NaN cannot be compared to other numeric operands, including another NaN or itself. The NaN encoding is:

0x7ff8000000000000L

## NEGATIVE_INFINITY

This constant returns the IEEE 754 value for negative infinity in double format. It is defined as follows:

```
public static final double NEGATIVE_INFINITY;
```

A negative infinity compares less-than any other value, except itself. The encoding for negative infinity is:

```
0xfff0000000000000L
```

## POSITIVE_INFINITY

This constant returns the IEEE 754 value for positive infinity in double format. It is defined as follows:

```
public static final double POSITIVE_INFINITY;
```

A positive infinity compares greater-than any other value, except itself. The encoding for positive infinity is:

```
0x7ff0000000000000L
```

The Class Double contains the following methods to test for these special encodings.

### public static boolean isInfinite(double v)

Argument v is the value to be tested. Returns true if the value is positive infinity or negative infinity; false otherwise.

### public boolean isInfinite()

Returns true if the value represented by this object is positive infinity or negative infinity; false otherwise.

### public static boolean isNaN(double v)

Argument v is the value to be tested. Returns true if the value of the argument is NaN; false otherwise.

### public boolean isNaN()

Returns true if the value represented by this object is NaN; false otherwise.

# java.lang Class Float

This class contains several methods for converting and manipulating data defined in IEEE 754 single format as well as methods for creating constants and special types.

The following constants are defined in the class:

## MAX_VALUE

This constant returns the largest magnitude that can be held in a variable of type float. The constant is defined as:

```
public final static float MAX_VALUE;
```

The largest value is the same for positive or negative numbers. MAX_VALUE returns:

$$3.40282346638528860e+38$$

## MIN_VALUE

This constant returns the smallest magnitude that can be held in a variable of type float. The constant is defined as:

```
public final static float MIN_VALUE;
```

The smallest value is the same for positive or negative numbers. MIN_VALUE returns:

$$1.40129846432481707e-45$$

## NaN

This constant returns an IEEE 754 Not-a-Number in float format. The constant is defined as follows:

```
public final static float NaN;
```

The value returned as a NaN cannot be compared to other numeric operands, including another NaN or itself. The NaN encoding float is:

$$0x7ffc00000$$

## NEGATIVE_INFINITY

This constant returns the IEEE 754 value for negative infinity in a type float. It is defined as follows:

```
public static final float NEGATIVE_INFINITY;
```

A negative infinity compares less-than any other value, except itself. The float encoding for negative infinity is:

$$0xff800000$$

## POSITIVE_INFINITY

This constant returns the IEEE 754 value for positive infinity in a type float. It is defined as follows:

```
public static final float POSITIVE_INFINITY;
```

A positive infinity compares greater-than any other value, except itself. The float encoding for positive infinity is:

$$0x7f800000$$

The Class Float also contains the following methods to test for these special encodings.

### public static boolean isInfinite(float v)

Argument v is the value to be tested. Returns true if the value is positive infinity or negative infinity; false otherwise.

### public boolean isInfinite()

Returns true if the value represented by this object is positive infinity or negative infinity; false otherwise.

### public static boolean isNaN(float v)

Argument v is the value to be tested. Returns true if the value of the argument is NaN; false otherwise.

### public boolean isNaN()

Returns true if the value represented by this object is NaN; false otherwise.

# Java Numeric Truncation

The class Math in the java.lang library contains several methods that allow control over truncation of floating-point values into integers. Although these methods are sometimes described as rounding methods, and two of them are named round(), they in fact perform IEEE 754 truncation operations. The truncation methods are named ceil(), floor(), rint(), and round(). Their operation is as follows:

### public static double ceil(double a)

Returns the smallest integer value that is closest to negative infinity and not less than the argument. The following are special cases:

1. If the argument is an integer, then the result is the same as the argument.
2. If the argument is a NaN, an infinity, positive zero, or negative zero, then the result is the same as the argument.
3. If the argument is less than zero but greater than -1.0, then the result is negative zero.

The methods only parameter is a value of type double. The method's name relates to the notion of a numeric ceiling.

### public static double floor(double a)

Returns the largest integer value that is closest to positive infinity and not greater than the argument. The following are special cases:

1. If the argument is an integer, then the result is the same as the argument.

2. If the argument is a NaN, an infinity, or positive zero, or negative zero, then the result is the same as the argument.

    The method's only parameter is a value of type double.

## public static double rint(double a)

Returns a double value that is closest in value to the argument and is an integer. If two double values that are integers are equally close to the value of the argument, then the result is the integer value that is even. The following are special cases:

1. If the argument is an integer, then the result is the same as the argument.

2. If the argument is NaN, or an infinity, or positive zero, or negative zero then the result is the same as the argument.

    The function's only parameter is a value of type double. Note that rint() returns an integer variable in a double type.

## public static long round(double a)

Returns the closest long to the argument. The result is rounded to an integer by adding 1/2, taking the floor of the result, and casting the result to type long. In other words, the result is equal to the value of the expression:

```
(long)Math.floor(a   0.5d)
```

The following are special cases:

1. If the argument is NaN, the result is 0.

2. If the argument is negative infinity or any value less than or equal to the value of Long.MIN_VALUE, the result is equal to the value of Long.MIN_VALUE.

3. If the argument is positive infinity or any value greater than or equal to the value of Long.MAX_VALUE, the result is equal to the value of Long.MAX_VALUE.

    The method's only parameter is of type double. The integer result is returned in a type long.

## public static int round(float a)

Returns the closest int to the argument. The result is rounded to an integer by adding 1/2, taking the floor of the result, and casting the result to type int. In other words, the result is equal to the value of the expression:

```
(int)Math.floor(a   0.5f)
```

The following are special cases:

1. If the argument is NaN, the result is 0.

2. If the argument is negative infinity or any value less than or equal to the value of Integer.MIN_VALUE, the result is equal to the value of Integer.MIN_VALUE.

3. If the argument is positive infinity or any value greater than or equal to the value of Integer.MAX_VALUE, the result is equal to the value of Integer.MAX_VALUE.

The method's only parameter is of type float. The integer result is returned in a type int.

# *Chapter 22*

# Variable-Precision Numeric Data

## High-Precision Arithmetic

The java.lang library provides two classes that allow the implementation of high-precision arithmetic. The BigDecimal class supports arbitrary-precision operations on signed decimal numbers, while the BigInteger does the same for integers. These classes allow the programmer to define the precision of decimal and integer values. The resulting numbers are never changed by the system and never overflow. On the other hand, the mathematical operations that can be applied to arbitrary-precision data is limited to basic arithmetic, conversions, comparisons, and rounding. The java libraries provide no trigonometry, logarithms, or exponential functions for arbitrary-precision data.

## BigDecimal Numbers

A BigDecimal object consists of an arbitrary-precision decimal number defined as an integer unscaled value and a non-negative 32-bit integer scale. The scale of a BigDecimal number is the number of digits to the right of the decimal point. For example, the number

```
123.556677
```

has a scale of 6, since there are six digits to the right of the decimal point. Zeros to the right of the scale digits are not truncated to reduce the scale; therefore, the numbers 2.0 and 2.00 are not considered equal by some operations of the BigDecimal class. Since the scale is a 32-bit integer number, the largest number of digits to the right of the decimal point is

```
68,719,476,735
```

Consider that the number

```
5.6677221133445533229988776666554433221133
```

has a scale of 40 digits, which is a very small fraction of the format's maximum range. This means that for most practical purposes this range can be considered of unlimited precision.

In addition to its high-precision, the BigDecimal class gives its users control over rounding behavior, by providing eight rounding modes. As discussed in Chapter 21, rounding control provides some interesting programming possibilities, including the use of boundary arithmetic.

## BigDecimal constructors

The BigDecimal class contains the following constructors:

### *BigDecimal(BigInteger val)*

Translates a BigInteger into a BigDecimal.

### *BigDecimal(BigInteger unscaledVal, int scale)*

Translates a BigInteger unscaled value and an int scale into a BigDecimal.

### *BigDecimal(double val)*

Translates a double into a BigDecimal.

### *BigDecimal(String val)*

Translates a string into a BigDecimal.

## Using the BigDecimal constructors

The first three constructors are used to convert from other numeric formats into the BigDecimal format. For example, to convert a value in double precision format you can code:

```
double aDbl = 1.23;
BigDecimal bigNum = new BigDecimal(aDbl);
```

At this point the variable bigNum contains the value of the closest double precision representation to the number 1.23. Since the value 1.23 cannot be exactly represented as a binary floating-point number, the value stored in bigNum is:

```
1.229999999999999982236431605997495353221893310546875
```

In order make sure of the value stored in a BigDecimal variable you must use the constructor that takes a string operand. For example:

```
bigNum = new BigDecimal("1.23");
```

This constructor translates the string operand into a BigDecimal value. The string consists of an optional positive or negative sign, or no sign for positive values, followed by a sequence of zero or more digits that form the integer part of the number, optionally followed by a decimal point, optionally followed by a fractional part, optionally followed by an exponent. The string must contain at least one digit in either the integer or the fractional part. The portion of the number formed by the sign, the integer and the fraction is referred to as the significand.

The exponent can consist of the character e or E, followed by one or more decimal digits. The value of the exponent must lie between Integer.MIN_VALUE and Integer.MAX_VALUE, inclusive.

The scale of the BigDecimal value produced by the constructor will be the number of digits in the fraction, or zero if the string contains no decimal point. If there is an exponent, the scale is adjusted by subtracting the exponent. If the resulting value is negative, the scale of the BigDecimal is zero. In any case the resulting BigDecimal is

```
significand * 10^exponent
```

For floats and doubles other that NAN, +INFINITY and -INFINITY, the string constructor is compatible with the values returned by Float.toString() and Double.toString(). Using the toString() methods is the recommended way to convert a float or double into a BigDecimal, as it avoids the unpredictability of the BigDecimal(double) constructor.

## BigDecimal scale operations

Two types of operations are provided for manipulating the scale of BigDecimal numbers: those that relate to setting and changing the scale and rounding controls, and those that move the decimal point.

### SetScale() method

The setScale() method is provided with two different signatures. One takes as parameters a scale and a rounding mode, and the other one just the scale. Recall that the scale is the number of representable digits to the right of the decimal point. The setScale() methods are as follows:

```
public BigDecimal setScale(int scale, int roundingMode)
```

Returns a BigDecimal whose scale and rounding mode are the specified values. The method returns a BigDecimal whose scale is the specified value, and whose unscaled value is determined by multiplying or dividing this

BigDecimal's unscaled value by the appropriate power of ten to maintain its overall value.

Throws:

1. ArithmeticException if scale is negative, or if roundingMode-
   ==ROUND_UNNECESSARY and the specified scaling operation would require rounding. Rounding modes are discussed later in this chapter.
2. IllegalArgumentException if roundingMode does not represent a valid
   rounding mode.

Examples of the scaling methods are provided in the context of round-ing operations later in this chapter.

```
public BigDecimal setScale(int scale)
```

Returns a BigDecimal whose scale is the specified value as described for the previous signature of this method. The call to this method can be used to reduce the scale if there are sufficiently many zeros at the end of its frac-tional part. This allows the rescaling without loss of precision.

### Scale() method

The scale() method is used to obtain the scale of a BigDecimal number. The method is documented as follows:

```
public int scale()
```

Returns the scale of a BigDecimal as a type int.

## BigDecimal point operations

Decimal point motion operations are provided by the methods movePointLeft() and movePointRight(). Both methods return a BigDecimal created from the operand by moving the decimal point a speci-fied distance in the specified direction. These methods change the value of a number without affecting its precision.

```
public BigDecimal movePointLeft(int n)
```

Returns a BigDecimal which is equivalent to the argument with the decimal point moved $n$ places to the left. If $n$ is non-negative, the method adds $n$ to the scale. If $n$ is negative, the method is equivalent to movePointRight(–n).

```
public BigDecimal movePointRight(int n)
```

Moves the decimal point the specified number of places to the right. If this BigDecimal's scale is $\geq n$, the method subtracts $n$ from the scale; otherwise, it sets the scale to zero, and multiplies the integer value by 10. If $n$ is negative, the call is equivalent to movePointLeft(-n).

## BigDecimal comparisons and conversions

Several methods of the BigDecimal class provide comparison of BigDecimal numbers with other objects, as well as conversion between BigDecimal numbers and other formats. The comparison methods are equals() and compareTo(), while the conversion methods are doubleValue(), floatValue(), intValue(), longValue(), toBigInteger(), valueOf(), toString(), and hashCode().

### *public boolean equals(Object x)*

Compares a BigDecimal with the object specified as an operand. This method considers two BigDecimal numbers equal if they are equal in value and scale only. Thus, equals returns that 3.0 is not equal to 3.00. The method returns if both BigDecimal objects are equal in value and scale, as in the following code fragment:

```
BigDecimal aNum = new BigDecimal ("3.45"); // String constructors
BigDecimal bNum = new BigDecimal ("3.450");
// Testing equals()
System.out.println(aNum.equals(bNum));      // FALSE
```

### *public int compareTo(BigDecimal val)*

Compares two BigDecimal with the specified BigDecimal independently of scale. In contrast with the equals() methods, compareTo() does not consider the scale of the operands when making comparisons. Also, compareTo() returns an integer instead of a boolean.

The compareTo() method can be used with any of the six boolean comparison operators (<, ==, >, >=, !=, <=). The general form is:

```
(x.compareTo(y) <op> 0)
```

where $x$ and $y$ are two BigDecimal numbers and <op> is one of the boolean operators. The method returns -1 if the first operator is less than the second one, 0 if both operators are equal, and 1 if the first one is greater than the second one. For example:

```
BigDecimal aNum = new BigDecimal ("3.45"); // String constructor
BigDecimal bNum = new BigDecimal ("3.450");
BigDecimal cNum = new BigDecimal ("5.0");
int numVal = 0;
// Testing compareTo()
System.out.println(aNum.compareTo(bNum) == 0); // TRUE
numVal =  aNum.compareTo(cNum);                 // -1
System.out.println(numVal);
```

### public double doubleValue()

Converts a BigDecimal to a double. If the BigDecimal operand is too large to represent, the method returns DOUBLE.NEGATIVE_INFINITY or DOUBLE.POSITIVE_INFINITY.

### public float floatValue()

Converts a BigDecimal operand to a float. If the BigDecimal is too large to represent as a float, the method returns FLOAT.NEGATIVE_INFINITY or FLOAT.POSITIVE_INFINITY.

### public int intValue()

Converts the BigDecimal operand to an int. The fractional part of the BigDecimal is discarded. If the resulting "BigInteger" is too large to fit in an int, the low-order 32 bits are returned.

### public long longValue()

Converts the BigDecimal operand to a long. The fractional part of the BigDecimal is discarded. If the resulting "BigInteger" is too large to fit in a long, the low-order 64 bits are returned.

### public BigInteger toBigInteger()

Converts the BigDecimal operand to a BigInteger. The fractional part of the BigDecimal is discarded. The BigInteger format is discussed later in this chapter.

### public static BigDecimal valueOf(long unscaledVal, int scale)

Translates a long unscaled value and an int scale into a BigDecimal. This method is provided in preference to a (long, int) constructor because it allows for reuse of common BigDecimals. For example:

```
// Testing valueOf()
System.out.println(BigDecimal.valueOf(2, 4));   // 0.0002
```

### public static BigDecimal valueOf(long val)

Translates a long value into a BigDecimal with a scale of zero. This method is provided in preference to a (long) constructor because it allows for reuse of common BigDecimals. For example:

```
// Testing valueOf()
System.out.println(BigDecimal.valueOf(1));      // 1
```

### public String toString()

Returns the string representation of the BigDecimal operand. A leading minus sign is used to indicate sign, and the number of digits to the right of the decimal point is used to indicate scale. This method is compatible with the constructor that uses a String argument.

### *public int hashCode()*

Returns the hash code for the BigDecimal operand. The hash code is an integer calculated from the number's value and scale. For this reason two numbers with the same value but different scales may have different hash codes. However, it is possible that two unequal big decimal numbers may have the same hash codes. Hash codes and hash tables are used in data processing.

## BigDecimal rounding controls

The class java.math contains several constants that are used to enable any one of several rounding modes. These constants are defined as static field variables of type int in the BigDecimal class. Table 22-1 lists the rounding mode constants.

### Table 22-1

*Rounding Mode Constants in BigDecimal Class*

| CONSTANT | ACTION |
| --- | --- |
| ROUND_CEILING | Round towards positive infinity |
| ROUND_DOWN | Round towards zero |
| ROUND_FLOOR | Round towards negative infinity |
| ROUND_HALF_DOWN | Round towards nearest value unless both values are equidistant, in which case round down |
| ROUND_HALF_EVEN | Round towards the nearest value unless both values are equidistant, in which case, round towards the even value |
| ROUND_HALF_UP | Round towards nearest value unless both values are equidistant, in which case round up |
| ROUND_UNNECESSARY | Assert that the requested operation hasan exact result, hence no rounding is necessary |
| ROUND_UP | Round away from zero |

The rounding control constants are typically used in methods that contain a rounding mode parameter, such as the setScale() and divide() methods of the BigDecimal class. For example, a method to change the scale and the rounding mode of a BigDecimal variable could be coded as follows:

```
static BigDecimal reScale(BigDecimal n,
                          int scale,
                          int roundingMode)
{
    return (n.setScale(scale, roundingMode));
}
```

This method would return the BigDecimal operand with a new scale and rounding mode. For example:

```
BigDecimal aNum = new BigDecimal ("3.45");
// Testing setScale() method and rounding mode constants
System.out.println(aNum);                        // 3.45
aNum = reScale(aNum, 1, BigDecimal.ROUND_UP);   // 3.5
System.out.println(aNum);
```

Since the scale() method returns the current scale of a BigDecimal number, the method reScale() could be modified to change the rounding mode only, as follows:

```
static BigDecimal reRound(BigDecimal n,
                          int roundingMode)
{
    return (n.setScale(n.scale(), roundingMode));
}
```

## BigDecimal Arithmetic

The BigDecimal class provides methods for performing basic arithmetic on BigDecimal numbers. Table 22-2 is a summary of these methods.

### Table 22-2
*Arithmetic Methods in BigDecimal Class*

---

**Abs()**
> Returns a BigDecimal whose value is the absolute value of this BigDecimal()

**add(BigDecimal val)**
> Returns a BigDecimal whose value is the sum of the argment and the operand

**divide(BigDecimal val, int roundingMode)**
> Returns a BigDecimal whose value is the quotient of the argument and the operand

**divide(BigDecimal val, int scale, int roundingMode)**
> Returns a BigDecimal whose value is the quotient of the argument and the operand and whose scale is as specified

**max(BigDecimal val)**
> Returns the maximum of this BigDecimal and val.

**min(BigDecimal val)**
> Returns the minimum of this BigDecimal and val

---

*(continues)*

**Table 22-2**

*Arithmetic Methods in BigDecimal Class (continued)*

---

**multiply(BigDecimal val)**
> Returns a BigDecimal whose value is the product of the argument and the operand

**negate()**
> Returns a BigDecimal whose value is the operand times −1

**int signum()**
> Returns -1, 0, or 1 if the value of the BigDecimal operand is negative, zero, or positive

**subtract(BigDecimal val)**
> Returns a BigDecimal whose value is the difference between the argument and the operand

---

Note in Table 22-2 that the arithmetic operations provided for BigDecimal numbers include addition, subtraction, multiplication, division, absolute value, maximum, minimum, sign extraction, and negation.

## A sample program

The following program demonstrates arithmetic on big decimal numbers by calculating the square root. The code requests user input for a string of digits representing the number and for the number's scale. The square root of the user's input is calculated using Newton's method and the results are displayed on the screen. The following is a listing of the source code.

```
class BigDSqrt
{
   public static void main(String[] args)
   {
        double value = 1.0;
        String numS;
        int scale = 30;
        BigDecimal v;

        System.out.println("Big decimal square root routine\n");
        numS = Keyin.inString("Enter value: ");
        scale = Keyin.inInt("Enter scale: ");
        // Convert value to big decimal format
        v = new BigDecimal(numS);
        System.out.println(sqrt(v, scale));
    }
   public static BigDecimal sqrt(BigDecimal n, int s)
   {
        BigDecimal TWO = BigDecimal.valueOf(2);
        // Obtain the first approximation
        BigDecimal x = n.divide(BigDecimal.valueOf(3), s,
          BigDecimal.ROUND_DOWN);
        BigDecimal lastX = BigDecimal.valueOf(0);
         // Proceed through 50 iterations
```

```
      for (int i=0; i<50; i++)
      {
        x = n.add(x.multiply(x)).divide(x.multiply(TWO), s,
            BigDecimal.ROUND_DOWN);
        if (x.compareTo(lastX) == 0)
            break;
      lastX = x;
    }
    return x;
  }
}
```

## On the Web

The BigDSqrt program is found in the Chapter 22 folder at www.crc-press.com.

# The BigInteger Class

The java.math library contains the BigInteger class which allows creation, manipulation, and basic arithmetic on arbitrary-precision integers. Integer numbers are less useful for scientific and engineering applications than the DigDecimal class described previously. However, Java's BigInteger class is not a mirror image of its BigDecimal counterpart. BigInteger implements operations that are not available for decimal numbers, in addition to the elementary ones that are available in both classes.

The BigInteger class provides methods that are analogs of the ones that the language provides for primitive integer operators. In addition, the BigInteger class provides operations for modular arithmetic, greatest common divisor calculation, testing and generating prime numbers, bit manipulations, and other operations not implemented for the primtive types.

## BigInteger numbers

Like the primitive integer data types, Java BigInteger numbers are represented in two's-complement form. Semantics of arithmetic operations are similar to the ones in Java integer arithmetic. For example, division by zero throws an ArithmeticException, and division of a negative by a positive yields a negative (or zero) remainder. One exception is the handling of overflow, which is not necessary for big integers since these numbers can be made as large as necessary to accommodate the results of an operation.

Bitwise shift operators are the same ones used in Java primitive data types. In this manner a right-shift with a negative shift distance results in a left shift, and vice-versa. Here again, the unsigned right shift operator (>>) is omitted since the operation is not necessary with the infinite word size provided by this class.

The bitwise logical operators and the comparison operators also mimic those of Java. The BigInteger class provides modular arithmetic operations to compute residues, perform exponentiation, and calculate multiplicative inverses. These methods return a non-negative result, between 0 and (modulus - 1), inclusive.

## BigInteger constructors

The BigInteger constructor is overloaded to provide several convenient ways of building big integer numbers. The constructor signatures are as follows:

### *BigInteger(byte[] val)*

Translates a byte array containing a two's-complement binary representation into a BigInteger. In this form of the constructor the big integer value is taken from the byte array val, which contains an integer in two's complement form. The bits are assumed to be in big-endian format. That is, val[0] contains the most-significant byte. The result is negative if the most-significant bit of val[0] is a 1 digit.

### *BigInteger(int signum, byte[] magnitude)*

Translates the sign-magnitude representation into a BigInteger. In this form of the constructor the big integer value is taken from the byte array magnitude, which must contain a nonnegative binary number. The bits are assumed to be in big-endian format, that is, magnitude [0] contains the most-significant byte. If signum is -1, the result is negative. If signum is 0, the magnitude argument must contain only zeros. If signum is 1, the result is positive.

### *BigInteger(int bitLength, int certainty, Random rnd)*

Constructs a randomly generated positive BigInteger that is probably prime, with the specified bitLength. In this form of the constructor the big integer value is initialized with bitLength number of random bits. The paramenter rnd is used to generate the random bits. The probability that the result is prime is controlled by the parameter certainty; larger values increase the probability of a prime number's being obtained. The larger the size of the certainty parameter the longer this constructor takes to complete.

### *BigInteger(int numBits, Random rnd)*

Constructs a randomly generated BigInteger, uniformly distributed over the range 0 to ($2^{numBits - 1}$), inclusive. In this form of the constructor the big integer value is initialized with numBits number of random bits. The parameter rnd is used to generate the random bits. The value is never negative.

### *BigInteger(String val)*

Translates the decimal String representation of a BigInteger into a BigInteger. In this form of the constructor val is parsed as a radix 10 number to obtain the big integer value. The first character can optionally be a negative sign. The parameter val must not contain spaces and must include at least one digit. This constructor form is compatible with the strings generated by the toString() method.

### *BigInteger(String val, int rdix)*

Translates the String representation of a BigInteger in the specified radix into a BigInteger. In this form of the constructor the parameter val is parsed as a radix rdix number to obtain the big integer value. The first character can optionally can be a negative sign. The string val must not contain spaces and must include at least one digit.

## BigInteger methods

There are over forty methods in the BigInteger class. Table 22-3 is summary of these methods.

**Table 22-3**

*Methods in the BigInteger Class*

| RETURNS | METHOD/ACTION |
|---|---|
| BigInteger | **abs()** <br> Returns a BigInteger whose value is the absolute value of this BigInteger |
| BigInteger | **add(BigInteger val)** <br> Returns a BigInteger whose value is (this val) |
| BigInteger | **and(BigInteger val)** <br> Returns a BigInteger whose value is (this & val) |
| BigInteger | **andNot(BigInteger val)** <br> Returns a BigInteger whose value is (this & ~val) |
| int | **bitCount()** <br> Returns the number of bits in the two's complement representation of this BigInteger that differ from its sign bit |

**(continues)**

**Table 22-3**

*Methods in the BigInteger Class (continued)*

| RETURNS | METHOD/ACTION |
| --- | --- |
| int | **bitLength()**<br>Returns the number of bits in the minimal two's-complement representation of this BigInteger, excluding a sign bit |
| BigInteger | **learBit(int n)**<br>Returns a BigInteger whose value is equivalent to this BigInteger with the designated bit cleared |
| int | **compareTo(BigInteger val)**<br>Compares this BigInteger with the specified BigInteger |
| int | **compareTo(Object o)**<br>Compares this BigInteger with the specified object |
| BigInteger | **divide(BigInteger val)**<br>Returns a BigInteger whose value is (this / val) |
| BigInteger[] | **divideAndRemainder(BigInteger val)**<br>Returns an array of two BigIntegers containing (this / val) followed by (this % val) |
| Double | **doubleValue()**<br>Converts this BigInteger to a double |
| boolean | **equals(Object x)**<br>Compares this BigInteger with the specified Object for equality |
| BigInteger | **flipBit(int n)**<br>Returns a BigInteger whose value is equivalent to this BigInteger with the designated bit flipped |
| Float | **floatValue()**<br>Converts this BigInteger to a float |
| BigInteger | **gcd(BigInteger val)**<br>Returns a BigInteger whose value is the greatest common divisor of abs(this) and abs(val) |
| int | **getLowestSetBit()**<br>Returns the index of the rightmost (lowest-order) one bit in this BigInteger (the number of zero bits to the right of the rightmost one bit) |
| int | **hashCode()**<br>Returns the hash code for this BigInteger |
| Int | **intValue()**<br>Converts this BigInteger to an int |
| boolean | **isProbablePrime(int certainty)**<br>Returns true if this BigInteger is probably prime, false if it's definitely composite |
| long | **longValue()**<br>Converts this BigInteger to a long |

*(continues)*

**Table 22-3**

*Methods in the BigInteger Class (continued)*

| RETURNS | METHOD/ACTION |
| --- | --- |
| BigInteger | **max(BigInteger val)**<br>Returns the maximum of this BigInteger and val |
| BigInteger | **min(BigInteger val)**<br>Returns the minimum of this BigInteger and val |
| BigInteger | **mod(BigInteger m)**<br>Returns a BigInteger whose value is (this mod m) |
| BigInteger | **modInverse(BigInteger m)**<br>Returns a BigInteger whose value is (this-1 mod m) |
| BigInteger | **modPow(BigInteger exponent, BigInteger m)**<br>Returns a BigInteger whose value is (thisexponent mod m) |
| BigInteger | **multiply(BigInteger val)**<br>Returns a BigInteger whose value is (this * val) |
| BigInteger | **negate()**<br>Returns a BigInteger whose value is (−this) |
| BigInteger | **not()**<br>Returns a BigInteger whose value is (~this) |
| BigInteger | **or(BigInteger val)**<br>Returns a BigInteger whose value is (this \| val) |
| BigInteger | **pow(int exponent)**<br>Returns a BigInteger whose value is (this.exponent) |
| BigInteger | **remainder(BigInteger val)**<br>Returns a BigInteger whose value is (this % val) |
| BigInteger | **setBit(int n)**<br>Returns a BigInteger whose value is equivalent to this BigInteger with the designated bit set |
| BigInteger | **shiftLeft(int n)**<br>Returns a BigInteger whose value is (this < n) |
| BigInteger | **shiftRight(int n)**<br>Returns a BigInteger whose value is (this > n) |
| int | **signum()**<br>Returns the sign of this BigInteger |
| BigInteger | **subtract(BigInteger val)**<br>Returns a BigInteger whose value is (this − val) |
| boolean | **testBit(int n)**<br>Returns true if and only if the designated bit is set |
| Byte[] | **toByteArray()**<br>Returns a byte array containing the two's-complement representation of this BigInteger |

*(continues)*

**Table 22-3**

*Methods in the BigInteger Class (continued)*

| RETURNS | METHOD/ACTION |
|---------|---------------|
| String | **toString()**<br>Returns the decimal String representation of this BigInteger |
| String | **toString(int radix)**<br>Returns the String representation of this BigInteger in the given radix |
| Static | **BigInteger valueOf(long val)**<br>Returns a BigInteger whose value is equal to that of the specified long |
| BigInteger | **xor(BigInteger val)**<br>Returns a BigInteger whose value is (this ^ val) |

## A sample program

The following program demonstrates arithmetic on big integer numbers by calculating the factorial. The following is a listing of the source code.

```
// Filename: BigIFact
// Reference: Chapter 22
// Description:
//          Demonstration of high-precision integer arithmetic
//          with the BigInteger class. Program calculates the
//          factorial of a big integer number
// Requires:
//          Keyin class in current directory

import java.math.*;
class BigIFact

{
   public static void main(String[] args)
   {
        int v;                                   // Input
        BigInteger p = BigInteger.valueOf(1);   // Factor

        System.out.println("Big integer factorial routine\n");
        v = Keyin.inInt("Enter value: ");
         // Calculate factorial by iteration
        for(int i = 1; i <= v; i++)
             p = p.multiply(BigInteger.valueOf(i));
        // Display result
        System.out.println(p);
     }
}
```

## On the Web

The program BigIFact.java can be found in the Chapter 22 folder at www.crcpress.com.

# Chapter 23

# Fundamental Operations

## Calculator Operations

In this chapter we look at basic mathematical calculations in Java. You can think of these operations as those typically found in scientific or engineering calculator. For the purpose of this chapter we classify the fundamental operations into the following groups:

1. Basic arithmetic: the calculation of absolute value, maximum and minimum, IEEE-style remainder, rounding operations, and obtaining the constants $\pi$ and e

2. Exponential functions: the calculation of powers and roots

3. Trigonometric functions: the calculation of trigonometric functions and arc-functions, conversions of radians to degrees and degrees to radians, and calculation of hyperbolic functions and arc-functions

4. Logarithms: the calculation of common and natural logarithms and the corresponding antilogarithms

5. Generation of random numbers

## Java Floating-Point Math

Most engineering calculations require decimal numbers. For this reason our emphasis in this chapter is on floating-point operations. These operations are located in several classes in the java.lang and java.math packages. Some of these classes have been discussed in previous chapters. In particular the classes Double and Float of java.lang, which were mentioned in Chapter 21, and the clases BigDecimal and BigInteger, which were the topic of Chapter 22. Here we are mainly concerned with the classes Math and StrictMath of java.math.

## Strict and non-strict math

Java supports two modes of floating point mathematics. One mode, called *strict* is designed to ensure portability of Java programs. The methods that provide strict mathematics are located in the StrictMath class of java.math.

The main purpose of Java strict math is to ensure that calculations produce identical results on any Java virtual machine. Non-strict arithmetic, on the other hand, can be implemented with more relaxed rules. That is, the designer of a Java virtual machine is allowed to use faster implementations for non-strict math functions, at the expense of producing slightly different results on different platforms.

The programmer can select strict or non-strict modes by means of the *strictfp* modifier. The modifier can be applied to a class, an interface, or a method. When a method is declared with the strictfp modifier, all the code is executed according to strict constraints. When used at the class or interface level, all code in the class or interface is evaluated according to strict math rules.

## Programmers note:

The StrictMath class was introduced in Java version 1.3. Previous versions of the JDK generate an error if StrictMath is referenced in code.

If your code requires exact bit-for-bit results on all Java virtual machines, then you should use the strictfp modifier. Note that implementing non-strict math is a developer's option. Therefore, it is possible that in a particular Java virtual machine strict and non-strict routines produce the same results.

At the application level strict math and non-strict math can be selected by referencing the corresponding parent classes: Math for non-strict code and StrictMath otherwise. For example, the following program calculates the square of the constant *e* using strict math.

```
// Java for Engineers
// Filename: StrictE
// Reference: Chapter 23
// Description:
//          Using strict math in applications.
//          Calculates e * e
// Requires:
//          Keyin class in current directory

import java.lang.*;
```

```
class StrictM
{
    public static void main(String[] args)
    {
        // Calculate E * E
        double e2 = StrictMath.E * StrictMath.E;

        System.out.println(e2);
    }
}
```

Alternatively, the strictfp operator can be used at the class or the method level. The program StrictPI.java, in the book's CD ROM, contains a class that is declared with the strictfp operator, as follows:

```
strictfp class StrictPI
```

## On the Web

The programs StrictE.java and StrictPI.java are located in the Chapter 23 folder at www.crcpress.com.

# Java Basic Arithmetic

The java.lang package contains several classes that provide basic arithmetic. The most important ones are the classes named Math and StrictMath. Both classes expose the same fields and methods, therefore the following descriptions apply to both Math, and StrictMath. As mentioned previously, strict mathematics can be enabled at the class or method level by means of the strictfp operator. In that case the methods and fields in java.lang.StrictMath are always used.

## Programmers note:

The so-called operator functions (+, −, *, /, and %) are Java language primitives and, therefore, not part of java.lang or any other Java package.

## Numeric constants

Two fields defined in Math and StrictMath allow declaring the common constants e and Pi. They are defined as follows:

### *public static final double E*

The value that is closer than any other to the base of the natural logarithms. The actual value is:

```
2.7182818284590452354
```

### *public static final double PI*

The double value that is closer than any other to the ratio of the circumference of a circle to its diameter. The actual value is:

```
3.14159265358979323846
```

## Absolute value

The method abs()returns the absolute value of the operand, which can be a double, a float, and int, or a long in the various implementations.

### *public static int abs(int a)*

Returns the absolute value of an int operand. If the argument is positive the same value is returned. If the argument is negative, the negation of the operand value is returned. If the argument is equal to the value of Integer.MIN_VALUE the result is that same value, which is negative.

### *public static long abs(long a)*

Returns the absolute value of a long operand. If the argument is not negative, the same value is returned. If the argument is negative, the negation of the argument is returned.

Note that if the argument is equal to the value of Long.MIN_VALUE the result is that same value, which is negative.

### *public static float abs(float a)*

Returns the absolute value of a float operand. If the argument is not negative, the same value is returned. If the argument is negative, the negation of the argument is returned. The following are special cases:

1. If the argument is positive zero or negative zero, the result is positive zero.

2. If the argument is infinite, the result is positive infinity.

3. If the argument is NaN, the result is NaN.

### *public static double abs(double a)*

Returns the absolute value of a double operand. If the argument is not negative, the same value is returned. If the argument is negative, the negation of the argument is returned. The following are special cases:

1. If the argument is positive zero or negative zero, the result is positive zero.

2. If the argument is infinite, the result is positive infinity.

3. If the argument is NaN, the result is NaN.

## Maximum and minimum

Two functions named max() and min() allow comparing two values to determine which is the greater or the smaller. The max() method returns the greater of two numbers, while the min() method determines the smaller. Both methods allow operands of type int, long, float, and double.

The general form of the max() and min() functions are as follows:

### *public static operand max(operand a, operand b)*

Operand can be of type int, long, float, or double. The max() method returns the greater of two values.

### *public static operand min(operand a, operand b)*

Operand can be of type int, long, float, or double. The min() method returns the smaller of two values.

## Rounding controls

Several methods in java.lang.Math and java.lang.StrictMath provide rounding controls over numeric operands. These methods round a floating-point value to a whole number. The methods are as follows:

### *public static double ceil(double a)*

Returns the smallest double value that is not less than the argument and is equal to an integer. The following are special cases:

1. If the argument value is already equal to an integer, then the result is the same as the argument.

2. If the argument is NaN or an infinity or positive zero or negative zero, then the result is the same as the argument.

3. If the argument value is less than zero but greater than -1.0, then the result is negative zero.

### *public static double floor(double a)*

Returns the largest double value that is not greater than the argument and is equal to an integer. The following are special cases:

1. If the argument is already equal to an integer, then the result is the same as the argument.

2. If the argument is NaN or an infinity or positive zero or negative zero, then the result is the same as the argument.

### public static double rint(double a)

Returns the double that is closest in value to a and is equal to an integer. If two double values that are integers are equally close to the value of the argument, the result is the integer value that is even. The following are special cases:

1. If the argument value is already equal to an integer, then the result is the same as the argument.

2. If the argument is NaN or infinity or positive zero or negative zero, then the result is the same as the argument.

### public static int round(float a)

Returns the closest int to the argument. The result is rounded to an integer by adding 1/2, taking the floor of the result, and casting the result to type int. The following are special cases:

1. If the argument is NaN, the result is 0.

2. If the argument is negative infinity or any value less than or equal to the value of Integer.MIN_VALUE, the result is equal to the value of Integer.MIN_VALUE.

3. If the argument is positive infinity or any value greater than or equal to the value of Integer.MAX_VALUE, the result is equal to the value of Integer.MAX_VALUE.

### public static long round(double a)

Returns the closest long to the argument. The result is rounded to an integer by adding 1/2, taking the floor of the result, and casting the result to type long. The following are special cases:

1. If the argument is NaN, the result is 0.

2. If the argument is negative infinity or any value less than or equal to the value of Long.MIN_VALUE, the result is equal to the value of Long.MIN_VALUE.

3. If the argument is positive infinity or any value greater than or equal to the value of Long.MAX_VALUE, the result is equal to the value of Long.MAX_VALUE.

## IEEE-style remainder

One method in the classes Math and StrictMath returns the remainder as defined by the IEEE 754 Standard. IEEE 754 requires that implementations must provide the add, subtract, multiply, divide, and remainder operations for any two operands of the same or different format.

The IEEE remainder, sometimes called the *exact remainder* is defined as follows:

When y not equal to 0, the remainder $r = x$ REM $y$ is defined by the mathematical relation:

$$r = x - y \times n$$

where $n$ is the integer nearest to the exact value of $x/y$. Whenever

$$\left| n - \frac{x}{y} \right| = \frac{1}{2}$$

then n is even. If $r = 0$ then the sign is that of $x$. In IEEE 754 precision control does not apply to the remainder operation.

The method is defined as follows:

### public static double IEEEremainder(double f1, double f2)

Computes the remainder operation on two arguments as prescribed by the IEEE 754 standard. The remainder value is mathematically equal to $f1 - f2 \times n$, $f1$ is the dividend, $f2$ is the divisor, and $n$ is the integer closest to the exact mathematical value of the quotient $f1/f2$. If two integers are equally close to $f1/f2$, then n is the integer that is even. If the remainder is zero, its sign is the same as the sign of the first argument. The following are special cases:

1. If either argument is NaN, or if the first argument is infinite, or if the second argument is positive zero or negative zero, then the result is NaN.

2. If the first argument is finite and the second argument is infinite, then the result is the same as the first argument.

# Exponential Function

The Math and StrictMath classes of the java.lang package provide methods to calculate powers and roots. These include the method pow() that returns a power function, the method sqrt() that returns the square root of the argument, and the method exp() which returns the constant e raised to a power. The methods are as follows:

### public static double pow(double a, double b)

Returns the value of the first argument raised to the power of the second argument, that is, the method calculates $a^b$. Because the exponent argument is a floating -point value, the pow() method can be used to calculate roots:

$$\sqrt[y]{x} = x^{\frac{1}{y}}$$

The laws of exponents apply to the arguments, therefore:

$$x^{-y} = \frac{1}{x^y}$$

The method has a long list of special cases.

1. If the second argument is positive or negative zero, then the result is 1.0.

2. If the second argument is 1.0, then the result is the same as the first argument.

3. If the second argument is NaN, then the result is NaN.

4. If the first argument is NaN and the second argument is nonzero, then the result is NaN.

5. If the absolute value of the first argument is greater than 1 and the second argument is positive infinity, or the absolute value of the first argument is less than 1 and the second argument is negative infinity, then the result is positive infinity.

6. If the absolute value of the first argument is greater than 1 and the second argument is negative infinity, or the absolute value of the first argument is less than 1 and the second argument is positive infinity, then the result is positive zero.

7. If the absolute value of the first argument equals 1 and the second argument is infinite, then the result is NaN.

8. If the first argument is positive zero and the second argument is greater than zero, or the first argument is positive infinity and the second argument is less than zero, then the result is positive zero.

9. If the first argument is positive zero and the second argument is less than zero, or the first argument is positive infinity and the second argument is greater than zero, then the result is positive infinity.

10. If the first argument is negative zero and the second argument is greater than zero, but not a finite odd integer, or the first argument is negative infinity and the second argument is less than zero but not a finite odd integer, then the result is positive zero.

11. If the first argument is negative zero and the second argument is a positive finite odd integer, or the first argument is negative infinity and the second argument is a negative finite odd integer, then the result is negative zero.

12. If the first argument is negative zero and the second argument is less than zero, but not a finite odd integer, or the first argument is negative infinity and the second argument is greater than zero, but not a finite odd integer, then the result is positive infinity.

13. If the first argument is negative zero and the second argument is a negative finite odd integer, or the first argument is negative infinity and the second argument is a positive finite odd integer, then the result is negative infinity.

14. If the first argument is less than zero and the second argument is a finite even integer, then the result is equal to the result of raising the absolute value of the first argument to the power of the second argument.

15. If the first argument is less than zero and the second argument is a finite odd integer, then the result is equal to the negative of the result of raising the absolute value of the first argument to the power of the second argument.

16. If the first argument is finite and less than zero and the second argument is finite and not an integer, then the result is NaN.

17. If both arguments are integers, then the result is exactly equal to the mathematical result of raising the first argument to the power of the second argument if that result can in fact be represented exactly as a double value.

The following program demonstrates the use of the pow() method.

```
// Java for Engineers
// Filename: ExpoDemo
// Reference: Chapter 23
// Description:
//              Using the pow() function

import java.lang.*;

strictfp class ExpoDemo
{
    public static void main(String[] args)
    {
        // Display the square root of 2 using sqrt()
        System.out.print("    sqrt(2.0) = ");
        System.out.println(Math.sqrt(2.0));

        // Calculate and display using pow()
        System.out.print("pow(2.0, 0.5) = ");
        System.out.println(Math.pow(2.0, 0.5));
        System.out.println();
    }
}
```

---
**On the Web**
---

The programExpoDemo.java is located in the Chapter 23 folder at www.crcpress.com.

---

### *public static double sqrt(double a)*

Returns the correctly rounded positive square root of a double value. The following are special cases:

1. If the argument is NaN or less than zero, then the result is NaN.

2. If the argument is positive infinity, then the result is positive infinity.

3. If the argument is positive zero or negative zero, then the result is the same as the argument.

Otherwise, the result is the double value closest to the true mathematical square root of the argument.

### *public static double exp(double a)*

Returns the constant e raised to the power of a double value. The following are special cases:

1. If the argument is NaN, the result is NaN.

2. If the argument is positive infinity, then the result is positive infinity.

3. If the argument is negative infinity, then the result is positive zero.

## Trigonometric Functions

Trigonometric methods in the classes Math and StrictMath provide for the calculation of trigonometric functions and arc-functions, as well as conversions of radians to degrees and degrees to radians. Table 23-1 describes the trigonometry-related functions.

The functions not included in the classes can be easily obtained by applying the corresponding identities, namely:

$$\sec \Theta = \frac{1}{\cos \Theta}$$

$$\csc \Theta = \frac{1}{\sin \Theta}$$

$$\cot \Theta = \frac{1}{\tan \Theta}$$

**Table 23-1**

*Trigonometric Method in Math and StrictMath Classes*

| RETURNS | METHOD/ACTION |
|---|---|
| static double | **sin(double a)**<br>Returns the trigonometric sine of an angle |
| static double | **cos(double a)**<br>Returns the trigonometric cosine of an angle |
| static double | **tan(double a)**<br>Returns the trigonometric tangent of an angle |
| static double | **asin(double a)**<br>Returns the arc sine of an angle, in the range<br>-π/2 through π/2 |
| static double | **acos(double a)**<br>Returns the arc cosine of an angle, in the<br>range of 0.0 through π |
| static double | **atan(double a)**<br>Returns the arc tangent of an angle, in the<br>range of −π/2 through π/2 |
| static double | **atan2(double a, double b)**<br>Converts rectangular coordinates (b, a) to<br>polar (r, θ) |
| static double | **toDegrees(double angrad)**<br>Converts an angle measured in radians to the<br>equivalent angle measured in degrees |
| static double | **toRadians(double angdeg)**<br>Converts an angle measured in degrees to<br>the equivalent angle measured in radians |

and the corresponding arc functions:

$$\sec^{-1}\Theta = \cos^{-1}\left(\frac{1}{\Theta}\right)$$

$$\csc^{-1}\Theta = \cos^{-1}\left(\frac{1}{\Theta}\right)$$

$$\cot^{-1}\Theta = \tan^{-1}\left(\frac{1}{\Theta}\right)$$

## Calculating trigonometric functions

The trigonometric functions in java.lang.Math receive as input an angle in radians. If input is in degrees, user code can convert to radians by calling the toRadians() method. By the same token, the trigonometric arc-functions return an angle in radians, which can be converted to degrees by means of the toDegrees() method. The following program shows the calculation of trigonometric functions and arc-functions.

```java
// Java for Engineers
// Filename: TrigFun
// Reference: Chapter 23
// Description:
//              Calculating trigonometric functions,
//              arcfunctions, and cofunctions.
// Requires:
//              Keyin class in current directory

import java.lang.*;

strictfp class TrigFun
{
    public static void main(String[] args)
    {
        double rads, degs, tanA, aTanA, coTanA;

// Obtain angle in degrees from user
        degs = Keyin.inDouble("Enter angle in degrees: ");
        // Convert degrees to radian
        rads = Math.toRadians(degs);

        // Calculate tangent
        tanA = Math.tan(rads);
        System.out.println("Tangent = " + tanA);

        // Calculate cotangent
        coTanA = 1.0/Math.tan(rads);
        System.out.println("Cotangent = " + coTanA);

        // Calculate arc-tangent
        rads = Math.atan(tanA);
        degs = Math.toDegrees(rads);
        System.out.println("Arc tangent: "  + degs);

        // Calculate arc-cotangent
        rads = Math.atan(1/coTanA);
        degs = Math.toDegrees(rads);
        System.out.println("Arc cotangent: "  + degs);

    }
}
```

## On the Web

The program TrigFun.java can be found in the Chapter 23 folder at www.crcpress.com.

## Hyperbolic functions and arc-functions

Engineering problems often require the evaluation of hyperbolic functions. These functions, called the hyperbolic tangent (tanh), hyperbolic sine (sinh), and hyperbolic cosine (cosh), have properties similar to the circular trigonometric functions, except that the hyperbolic functions are related to the hyperbola rather than to the circle. However, the hyperbolic functions cannot be readily derived from their trigonometric counterparts. Instead, they are expressed by the following formulas

$$\sinh(x) = \frac{e^x - e^{-x}}{2}$$

$$\cosh(x) = \frac{e^x + e^{-x}}{2}$$

$$\tanh(x) = \frac{e^x - e^{-x}}{e^x + e^{-x}}$$

$$\tanh(x) = \frac{\sinh(x)}{\cosh(x)}$$

In evaluating the hyperbolic functions code can make use of the exp() method in java.lang.Math previously discussed. The exp() method returns a power of e, which allows estimating the numerator in the sinh and cosh.

Hyperbolic arc-tangent functions can be calculated according to the following formulas:

$$\sinh^{-1}(x) = \ln(x + \sqrt{x^2 + 1}$$

$$\cosh^{-1}(x) = \ln(x + \sqrt{x^2 - 1}$$

$$\tanh^{-1}(x) = \frac{1}{2}\ln\left(\frac{1+x}{1-x}\right)$$

Here again the input angle is in radians. The following program demonstrates the calculation of hyperbolic functions and arc-functions.

```
// Java for Engineers
// Filename: HypFun
// Reference: Chapter 23
// Description:
//              Caculating hyperbolic functions
// Requires:
//              Keyin class in current directory

import java.lang.*;

strictfp class HypFun
{
    public static void main(String[] args)
    {
        double rads, degs, sinHA, cosHA, tanHA, asinHA;

        // Obtain angle in degrees from user
        degs = Keyin.inDouble("Enter angle in degrees: ");
        // Convert degrees to radian
        rads = Math.toRadians(degs);

        // Calculate hyperbolic sine
        sinHA = (Math.exp(rads) - Math.exp(-rads))/2;
        System.out.println("Hyperbolic sine = "  + sinHA);

        // Calculate Hyperbolic cosine
        cosHA = (Math.exp(rads) + Math.exp(-rads))/2;
        System.out.println("Hyperbolic cosine = "  + cosHA);

        // Calculate hyperbolic tangent
        tanHA = sinHA/ cosHA;
        System.out.println("Hyperbolic tangent = " + tanHA);

        // Calculate hyperbolic arc-sine
        asinHA = Math.log(sinHA + Math.sqrt((sinHA * sinHA)+ 1.0));
        degs = Math.toDegrees(asinHA);
        System.out.println("Arc hyperbolic sine = " + degs);
    }
}
```

## On the Web

The program HypFun.java can be found in the Chapter 23 folder at www.crcpress.com.

## Cartesian and polar coordinates

In mathematics the study of complex numbers leads directly to an alternative plane of trigonometric representation, usually called the polar coordinate system. Conventionally, the polar coordinate system is depicted as based on a point, called the *pole*, located at the origin of the Cartesian plane, and a ray from this pole, called the *polar axis*. The polar axis is assumed to lie in the positive direction of the *x*-axis. A point in the polar coordinate system is defined by its directed angle (called the vectorial angle) from the polar axis, and its directed distance from the pole, called the radius vector. Figure 23-1 shows the elements of the polar and Cartesian coordinate systems.

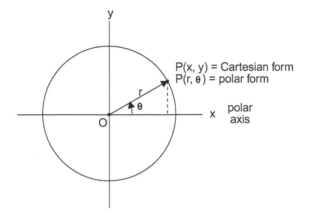

**Figure 23-1** *Polar and Cartesian Coordinate Systems*

Engineering applications often require converting coordinate pairs between the polar and the Cartesian systems. Cartesian coordinates are also called rectangular coordinates. The following formulas express polar coordinates from the rectangular form:

The method atan2() in java.lang.Math returns the vectorial angle expressed by the first formula from the rectangular coordinates. The radius

$$\tan \Theta = \frac{y}{x}$$

$$r = \sqrt{x^2 + y^2}$$

vector (r) can be calculated with the second formula.

The reverse process is obtaining the rectangular coordinates from the polar form. The following formulas can be used:

$$x = r \cos \Theta$$

$$y = r \sin \Theta$$

where $r$ is the radius vector and $\theta$ is the vectorial angle. The following program demonstrates conversion from Cartesian to polar coordinates and vice versa.

```java
// Java for Engineers
// Filename: CartPol
// Reference: Chapter 23
// Description:
//              Conversion between polar and rectangular
//              coordinates
// Requires:
//              Keyin class in current directory

import java.lang.*;

strictfp class CartPol
{
    public static void main(String[] args)
    {
        double x, y, vA, degs, radVec;

        // Obtain rectangular coordinates from user
        x = Keyin.inDouble("Enter x: ");
        y = Keyin.inDouble("Enter y: ");

        // Convert rectangular to polar coordinates
        vA = Math.atan2(x, y);
        degs = Math.toDegrees(vA);
        System.out.println("Vectorial angle = " + degs);
        // Calculate radius vector
        radVec = Math.sqrt((x * x)+(y * y));
        System.out.println("Radius vector = " + radVec);

        // Convert polar back to rectangular coordinates
        x = radVec * Math.cos(vA);
        System.out.println("x coodinate = " + x);
        y = radVec * Math.sin(vA);
        System.out.println("y coordinate = " + y);
    }
}
```

## On the Web

The program CartPol.java can be found in the Chapter 23 folder at www.crcpress.com.

# Logarithmic Functions

The classes java.lang.Math and java.lang.StrictMath contain a single method that relates to logarithms: log(). This method returns the natural logarithm (base e) of the double argument. However, the logarithmic formulas and identities allow using the natural logarithm to obtain logs to other bases, as well as calculating anti-logarithms. The following formula

$$\log_n(x) = \frac{\log_e(x)}{\log_e(n)}$$

allows using the natural log to obtain logs to other bases:

$$\log_{10}(x) = \frac{\log_e(x)}{\log_e(10)}$$

$$\log_2(x) = \frac{\log_e(x)}{\log_e(2)}$$

For example, to obtain the common logarithm (base 10) and the binary logarithm (base 2) we can calculate:

## Calculating antilogarithms

$$\mathrm{alog}_b(x) = b^x$$

Antilogarithms are the inverse function of the logarithm. The following formula generalizes antilogarithms to any base (b):

$$\mathrm{alog}_{10}(x) = 10^x$$

$$\mathrm{a}\log_e(x) = e^x$$

The natural (base e) and common (base 10) antilogarithms are defined as follows:

The following program uses the preceding formulas to calculate natural and common logarithms and antilogarithms.

```
// Java for Engineers
// Filename: Logs
// Reference: Chapter 23
// Description:
//              Conversion between polar and rectangular
//              coordinates
```

```
// Requires:
//              Keyin class in current directory

import java.lang.*;

strictfp class Logs
{
    public static void main(String[] args)
    {
        double num, loge, log10, aloge, alog10;

        // Obtain input from user
        num = Keyin.inDouble("Enter number: ");

        // Calculate and display the natural logarithm
        loge = Math.log(num);
        System.out.println("log base e = " + loge);
        // Calculate the common log
        log10 = Math.log(num)/Math.log(10.0);
        System.out.println("log base 10 = " + log10);

        // Calculate the antilogarithm of log base e
        aloge = Math.exp(loge);
        System.out.println("antilog of log base e = " + aloge);

        // Calculate the antilogarithm of log base 10
        alog10 = Math.pow(10.0, log10);
        System.out.println("anitlog of log base 10 = " + alog10);
    }
}
```

## On the Web

The program named Logs.java is found in the Chapter 23 folder at www.crcpress.com.

# Random Numbers

In computer games and in scientific and engineering simulations it is some-times necessary to obtain a number, or set of numbers, at random. Computers can be programmed to generate random numbers; however, their values may repeat after a certain number of iterations. It has been proven that true randomness requires mechanical devices. For this reason computers are often said to produce pseudo-random numbers. However, these pseudo-random numbers are often of sufficient quality to be useful in many applications.

Java provides several mechanisms for obtaining random numbers. The class java.util.Random contains ten methods that relate to the generation of random numbers. The classes java.lang.Math and java.lang.StrictMath contain a method random() that returns a pseudo-random number. This method is simple to use and produces satisfactory results for many applications.

## Producing pseudo-random numbers

How much programming is put into a random number generator depends on the randomness tests that the results must pass. The most basic pseudo-random generator can be based on the random() method of the Math and StrictMath classes. This method is documented as follows:

### *public static double random()*

Returns a pseudo-random double value ($r$) with a positive sign in the range $0.0 >= r < 1.0$. Returned values are uniform distributed over the range. When this method is first called, it creates a single new pseudo-random-number generator, as if by a call to:

```
new java.util.Random()
```

Thereafter the new pseudo-random-number generator is used for all calls to this method, but nowhere else.

Alternatively, you can use method in java.util.Random to generate random numbers. This approach is more complicated but ensures a better distribution of the random numbers. The method nextDouble() returns the next pseudo-random number uniformly distributed between 0.0 and 1.0. The method nextGaussian() generates a bell-curve distribution with a mean of 0.0 and a standard deviation of 1.0. In other words, nextDouble() produces a flat distribution curve and nextGaussian() produces a "normal" distribution curve.

The following program uses the random() method of java.lang.Math and java.lang.StrictMath to generate 10000 random numbers. The numbers are scaled to the range 0 to 9. The random numbers produced are classified according to their value in order to compare their frequency. The result is a flat distribution like the ones produced by the nextDouble() method.

```
// Java for Engineers
// Filename: RandNum
// Reference: Chapter 23
// Description:
//           Generating random numbers

import java.lang.*;
```

```
class RandNum
{
    public static void main(String[] args)
    {
        int num;
        int[]  dist = new int[10];   // Storage for distribution

        // Generate 10000 random numbers using Math.random()
        for(int x = 0; x < 10000; x++)
        {
            num = (int)(Math.floor(Math.random() * 10));
            dist[num]++;
        }
        // Display distribution of random integers in the range
        // 0 to 9
        System.out.println("Distribution using Math.random() ");

        for(int k = 0; k < 10; k++)
            System.out.print(k + "\t");
        // Display results
        for(int y = 0; y < 10; y++)
        {
            System.out.print(dist[y] + "\t");
        }
        System.out.println();
    }
}
```

## On the Web

The program RandNum.java is located in the Chapter 23 folder at www.crcpress.com.

# Chapter 24

# Java Math for Engineers

## Java Numerical Primitives

This chapter contains an assortment of numerical routines and primitives that are often required in solving engineering problems. The chapter serves a double purpose. The first one is to provide a small library of Java primitives. Second, and more important, to demonstrate how you can use your knowledge of the Java language to solve problems that are expressed in formulas and equations.

## Factorial

The factorial of a number is the product of all positive integers less than or equal to the number, for example:

```
5! = 5 * 4 * 3 * 2 * 1 = 120
```

A typical computer algorithms for the calculation of factorials is recursive. The recursive definition of the factorial function is as follows:

```
0! = 1
n! = n * (n - 1)! for n > 0
```

In Java code a recursive factorial function can be coded as follows:

```java
int Factorial(int n)
{
   if(n == 0)
      return 1;
   else
      return n * Factorial(n - 1);
}
```

Recursive methods, although elegant, often show much worse performance than those that use conventional iteration. The following program calculates the factorial function with a while loop that contains a single line of code.

```java
// Java for Engineers
// Filename: Factorial
// Reference: Chapter 23
// Description:
//              Non-recursive calculation of factorial
// Requires:
//              Keyin class in current directory

import java.lang.*;

class Factorial
{
    public static void main(String[] args)
    {
        int num;
        int prod = 1;
        int factor = 1;

        // Get user input
        num = Keyin.inInt("Enter factorial value: ");

        // Factorial calculation
        while(factor <= num)
            prod *= factor++;

        System.out.println("Factorial " + num + " is " + prod);
    }
}
```

## On the Web

The program Factorial.java is found in the Chapter 24 folder at www.crcpress.com.

# Evaluating Numeric Results

Java code can perform operations on numbers that produce unexpected, unacceptable, or invalid results. For example, a program can accidentally or unintentionally perform integer division by zero, which ends with Java abruptly throwing an arithmetic exception, because division by zero is mathematically undefined and thus is considered a logic error.

## Floating-point errors

Floating-point numbers are defined over an almost unlimited range. Therefore floating-point operations do not throw arithmetic exceptions. Instead, they signal errors by producing error constants. For example, if you divide by an integer value of zero the program stops abruptly, generating the message:

```
ArithmeticException: /by zero at ...
```

On the other hand, if you divide a floating-point number by zero the result is the constant POSITIVE_INFINITY if the dividend is a positive number, or the constant NEGATIVE_INFINITY if the dividend is a negative number. If the result is otherwise invalid a floating-point operation produces NaN (Not a Number).

The constants NaN, POSITIVE_INFINITY, and NEGATIVE_INFINITY are defined in the wrapper classes Double and Float of the java.lang package. In addition, these classes provide methods that test whether a value is a NaN or an Infinity. Providing a method to test for a NaN is necessary because NaNs have the property of not being equal to themselves. The expression

```
if(val == Double.NaN)
```

will never evaluate to true. The following program demonstrates error detection of floating-point results.

```
// Java for Engineers
// Filename: FpError
// Reference: Chapter 24
// Description:
//            Floating-pioint error diagnostics
// Requires:
//            Keyin class in current directory

import java.lang.*;

class FpError
{
 public static void main(String[] args)
 {
    double res;
    double divisor = 0;
    double dividend, root;

    // Get user input for numerator
    System.out.println("Forcing division by zero error");
    dividend = Keyin.inDouble("Enter dividend: ");
    res = dividend/divisor;
    // Test for negative invifinity
```

```
    if(res == Double.NEGATIVE_INFINITY)
        System.out.println("result is NEGATIVE_INFINITY");
    if(res == Double.POSITIVE_INFINITY)
        System.out.println("result is POSITIVE_INFINITY");
    // Test for either infinity
    if(Double.isInfinite(res))
        System.out.println("result is infinite");

    // Get user input for square root
    System.out.println("\nCalculating square root (try negative)");
    root = Keyin.inDouble("Enter root: ");
    res = Math.sqrt(root);
    if(Double.isNaN(res))
        System.out.println("result is Nan");
    else
        System.out.println("Square root = " + res);
    }
}
```

## On the Web

The program FpError.java is found in the Chapter 24 folder at www.crcpress.com.

# Comparing Floating-Point Numbers

The comparison operator (==) can be used for comparing double or float values with finite operands, but the results are not always as expected. Consider the following code fragment:

```
double num1 = -0.0;
double num2 = 0.0;

if(num1 == num2)
    System.out.println("numbers are equal");
else
    System.out.println("numbers not equal");
```

The result of this test is that negative zero and positive zero are reported as equal values. In the preceding section you saw that comparisons may also fail when one or both operands are NaNs. The class java.lang.Object provides a method named equals() that allows comparing two objects. This method is overridden in the subclasses of Object, such as Byte, Short, Integer, Long, Double, Float, BigDecimal, and BigInteger. Therefore, the equals() method can be used to compare numeric values of any type. The equals() method is defined in the java.lang.Object as follows:

```
public boolean equals(Object obj)
```

Indicates whether some other object is equal to this one, according to the following rules.

1. The comparison is reflexive, that is, for any reference value x, x.equals(x) returns true.

2. The comparison is symmetric, that is, for any reference values x and y, x.equals(y) returns true if and only if y.equals(x) returns true.

3. The comparison is transitive, that is, for any reference values x, y, and z, if x.equals(y) returns true and y.equals(z) returns true, then x.equals(z) returns true.

4. The comparison is consistent, that is, for any reference values x and y, multiple invocations of x.equals(y) consistently return true or consistently return false, provided no information used in equals comparisons on the object is modified.

5. For any non-null reference value x, x.equals(null) returns false.

6. The equals() method implements the most discriminating possible equivalence relation on objects; that is, for any reference values x and y, this method returns true if and only if x and y refer to the same object (x==y has the value true).

In the implementation of equals() in the classes Double and Float the method returns true if the two values are the same bit for bit. In other words, equals() returns true if and only if the numbers are the same, or if both are both NaN.

## Comparisons in IEEE 754

The IEEE 754 Standard specifies that comparisons of floating point numbers are exact and never underflow or overflow. The standard defines four mutually exclusive relations: less than, equal, greater than, and unordered. The unordered case arises when at least one operand is a NaN. The standard states that every NaN shall compare unordered with everything, including itself and that comparisons shall ignore the sign of zero, so +0 = -0. Implementations can return one of the four relationships (less than, equal, greater than, or unordered), or return true or false to predicates that name the specific comparisons. Java adopts this second option.

The equals() methods of java.lang.Double and java.lang.Float do not conform to the requirements of IEEE 754 in regards to comparisons. Comparison of a negative zero to a positive zero returns false. Furthermore, two NaN doubles are considered equal no matter their origin. The following program demonstrates comparisons using the == operator and the methods of java.lang.

```
// Java for Engineers
// Filename: FpComp
// Reference: Chapter 24
// Description:
//              Floating-pioint comparisons
// Requires:
//              Keyin class in current directory

import java.lang.*;

class FpComp
{
    public static void main(String[] args)
    {

        double num1 = -0.0;
        double num2 = 0.0;
        double sqrPos = Math.sqrt(4.0);
        double sqrNeg1 = Math.sqrt(-4.0);
        double sqrNeg2 = Math.sqrt(-9.0);

        // Comparing signed zeros using the == operator
        System.out.println("Using == to compare 0 and -0 ");
        if(num1 == num2)
            System.out.println("numbers are equal");
        else
            System.out.println("numbers are not equal");

        // Comparing using the equals() method
        // First convert primtive doubles to Double objects
        Double n1 = new Double(num1);
        Double n2 = new Double(num2);
        System.out.println("Using equals() to compare 0 and -0");
        if(n1.equals(n2))
            System.out.println("numbers are equal");
        else
            System.out.println("numbers are not equal");

        // Comparing NanS
        Double sp1 = new Double(sqrPos);
        Double sn1 = new Double(sqrNeg1);
        Double sn2 = new Double(sqrNeg2);
        System.out.println("Using equals() to compare two NaNs ");
        if(sn1.equals(sn2))
            System.out.println("NaNs are equal");
        else
            System.out.println("NaNs are not equal");
    }
}
```

When the program executes the following output is produced:

```
Using == to compare 0 and -0
numbers are equal
Using equals() to compare 0 and -0
numbers are not equal
Using equals() to compare two NaNs
NaNs are equal
```

## On the Web

The program FpComp.java is located in the Chapter 24 folder at www.crcpress.com.

## Weighted comparisons

Java comparisons in regards to valid numeric values (not NaNs or infinities) of primitive floating point types, or of floating-point objects of the classes Double and Float, return true if both values are bit-by-bit identical. This is often undesirable in engineering or scientific applications in which different routes used in calculations can lead to small differences. In other words, the code needs to determine not if two values are identically equal, but if they are approximately equal to some pre-determined degree.

The Greek letter epsilon is sometimes used in mathematics to define a small quantity. In this sense we can describe the weighted equality of two operands if their values are within some tolerance, represented as epsilon. If the value of epsilon is defined as a constant we can develop an overloaded version of the equals() method to test for weighted equality. For example:

```
final static double EPSILON = 1.0E-12;
// Method overloading equals()
public static boolean equals(double v1, double v2, double e)
{
    return Math.abs(v1 - v2) < e;
}
```

In this case the method calculates the absolute difference between the two operands and returns true if this differences is smaller than the value defined for the constant passed as the third argument. The following program demonstrates the difference between absolute and weighted equality.

```
// Java for Engineers
// Filename: WtComp
// Reference: Chapter 24
// Description:
//          Weighted floating-pioint comparisons
```

```
import java.lang.*;

class WtComp
{
    public static boolean equals(double v1,  // First argument
                                 double v2,  // Second argument
                                 double e)   // Epsilon
    {
       return Math.abs(v1 - v2) < e;
    }

    public static void main(String[] args)
    {

        double a = 9.33333333333000;
        double b = 9.33333333333333;
        final double EPSILON = 1.0E-10;

        if(equals(a, b, EPSILON))
            System.out.println("values are equal");
        else
            System.out.println("values are not equal");
    }
}
```

---

## On the Web

---

The program WtComp.java is found in the Chapter 24 folder at www.crcpress.com.

---

## Bit-by-Bit operations

In Chapter 21 (Table 21-2 and Figure 21-1) you saw how floating-point numbers are encoded in the IEEE 754 double and single formats. Java's double and float types correspond bit-by-bit to IEEE 754 double and single basic and double basic formats. The classes java.lang.Double and java.lang.Float contain methods that allow inspecting and manipulating the individual bits and bit fields of a floating-point number. Java bit encoding for double and float formats is shown in Figure 24-1.

The following methods in java.lang.Double relate to bit conversions of floating-point values.

### *public static long doubleToLongBits(double value)*

Returns the bit layout of the specified floating-point value according to IEEE 754. Table 24-1 shows the masks that can be used to select the individual bits and bit fields.

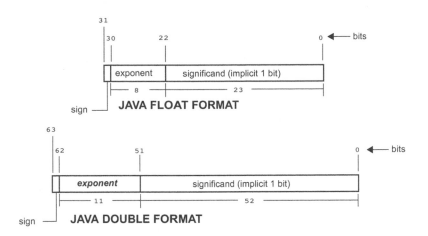

**Figure 24-1** *Bit Map for Java Float and Double Format*

**Table 24-1**

*Bit- and Bit-Field Masks for Double Format*

| BIT/BIT FIELD | MEANING | MASK |
| --- | --- | --- |
| 63 | sign | 0x8000000000000000L |
| 62–52 | exponent | 0x7ff0000000000000L |
| 51–0 | significand | 0x000fffffffffffffL |

The following are special encodings:

1. Positive infinity is represented as 0x7ff0000000000000L.

2. Negative infinity is represented as 0xfff0000000000000L.

3. All NaNs are represented as 0x7ff8000000000000L.

In all cases, the result is a long integer that when given to the long-BitsToDouble(long) method, will produce a floating-point value equal to the argument of doubleToLongBits.

### public static long doubleToRawLongBits(double value)

This method is similar to doubleToLongBits() except that if the argument is a NaN the result is the long integer representing the actual NaN value. Unlike the doubleToLongBits, the doubleToRawLongBits method does not collapse NaN values.

### *public static double longBitsToDouble(long bits)*

Returns the double corresponding to a given bit map. The argument is considered to be a representation of a floating-point value according to the IEEE 754 floating-point double precision layout. The special encodings produce the following results:

1. The value 0x7ff0000000000000L produces a positive infinity.

2. The value 0xfff0000000000000L produces negative infinity.

3. If the argument is any value in the range 0x7ff0000000000001L through 0x7fffffffffffffffL or in the range 0xfff0000000000001L through 0xffffffffffffffffL, the result is NaN.

---

### Programmers note

---

Contrary to the requirements of IEEE 754, Java NaN values of type double are lumped together into a single representation. Distinct values of NaN are only accessible by use of the Double.double-ToRawLongBits method.

---

The following program shows unpacking the bit fields of a floating-point number in double format.

```
// Reference: Chapter 24
// Description:
//              Bit-level unpacking of floating-pioint data
// Requires:
//              Keyin class in current directory

import java.lang.*;

class BitOps
{
    public static void main(String[] args)
    {
        // Definition of bit field masks for double
        final long SIGN = 0x8000000000000000L;
        final long EXPN = 0x7ff0000000000000L;
        final long SGNF = 0x000fffffffffffffL;
        final long BIT1 = 0x8000000000000000L;
        // Storage for bit fields
        long s;             // Sign
        long e;             // Exponent field
        long m;             // Significand (mantissa) field
        String eS;          // For conversions

        double num;
        long binVal;
```

```
      long t;

      // Get user input
      num = Keyin.inDouble("Enter a floating-point double: ");
      binVal = Double.doubleToRawLongBits(num);

      // Display hex bits
      System.out.println("As long = " + Long.toHexString(binVal));

      // Display bit fields of double format
      s = binVal & SIGN;
      if(s != 0)
         System.out.println("Sign = -");
      else
         System.out.println("Sign = +");

      // Mask out exponent field
      e = (binVal & EXPN);
      eS = Long.toHexString(e);
      System.out.println("Exponent = " + eS);

      // Mask out significand field
      m = (binVal & SGNF);
      eS = Long.toHexString(m);
      System.out.println("Significand = " + eS);

      System.out.println("\nFields in binary");
      if(s != 0)
         System.out.println("Sign bit = 1");
      else
         System.out.println("Sign bit = 0");

      // Display binary exponent
      // Eliminate sign bit
      e = e < 1;
      System.out.print("Exponent = ");
      for(int k = 0; k < 11; k++)
      {
          t = e & BIT1;
          // System.out.println(Long.toHexString(t));
          if(t != 0)
              System.out.print("1");
          else
              System.out.print("0");
          e = e < 1;
      }
      System.out.println("\n               |-11 bits-|");
      // Display binary significand
      // Eliminate exponent and sign bits
      m = m < 12;
      System.out.print("Significand = 1.");
      for(int j = 0; j < 51; j++)
      {
          t = m & BIT1;
```

```
            if(t != 0)
                System.out.print("1");
            else
                System.out.print("0");
            m = m < 1;
        }
        System.out.println("\n                      ^  |");
        System.out.println("implicit bit -|  | --- 52 bits ->");
    }
}
```

When the program executes with an input of -127.375 the following output is produced:

```
As long = c05fd80000000000
Sign = -
Exponent = 4050000000000000
Significand = fd80000000000

Fields in binary
Sign bit = 1
Exponent = 10000000101
            |-11 bits-|
Significand = 1.1111110110000000000000000000000000000000000000000000
                  ^ |
implicit bit -|  | --- 52 bits ->
```

---

## On the Web

---

The program BitOps.java is located in the Chapter 24 folder at www.crcpress.com.

---

## Conversion Operations

Code often needs to convert a floating-point value into an integer. One method is by typecasting, for example:

```
double a = 1.998899;
long b = (long) a;         // b = 1
```

In this case Java truncates the integer portion of the double variable and uses it for the value of the integer variable. In some cases this conversion may be acceptable, but more often you need to obtain the value of the integer that is closest to the floating-point number. The round() method of java.lang.Math returns the closest double to the argument if the argument is a double, and the closest int if the argument is a float. The round() method was described in Chapter 23. The following fragment shows the use of the round() method:

```
double a = 1.998899;
long b = Math.round(a);      // b = 2
```

The rint() method also rounds the double operand to an integer but returns the result as a double. The methods floor() and ceil() of java.lang.Math allow obtaining the largest and the smallest integers of a double value. Both methods return a double integer, which can then be typecast into one of the integer formats. These methods are described in Chapter 23.

## Integer and fractional parts

Rational and irrational numbers must often be separated into their integer and fractional parts. Obtaining the integer part of a floating-point value is easily accomplished by typecasting. Note that the round() method cannot be used in this case since you actually want to chop off the integer part. The fractional part can be obtained by subtracting the integer part from the original number. The following program shows the operations.

```
// Java for Engineers
// Filename: IntFrac
// Reference: Chapter 24
// Description:
//            Obtaining the integer and fractional parts
// Requires:
//            Keyin class in current directory
import java.lang.*;

class IntFrac
{
   public static void main(String[] args)
   {

        double num;
        long iPart;
        double fPart;

        // Get user input
        num = Keyin.inDouble("Enter a floating-point value: ");
        iPart = (int)num;
        fPart = num - iPart;
        System.out.println("Integer part = " + iPart);
        System.out.println("Fractional part = " + fPart);
   }
}
```

## On the Web

The program IntFrac.java is found in the Chapter 24 folder at www.crcpress.com.

# Solving Triangles

Many engineering problems require the solution of triangles. The programming required is simple and straightforward. The following examples are provided as illustrations of applying Java code to the solution of simple equations.

## Pythagoras' theorem

One of the theorems of Euclidean geometry, usually attributed to the Greek mathematician Pythagoras, states the relationship between the sides of a right triangle, as shown in Figure 24-2.

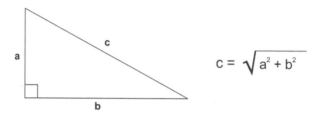

**Figure 24-2** *Pythagoras' Theorem*

If the values of sides *a* and *b* in Figure 24-2 are stored in variables of type double, then the hypotenuse can be calculated as follows:

```
double a, b, c;          // Sides a, b, and c
. . .
c = Math.sqrt((a * a)+(b * b));
```

## Side-angle problems

Sometimes the solution of a right triangle is required in terms of one side and the adjacent angle. The tangent function can be applied to this case, as shown in Figure 24-3.

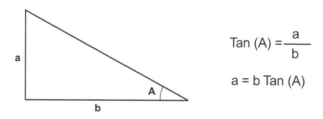

**Figure 24-3** *Side-Angle Formula for Right Triangle*

The following program solves right triangles by means of Pythagoras' theorem and by applying the side/angle formula.

```java
// Java for Engineers
// Filename: TrigSolv
// Reference: Chapter 24
// Description:
//              Solving right triangles
// Requires:
//              Keyin class in current directory

import java.lang.*;

strictfp class TrigSolv
{
  public static void main(String[] args)
  {

      double a, b, c, angleA, radA;

      // Pythagoras' Theorem
      // Obtain sides from user
      System.out.println("Side c in terms of sides a and b");
      a = Keyin.inDouble("Enter side a: ");
      b = Keyin.inDouble("Enter side b: ");
      c = Math.sqrt((a * a)+(b * b));
      System.out.println("Side c = " + c);

      // Side-angle formula
      System.out.println("Side c in terms of side b and angle A");
      b = Keyin.inDouble("Enter side b: ");
      angleA = Keyin.inDouble("Enter angle A: ");
      radA = Math.toRadians(angleA);
      c = b * Math.tan(radA);
      System.out.println("Side c = " + c);
  }
}
```

## On the Web

The program named TrigSolv.java is found in the Chapter 24 folder at www.crcpress.com.

# Solving Quadratic Equations

The general quadratic equation is expressed by the formula:

$$ax^2 + bx + c = 0$$

where the coefficients $a$, $b$, and $c$ are constants. The solution a quadratic equation can be attempted by applying the standard quadratic formula:

$$x = \frac{-b \pm \sqrt{b^2 - 4ac}}{2a}$$

In the quadratic equation the term

$$\sqrt{b^2 - 4ac}$$

is called the discriminant. The value of the discriminant is used to determine if the solution set has two equal real roots, two different real roots, or no real roots. The following program attempts to find the real roots of a quadratic equation (if they exist) by solving the quadratic formula.

```
// Java for Engineers
// Filename: QuadSolv
// Reference: Chapter 24
// Description:
//              Applying the quadratic formula
// Requires:
//              Keyin class in current directory

import java.lang.*;

strictfp class QuadSolv
{
    public static void main(String[] args)
    {

        double a, b, c, discr, root1, root2;

        // Apllying the quadratic formula
        // Obtain sides from user
        System.out.println("Applying the quadratic formula");
        a = Keyin.inDouble("Enter a: ");
        b = Keyin.inDouble("Enter b: ");
        c = Keyin.inDouble("Enter c: ");

        // Solve the discriminant (SQRT (b^2 - 4ac)
        discr = Math.sqrt((b * b) - (4 * a * c));
        System.out.println("Discriminant = " + discr);
        // Determine number of roots
```

```
// if discr > 0 equation has 2 real roots
// if discr == 0 equation has a repeated real root
// if discr < 0 equation has imaginary roots
// if discr is NaN equation has no roots

// Test for NaN
if(Double.isNaN(discr))
   System.out.println("Equation has no roots");

if(discr > 0)
{
   System.out.println("Equation has 2 roots");
   root1 = (-b + discr)/2 * a;
   root2 = (-b - discr)/2 * a;
   System.out.println("First root = " + root1);
   System.out.println("Second roor = " + root2);
}

if(discr == 0)
{
   System.out.println("Equation has 1 root");
   root1 = (-b + discr)/2 * a;
   System.out.println("Root = " + root1);
}

if(discr < 0)
   System.out.println("Equation has imaginary roots");

}
}
```

## On the Web

The program QuadSolv.java can be found in the Chapter 24 folder at www.crcpress.com.

# Chapter 25

# Introducing Computer Graphics

## Developing Graphical Applications

The programs developed so far provide output in text form only. Because of its simplicity, this approach is useful when developing console-based applications that communicate with the user with simple text commands and do not require graphics. However, text-based programs are almost an anachronism, since most programs developed today communicate with the user by means of graphics devices, such as the mouse, and are capable of outputting graphics.

In this chapter we provide a brief overview of computer graphics. Graphics programming is a complex and elaborate subject, but elementary graphics in Java are not difficult.

## Origin of Computer Graphics

During the late 1950s IBM and other companies invented and developed several technologies that simplified computer use and programming. Originally, computer input and output consisted of punched cards and paper tape. The introduction of teletype machines (called TTYs) as an input and output device was a major advance. A TTY has a typewriter-like keyboard and produces a paper printout as well as a strip of paper or mylar tape in which data is encoded in rows of punched holes. These tapes provide a convenient way for transferring data and programs from the TTY into the computer.

Soon thereafter the Cathode Ray Tube, already in use in commercial television, was adapted to displaying computer data. At first it was referred to as a *glass teletype*. An added bonus was that the CRT could also be used to display pictures.

Other devices designed to facilitate input and output are the the lightpen, the touch screen, the graphic tablet, the joystick, and the mouse. All of these devices allow the user to visually interact with the machine.

The original idea for a computer with which the user communicates graphically came from the work of Allan Kay at the Xerox Palo Alto Research Center. Dr. Kay's work was an attempt at a computer that could be used by children too young to read or to type commands in text form. One approach was based on small screen objects, called *icons*, that represent some object familiar to the child. A mechanical device (which later became the mouse) allowed moving these graphics objects on the screen.

Interactive graphics and the graphical user interface were not an instant success. It was Apple Computers that first developed an operating system that supported graphical, mouse-controlled, icon-based user interaction. The first machine to fully implement the technology was the Macintosh computer. Not long afterward Microsoft developed a graphical operating system for the PC, called Windows.

## Text-based and graphical systems

Operating systems can be classified into two types: single-user, single-task, command-driven systems, like DOS, and multiple-task, GUI-based systems, such as Windows, XWindows, or the Macintosh. DOS-like, command-driven, systems allow unrestricted access to machine resources. Once an application code gains control, it can do whatever it pleases. Its only limitations are the hardware capabilities and the programmer's skills.

Although DOS-like operating systems often list rules that well-behaved programs should follow, there is no way of enforcing these rules. Intentionally or accidentally, programs can raise havoc by deleting or modifying files, interfering with other applications, or even damaging the hardware. A single-user, single task program has total control over all system resources. It can allocate all memory to itself, set up the input and output devices, directly control the printer and the communications lines, and manage the mouse and the keyboard. In this environment there are no shared resources, since a single program executes in the machine and the operating system is dormant while an application is in control.

On the other hand, multitasking systems such as Windows, must share resources between several applications. Memory, CPU time, display hardware, communications lines and devices, mouse, keyboard, and disk storage are all shared. Each program operates in its own private memory space, with limited access to other memory areas. Hardware devices are controlled by the operating system, which grants access to applications at its discretion and under its control. The library of services that is made available to applications by a multitasking operating system is often called the *application programming interface*, or API. Figure 25-1 shows how single-tasking and multitasking programs access system resources.

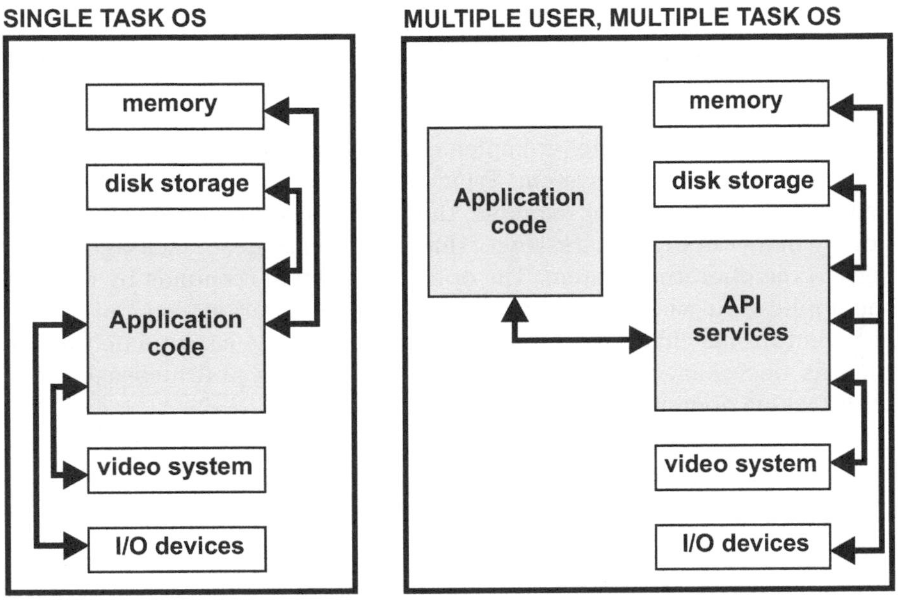

**SINGLE TASK OS**  **MULTIPLE USER, MULTIPLE TASK OS**

**Figure 25-1** *Access to System Resources*

Multitasking operating systems have text-based or graphical interfaces. In the first case we say that the system is command-driven, which means that operating system services and functions are accessed by commands entered from the console. In the second case we describe the system as having a graphical user interface or GUI.

The paradigm that defines a single-user command-driven operating system is quite different from the one for a GUI-based multitasking system. A preemptive multitasking operating system switches the foreground (CPU access) from one application to another. If an application misbehaves, the operating system can turn it off. In this model it is the operating system that is "the god of the machine," not the running program.

# Event-Driven Programming

The programming model that describes the interaction between the application and a multitasking operating system is sometimes called *event-driven programming*. The event-driven term relates to the fact that synchronization between the operating system and the application is in the form of *events*. For example, *a user event* takes place when the user initiates an action to change the size of the program window. In response to this user event, the operating system proceeds to change the window's size by means of a system event. The application is notified of the system event so that it can initiate additional actions. This in turn generates another chain of events.

The event-driven model is implemented by messages passed between the application and the system. Typically each event, or group of events, generates a message. For example, the user drags the corner of the program window in order to resize it. This event generates a message that is sent to the operating system. The operating system responds by resizing the application window. It then informs the application that the size of the window has changed so that the application code can update the display as necessary. Figure 25-2 shows the actions and messages in a multitasking operating system environment.

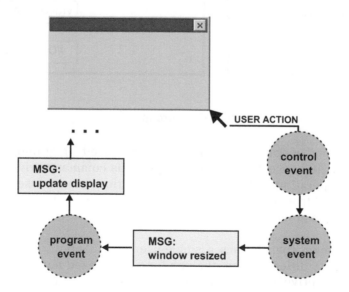

**Figure 25-2** *Event-Driven Model*

## Event manager and event handler

The event-driven application is passive since the program does not monitor devices directly. The task of detecting input is left to the operating system The application stays dormant until it is notified that a user event has taken place, as shown in Figure 25-2. The operating system is the event handler, and the application the event manager.

Events are loosely classified into several types: system events, control events, and program events. One event often triggers another one of the same type, or of a different type. A system event can generate a control event. Or a program event can be the cause of a system event, which, in turn, generates another system event, and so forth.

# The Main Window

The main window is an application's principal means of input and output and its only access to the video display. In Java the program's main window is called the frame.

The following are the fundamental building blocks of a window:

- The main window has a *title bar*. The title bar can display a caption or it can be blank.

- In the right-hand side of the title bar there are usually buttons to minimize, maximize, and close the program window. The application can select which, if any, of these control buttons are displayed.

- The optional *menu bar* is located below the title bar. A typical menu bar contains one or more *drop-down menus*. Each drop-down menu consists of commands that are activated by a mouse click or by using the Alt key and the underlined letter code. Menu commands that expand into submenus are usually indicated by trailing ellipses.

- The program *main window*, as well as many input/output controls, can have vertical or horizontal *scroll bars*. The operating system notifies the application of user's action on the scroll bars, but the application must provide the required processing.

- The screen zone assigned to each program window is called the *client area*. The dimensions and graphics attributes of the client area can be obtained from the operating system.

Figure 25-3, on the next page, shows the basic components of a program window.

## Controls

The program window in Figure 25-3 contains several controls: the buttons on the title bar, the menu items and menu commands, and the scroll bars. Buttons, scroll bars, and menu commands are just a few of the many control components that are available in a graphics application. The components that are used in implementing input/output and program manipulation operations are generically called controls.

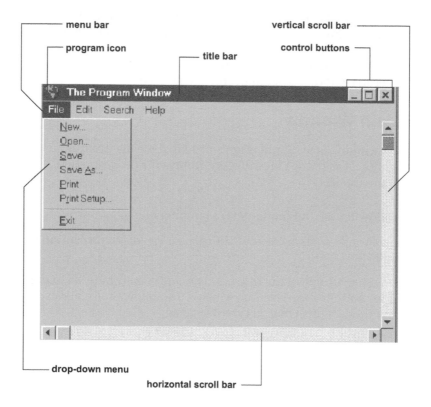

**Figure 25-3** *Components of a Program Window*

## Incidentally...

Some controls have been around since the original GUI operating systems.

# Chapter 26

# Java Graphics

## The Greatest Challenge

The greatest challenge that confronted the creators of the Java programming language was the implementation of a cross-platform Graphical User Interface. Windowing environments, such as MAC OS, X-Windows, and the various versions of Microsoft Windows, all have unique features. The creators of Java had to find the common elements in all platforms while ignoring the features that were exclusive of a particular one. In other words, they had to find the common graphics functionality, while making sure that Java virtual machines would accommodate the unavoidable differences. A task indeed!

The first implementation of a Java GUI was called the Java Abstract Windowing Toolkit, or AWT. The original version had major shortcomings and several nasty bugs, most of which have been fixed.

## Applets and applications

The World Wide Web was at the origin of the Java language and continues to be one of its principal fields of application. Small Java programs, called *applets*, execute within a Web browser, such as Netscape Navigator or Internet Explorer. These programs expand the functionality of the browser by providing the logic and data processing capabilities of Java.

Most of the support required for Java graphics at the applet level is located within the browser. This means that the browser itself must solve all of the platform-dependency issues. Java applications, on the other hand, are full-fledged Java programs that are executed by the Java interpreter. In this book we consider only Java applications.

301

# The Java Foundation Classes

Graphics programming in Java is by means of packages called the *Java Foundations Classes*. In Java 1.2 the foundations classes include the following APIs:

1. Abstract Windows Toolkit or AWT

2. Swing components

3. Java 2D

4. Java accessibility

Of these, the Java Accessibility API package supports handicap assistive technologies such as screen readers, screen magnifiers, etc. The classes that more directly relate to conventional graphics (AWT, Swing, and Java 2D) are briefly discussed in the following sections.

## AWT

The Abstract Windows Toolkit (AWT) is the core package for implementing graphics. The AWT contains classes for creating and operating a Graphical User Interface and for performing drawing and painting operations. In addition, the current versions of the AWT provide support for clipboard-based transfers, for image manipulations, fonts, printing, 2D geometrical operations, input, and provides an event handling mechanism.

One of the most useful classes of the AWT is java.awt.Component. A component can be a button, a menu, a scrollbar, or any graphical element that is displayed on the screen and that can interact with the user. In Microsoft Windows components are called *controls*. The Component class is currently extended by sixty-six classes.

## Swing

The designers of the AWT decided to use the functionality of the underlying operating systems instead of coding the user interface toolkit from scratch. For this reason, the AWT is actually a thin software layer that provides access to the system's application programming interface. The underlying code that provides the specific windowing functions are called *peer classes*. For example, if a Java application uses the AWT to create a button control, the resulting component would be a standard Windows button, a Macintosh button, or a Motif button according to the operating system on which the application executes.

---
### Programmers note
---

Java documentation refers to elements that use the underlying APIs as heavyweight components and those that are totally implemented in Java code as lightweight components. In this sense the AWT consists of all heavyweight components. The Swing components, on the other hand, are mostly lightweight.

---

A mechanism called "peers" facilitated the development of the original Java toolkits and gave applications the look-and-feel of their host operating system. However, the use of peers brings about a performance penalty for Java applications and has been the source of bugs and system dependecies. Java 1.2 addressed these problems by means of a new set of APIs called Swing.

In contrast with API components, Swing components are designed to work the same on all platforms. Swing components add functionality to the AWT methods. The swing interface makes it possible to select an application's "look and feel." For example, a program using Swing components can look like a Win32, a Motif, or a Mac program. In addition swing implements a new graphics rendering paradigm called a Model-View-Controller (MVC) architecture. In this scheme each component has an associated Model class and an interface it uses. In this book graphics coverage is restricted to the AWT. We do not cover swing.

## Java 2D

Java 2D is the name of an extension of the AWT that includes enhanced graphics, text operations, image handling, color definition and composition, hit detection, and device-independent printing. The class Graphics2D, which extends the AWT Graphics class, is the fundamental class of Java 2D.

Applications that use Java 2D functionality start by creating an object of the Graphics class, then casting it into one of the Graphics2D classes. The result is that the methods of both classes, Graphics and Graphics2D, become accessible to code. In this book you will see how the Graphics and Graphics2D classes are used to implement GUIs and graphics output.

Java proposes to be a portable language, but the graphics platforms present the biggest challenge to this portability. The hardware variations and the uniqueness of the various operating systems result in GUIs with substantial differences. Windows, Macintosh, xWindows, and Motif, among others, present individualities that are often difficult for Java to accommodate. The Java AWT provides facilities for manipulating images and generating graphics across all supported platforms. The results are not always perfect, but very often they are good enough for the task at hand. In any case, regarding portable graphics, Java is still "the only game in town."

# The Frame Concept

In Java graphics a *frame* is a top-level window. The Java frame includes the window's title bar and border. The Frame object can resize itself when the user drags the edge or the corner of the window. A frame is repositioned when the user drags it to another place in the desktop. A frame can contain other graphics objects, such as text, buttons, and controls.

Java AWT contains a Frame class that provides much of the functionality needed to implement a typical application window. The default frame has a title bar and a border. Applications are expected to provide processing for handling events such as the user resizing or closing the frame. This means that if your code does not provide processing for closing a frame, then the program window can only be closed by system-level commands. In Windows, the system command for closing a frame is <Ctrl-Alt-Del> keystrokes. This is not only inconvenient, but can also lead to an unexpected system reboot with possible loss of data. Later in this chapter we develop code to create frames that can be closed by the user.

The Java Frame class is located in a class hierarchy with the Component class at its highest level. We concentrate out attention on the core classes: Frame, Window, Container, and Component.

## AWT frame class

The Frame class is used to create a window with a title bar, a border and an optional menu bar. A frame can also contain gadgets such as buttons to resize, minimize, or maximize the window. The Frame class, which extends Window, provides methods for configuring and manipulating frames. Table 26-1 lists some of the most used methods in the Frame class.

## Window class

A window object represents a top-level window with no border or menu. When a window object is constructed it must have either a frame, a dialog, or another window object as its owner. Window object generate events to signal that the window has been opened or closed. Table 26-2 lists some of the most used methods in the Window class.

**Table 26-1**

*Commonly Used Methods of the Frame Class*

| RETURNS | NAME | DESCRIPTION |
|---|---|---|
| void | **addNotify()** | Makes thes Frame displayable by connecting it to a native screen resource. |
| static Frame[] | **getFrames()** | Returns an array containing all frames created by the application. |
| Image | **getIconImage()** | Gets the image to be displayed in the minimized icon. |
| MenuBar | **getMenuBar()** | Gets the frame's menu bar. |
| int | **getState()** | Gets the frame's state. |
| String | **getTitle()** | Gets the frame's title. |
| boolean | **isResizable()** | Indicates whether the frame is resizable by the user. |
| String | **paramString()** | Returns theparameter string. |
| void | **remove(MenuComponent m)** | Removes the frame's Menu bar. |
| void | **removeNotify()** | Makes the Frame un-displayable by removing its connection to its native screen resource. |
| void | **setIconImage(Image image)** | Sets the image to be displayed in the minimized icon for this frame. |
| void | **setMenuBar(MenuBar mb)** | Sets the menu bar for this frame to the specified menu bar. |
| void | **setResizable(boolean resizable)** | Sets whether this frame is resizable by the user. |
| void | **setState(int state)** | Sets the frame's state. |
| void | **setTitle(String title)** | Sets the frame's title. |

**Table 26-2**

*Commonly Used Methods of the Window Class*

| RETURNS | 6NAME | DESCRIPTION |
|---|---|---|
| void | **addNotify()** | Makes this Window displayable by creating the connection to its native screen resource. |
| void | **addWindowListener(WindowListener l)** | Adds a window listener to receive events from this window. |
| void | **dispose()** | Releases all of the native screen resources used by this Window. |

*(continues)*

**Table 26-2**

*Commonly Used Methods of the Window Class (continued)*

| RETURNS | NAME | DESCRIPTION |
|---|---|---|
| Locale | **getLocale()** | Gets the Locale object that is associated with this window, if one has been defined. |
| indow[] | **getOwnedWindows()** | Return an array containing all the windows thls window currently owns. |
| Window | **getOwner()** | Returns the owner of this window. |
| void | **hide()** | Hide this Window. |
| boolean | **isShowing()** | Checks if this Window is currently displayed. |
| void | **pack()** | Causes this Window to be sized to fit the preferred size and layouts of its subcomponents. |
| protected void | **processEvent(AWTEvent e)** | Processes events on this window. |
| protected void | **processWindowEvent(WindowEvent e)** | Processes window events occurring on this window by dispatching them to any registered WindowListener object. |
| void | **removeWindowListener(WindowListener l)** | Removes the specified window listener. |
| void | **setCursor(Cursor cursor)** | Set the cursor image to a specified cursor. |
| void | **show()** | Makes the Window visible. |
| void | **toBack()** | Sends this window to the back. |
| void | **toFront()** | Brings this window to the front. |

## Container class

The java.awt.Container class defines a generic container object that can contain other containers or components. A Java container object is a rectangular area in which other program elements can be placed. The Container class is a subclass of Component. This means that container objects can be nested one inside the other one. The Container class contains over 50 methods. Table 26-3 is a selection of some of the most frequently used methods in the Container class.

**Table 26-3**

*Commonly Used Methods of the Container Class*

| RETURNS | NAME | DESCRIPTION |
|---|---|---|
| Component | **add(Component comp)** | Adds the specified component to this container. |
| Component | **add(Component comp, int index)** | Adds the specified component to this container at the given position. |
| void | **add(Component comp, Object constraints)** | Adds the specified component to the end of this container with the given constraints. |
| void | **add(Component comp, Object constraints, int index)** | Adds the specified component to this container with the specified constraints at the specified location. |
| Component | **add(String name, Component comp)** | Adds the component specified by its name to this container. |
| void | **addContainerListener(ContainerListener l)** | Adds the specified container listener to receive container events from this container. |
| void | **addNotify()** | Makes this Container displayable by connecting it to a native screen resource. |
| Component | **findComponentAt(int x, int y)** | Locates the child component that contains the specified position. |
| Component | **findComponentAt(Point p)** | Locates the child component that contains the specified point. |
| float | **getAlignmentX()** | Returns the x axis alignment. |
| float | **getAlignmentY()** | Returns the y axis alignment. |
| Component | **getComponent(int n)** | Returns the nth component in this container. |
| Component | **getComponentAt(int x, int y)** | Locates the component that contains the specified x,y position. |
| Component | **getComponentAt(Point p)** | Gets the component that contains the specified point. |

*(continues)*

**Table 26-3**

*Commonly Used Methods of the Container Class (continued)*

| RETURNS | NAME | DESCRIPTION |
|---|---|---|
| int | **getComponentCount()** | Gets the number of components in the panel. |
| Component[] | **getComponents()** | Gets all the components in this container. |
| Insets | **getInsets()** | Determines the size of the container's border. |
| LayoutManager | **getLayout()** | Gets the layout manager for this container. |
| Dimension | **getMaximumSize()** | Returns the container's maximum size. |
| Dimension | **getMinimumSize()** | Returns the container's minimum size. |
| Dimension | **getPreferredSize()** | Returns the preferred size of this container. |
| void | **invalidate()** | Invalidates the container. |
| boolean | **isAncestorOf(Component c)** | Checks if the component is contained in the component hierarchy of this container. |
| void | **list (PrintStream out, int indent)** | Prints a listing of this container to the specified output stream. |
| void | **list (PrintWriter out, int indent)** | Prints out a list, starting at the specified indention, to the specified print writer. |
| void | **paint (Graphics g)** | Paints the container. |
| void | **paintComponents(Graphics g)** | Paints each of the components in this container. |
| protected | **String paramString()** | Returns the parameter string for the state of this container. |
| void | **print(Graphics g)** | Prints the container. |
| void | **printComponents(Graphics g)** | Prints each of the components in this container. |

*(continues)*

**Table 26-3**

*Commonly Used Methods of the Container Class (continued)*

| RETURNS | NAME | DESCRIPTION |
|---|---|---|
| protected void | **processContainerEvent(ContainerEvent e)** | Processes container events occurring on this container by dispatching them to any registered ContainerListener objects. |
| protected void | **processEvent(AWTEvent e)** | Processes events on this container. |
| void | **remove(Component comp)** | Removes the specified component from this container. |
| void | **remove(int index)** | Removes the component specified by index. |
| void | **removeAll()** | Removes all the components from this container. |
| void | **removeContainerListener(ContainerListener l)** | Removes the specified container listener. |
| void | **removeNotify()** | Makes this Container undisplayable by removing its connection to its native screen resource. |
| void | **setCursor(Cursor cursor)** | Sets the cursor image to the specified cursor. |
| void | **setFont(Font f)** | Sets the font of this container. |
| void | **setLayout(LayoutManager mgr)** | Sets the layout manager for this container. |
| void | **update(Graphics g)** | Updates the container. |
| void protected | **validate()** | Validates this container. |

The highest level class in the hierarchy is named Component. The Java Component class defines objects that can be displayed on the screen and interact with the user. The notion of a component is similar to that of a Windows control. Examples of components are buttons, checkboxes, scrollbars, and menus. The graphical user interface is implemented by means of components. The Component class is one of the richest in the AWT. You should consult the Java documentation to inspect the methods in this class.

# The Java Graphics Application

Java graphics applications must provide processing for handling events such as the user closing the frame. If this logic is not provided by your program, then the window can only be closed by system-level commands, which is both inconvenient and awkward.

To create a frame that can be closed by means of the control button requires implementing event-handlers and using event-handling code. With the previous version of the AWT this task posed no great problems, since the event handling model was simple and intuitive. But, this model, which was based on inheritance, had serious limitations. This led to the adoption of a more complex delegation-based model. Although code that uses the old model still works in Java 1.2, Java has declared that this support will end in the near future.

In order to make the frames "closeable" we use a class called ActiveFrame. Since ActiveFrame extends Frame, all the methods of the Frame class remain available to our code.

An ActiveFrame object has the following properties:

• The frame's default size is 300 by 200 pixels

• The default location is the top left screen corner

• The title bar displays the name of the class

## The ActiveFrame class

Creating code that can process windows events requires creating a WindowListener object. This is done by means of the WindowAdapter class which is part of the java.lang package. The windowClosing() method of the WindowAdapter class takes a WindowEvent object as a parameter. This method is invoked when the application window is being closed thus providing implementation of a "user-closeable" window. The ActiveFrame class, listed below, extends the Java Frame class and provides the necessary code for conventional closing of the program window. ActiveFrame is defined as follows:

```
import java.awt.*;
import java.awt.event.*;

public class ActiveFrame extends Frame
{
  //***************************
  //       Constructors
  //***************************
```

```
  public ActiveFrame()
   {  addWindowListener
     (new WindowAdapter()
        { public void windowClosing(WindowEvent e)
           { System.exit(0);}
        }
     );
     setSize(300, 250);
     setTitle(getClass().getName());
   }
}
```

In addition to creating a closeable window, the ActiveFrame class sets the window size to 300 by 250 pixels and displays the name of the driving class as the program title. Your code can modify these default values. The following program, named Closeable.java, creates a program window using the ActiveFrame class.

```
//*************************************************************
//*************************************************************
// Project: Java for Engineers
// Program: Closeable.java
// Reference: Chapter 26
// Topics:
//      1. Extending the java Frame class with ActiveFrame.
//         ActiveFrame provides additional processing logic
//         for closing the program window without having to
//         re-boot.
//      2. Calling methods in the superclasses.
//      3. Displaying the frame using the show() method of
//         the Window class.
//*************************************************************
// Requires:
//      1. ActiveFrame class in the current directory
//*************************************************************
//*************************************************************
import java.awt.*;
import ActiveFrame;

//********************************************
//********************************************
//              driving class
//********************************************
//********************************************

public class Closeable extends ActiveFrame
{
// By extending ActiveFrame we make accessible all its
// methods and those of its superclasses (Object, Component,
// Container, Window, and Frame).
//*************************
//           main
//*************************
```

```
public static void main(String[] args)
{
    // Create an object of the class GFrame. We can use
    // this object to access the methods in GFrame and
    // its superclasses

    Closeable aframe = new Closeable();

    // Use methods in the Component class
    // to modify object's default dimensions and screen
    // and the setTitle() method of the Frame class to change
    // the window title
    aframe.setSize(400, 300);                 // Set frame size
    aframe.setLocation(200, 100);             // Set frame location
    aframe.setTitle("Closeable Frame Demo");  // Titlebar text

    // Display the frame using the show() method of the Window
      // class
    aframe.show();
    }
}
```

The resulting window overrides the default size defined in the ActiveFrame class, which is of 300 by 250 pixels. Also the program's title, as displayed in the title bar, is changed. Because we have extended ActiveFrame, the program window can be closed by clicking the X button on the title bar or by means of the Close command in the system menu. Figure 26-1 is a screen snapshot of the resulting program window.

**Figure 26-1** *Screen Snapshot of the Closeable Program*

The Closeable program provides a simple shell in which to create a graphics window using the ActiveFrame class. In your own programs you will probably need to configure the Window to suit your purposes. For example, if your program needs to execute in a window of a size different than the one in the sample code, or if it is initially located at a different position in the desktop area, you would most likely use your own window title. All of these and many other program parameters can be changed by means of the corresponding methods of its superclasses, namely, Component, Container, Window, and Frame. For example, you can resize the program window by calling the setSize() method of the Component class, as shown in the Closeable program.

---

## On the Web

---

The program Closeable.java is located in the Chapter 26 folder at www.crcpress.com. Also in this folder is the source for ActiveFrame.java.

---

# The Display Context

A Windows data structure that stores information about a particular device, such as the video display or a printer, is called a *device context*. The Java counterpart for a device context is an object of the Graphics class. The Graphics object contains information that is necessary for drawing operations, such as:

- The object that is to receive the drawing. This is normally a Component, but it can also be an off-screen image.

- A coordinate translation mode that controls the object's position on the screen.

- A clipping rectangle that limits output to the current frame.

- A color used for drawing.

- A font used for text output.

Every Java program that renders text or graphics in a frame must reference a Graphics object. The Graphics class, which is part of the AWT, contains over 35 methods, which can be used to draw lines, arcs, rectangles, characters, bytes, bitmaps (called images in Java), ellipses, polylines, among many graphic objects. The Graphics class is an abstract class so you cannot instantiate objects of this class directly.

## The update() and paint() methods

Java programs that use the AWT are event-driven. The programmer codes the operations that draw on the program's client area but does not perform the drawing directly. Instead the code waits for a system or user generated event to draw to the window. This event can be the program window being displayed for the first time, or the program window being uncovered, resized, minimized, maximized, or otherwise modified by the user. When the Java event handler needs to redraw a window, it triggers a call to a method called update() which is located in the Component class. The update() method erases the window background and then calls the paint() method in the Java Canvas class. A typical application redefines the paint() method so that it receives control whenever the program's window requires updating. The paint() method receives a Graphics object as its only parameter. For example:

```
public void paint(Graphics g)
{
    g.drawString("Hello World!!!", 50, 100);
}
```

In this case the code has redefined paint() with its own version so that it receives control whenever a screen update is required. The only output operation in this case is displaying a message on the screen using the drawString() method of the Graphics class. The second and third parameters to drawString() are the $x$ and $y$ pixel coordinates in the client area.

## Manipulating fonts

A font is a set of characters of the same typeface, style, and size. In the AWT the typefaces available are SansSerif, Serif, Monospaced, Dialog, and Windows Dialog. The sytles are bold, italic, bold-italic, and plain. The size is expressed in units called *points*, each point being 1/72th of an inch.

In Java an attribute of the Graphics object is the default font that is used in drawing text to the screen. Applications can select other fonts and point sizes by instantiating an object of the Font class. The Font constructor is as follows:

```
    public Font(String name, int style, int size)
                -----------    ---------   --------
        FONT NAME: ---- |              |              |------ point size
        SansSerif                 |------------ STYLES:
        Serif                                   BOLD
        Monospaced                              ITALIC
        Dialog                                  BOLD | ITALIC
        Dialog input                            PLAIN
```

An application can create a font object as follows:

```
Font f = new Font("SansSerif", Font.BOLD, 14);
```

The font is then installed in the device context using the setFont() method of the Component class, as follows:

```
g.setFont(f);
```

The following program, named Text.java, demonstrates the fundamental manipulations required for a Java graphics application that displays text to the screen.

```
//*************************************************************
// Project: Java for Engineers
// Program: Text.java
// Reference: Chapter 26
// Topics:
//        1. Instantiating a Graphics object
//        2. Redefining the paint() method
//        3. Changing fonts
//        4. Displaying a text message
//*************************************************************
// Requires:
//        1. ActiveFrame class in the current directory
//*************************************************************
//*************************************************************
import java.awt.*;
//*********************************************
//*********************************************
//             driving class
//*********************************************
//*********************************************
public class Text extends ActiveFrame
{
    //*********************************
    //       redefinition of paint()
    //*********************************
    // The paint() method of the Java AWT Canvas class
    // fills the Window's client area with the default
    // color. An application can redefine paint() in
    // order to output graphics to the display.
    // The following code redefines paint(), which receives
    // a Graphics object as a parameter, and then uses
    // the drawString method of the Graphics class to
    // display a message on the screen.

    public void paint(Graphics g)
    {
        // Define a monospaced, bold, 16-point font
        Font f = new Font("Monospaced", Font.BOLD, 16);
        // Set the font in the device context
        g.setFont(f);
        // Display a text string
```

```
        g.drawString("Hello Engineers, this is Java", 50,
                     100);
    }
    //***************************
    //          main
    //***************************
    public static void main(String[] args)
    {
        // Create an object of the class WindowText
        Text aframe = new Text();

        // Use methods in superclasses to modify object's default
        // size, location, and program title
        aframe.setSize(500, 300);              // Set frame size
        aframe.setLocation(200, 100);          // Set frame location
        aframe.setTitle("Text Demo Program"); // Titlebar text

        // Display frame calling the show() method of the Window
        // class
        aframe.show();

    }
}
```

Figure 26-2 is a screen snapshot of the Text program.

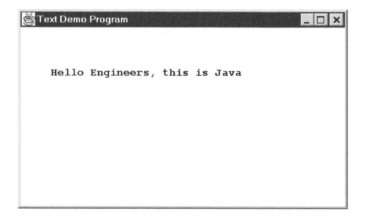

**Figure 26-2** *Snapshot of the Text.Program*

## On the Web

The program Text.java is located in the Chapter 26 folder at www.crcpress.com.

# *Chapter 27*

# Displaying Graphic Images

## Vector and Raster Graphics

Two technologies are used in creating and displaying images on the graphics screen, they are called *vector* and *raster graphics*. As the name implies, vector images are described mathematically. In vector graphics a straight line is defined by the screen location of its start and end points, while circles and ellipses are defined by the dimension and coordinates of the rectangle that tightly contains the figure. In other words, in vector graphics a complex graphical object consists of the descriptions of all the simpler component that form it. Since vector-defined objects are a numerical expression, the objects can be manipulated by transforming the values that represent it. Thus, vector images can be moved, scaled, and rotated on the screen by performing mathematical operations on its data.

Raster graphics, on the other hand, consist of images defined in terms of their individual screen dots. The pattern of dots is arranged in rows and columns; each dot usually associated with a color attribute. AWT and other Java graphics packages support both vector and raster graphics.

## The frame origin

Before you attempt to draw graphics objects on the video display you must consider a peculiarity of Java graphics. There is a geometrical issue that should be addressed before we attempt to draw graphic objects on the video display. Figure 27-1 shows a typical Java frame.

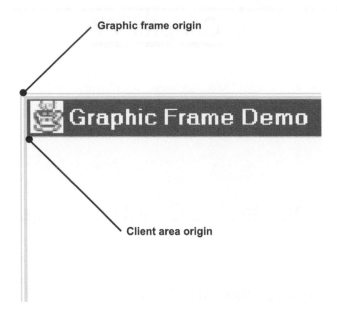

**Figure 27-1** *Frame and the Client Area Origin*

The concept of a Java program frame includes the title bar and the window border, as shown in Figure 27-1. Since applications cannot draw on the title bar or the border, it is useful to change the frame origin to the top-left corner of the client area, which is the screen area that applications can access. In order to translate the drawing origin from the frame area to the client area you can use the translate() method of the graphics class. The method receives two parameters which represent the $x$ and the $y$ values by which the origin is to be moved. The size of the title bar and the frame border can be obtained with the getInsets() method of the Container class, as follows:

```
getInstets().left -> returns the width of the border

getInsets().top   -> returns the width of the titlebar
```

The call to translate() is made as follows:

```
g.translate(getInsets().left, getInsets().top);
```

After the translate() method executes, the origin of the drawing is located at the top left corner of the application's client area.

## Color and Java graphics

In Java graphics the video display color is an attribute of the graphics object. Once a color is set, it is used for all drawing operations that follow. To draw in multiple colors you must select them in succession. The Color class Java's AWT encapsulates colors. Several methods are available for defining colors. One of them is based on the pre-defined color names, shown in Table 27-1.

### Table 27-1
*Java Standard Colors*

| | | |
|---|---|---|
| black | green | red |
| blue | lightGray | white |
| cyan | magenta | yellow |
| darkGray | orange | gray |
| pink | | |

## RGB color designation

Based on the physics of light, a color can also be defined by its red, green, and blue components. This method is called the RGB color format. Constructors of the Color class allows a custom color to be created by specifying its red, green, and blue components. In one constructor the RGB values are specified as floating point numbers in the range 0.0 to 1.0. Another constructor allows specifying the RGB value with integers. A third constructor reflects the architecture of the most common video cards which use a byte value to encode each of the RGB components. Using this third constructor you can create objects of the Color class, as follows:

```
Color aRed = new Color(200, 0, 0);
Color lightBlue = new Color(0, 0, 210);
Color pink = new Color(200, 50, 50);
Color blackest = new Color(0, 0, 0);
Color whitest = new Color(255, 255, 255);
```

Once a color has been defined, its name can be used to install it as an attribute of the Java graphics object by means of the setColor() method. The method takes a Color object as a parameter, which can be a color created using one of the pre-defined color names in Table 27-1, or it can also be a named color using one of the other constructors. For example:

```
g.setColor(aRed);
g.setColor(Color.orange);
```

You can also create a customized color and install it as an attribute of the graphics object in the same statement:

```
g.setColor(new Color(0, 128, 128));
```

# The Java Graphics Class

The Java Graphics class is an abstract base class that allows applications to draw onto the various devices, as well as creating off-screen images. A Graphics object contains information that defines the basic rendering operations. This state information includes the following properties:

- The Component object on which drawing takes place

- A translation origin for rendering and for clipping coordinates

- The current clipping rectangle

- The current color

- The current font

- The current logical pixel operation function

- The current XOR alternation color

Some of these attributes, such as the Component, the translation origin, the color and the font, have already been mentioned. In Java, rendering operations modify only pixels which lie within the area bounded by the current clipping rectangle, one of the attributes of the graphics object. Table 27-2 lists some of the methods in the Java Graphics class.

**Table 27-2**

*Commonly Used Method the Graphics Class*

| RETURNS | METHOD/ACTION |
|---|---|
| abstract void | **clearRect(int x, int y, int width, int height)** Clears the specified rectangle by filling it with the current background color. |
| abstract void | **clipRect(int x, int y, int width, int height)** Intersects the current clip with the specified rectangle. |
| abstract void | **copyArea(int x, int y, int width, int height, int dx, int dy)** Copies an area of the component distance in dx and dy. |
| abstract Graphics | **create()** Creates a new Graphics object that is a copy of the current one. |
| Graphics | **create(int x, int y, int width, int height)** Creates a new Graphics object based on this Graphics object, but with a new translation and clip area. |

*(continues)*

**Table 27-2**

*Commonly Used Method the Graphics Class (continued)*

| RETURNS | METHOD/ACTION |
| --- | --- |
| void | **dispose()**<br>Disposes of this graphics context and releases any System resources that it is using. |
| Abstract<br>void | **drawArc(int x, int y, int width, int height,<br>                int startAngle, int arcAngle)**<br>Draws the outline of a circular or elliptical arc defined by the specified rectangle. |
| void | **drawBytes(byte[] data, int offset, int length, int x,<br>           int y)**<br>Draws the text given by the specified byte array using the current color and font. |
| void | **drawChars(char[] data, int offset, int length, int x,<br>           int y)**<br>Draws the text in the specified character array, using the current font and color. |
| abstract<br>void | **drawLine(int x1, int y1, int x2, int y2)**<br>Draws a line, using the current color, between point (x1, y1) and  point (x2, y2). |
| abstract<br>void | **drawOval(int x, int y, int width, int height)**<br>Draws the outline of an oval defined by its bounding rectangle. |
| abstract<br>void | **drawPolygon(int[] xPoints, int[] yPoints,<br>int nPoints)**<br>Draws a closed polygon defined by arrays of x and y coordinates. |
| void | **drawPolygon(Polygon p)**<br>Draws the outline of a polygon defined by the specified polygon object. |
| abstract<br>void | **drawPolyline(int[] xPoints, int[] yPoints, int nPoints)**<br>Draws a sequence of connected lines defined by the corresponding arrays of x and y coordinates. |
| void | **drawRect(int x, int y, int width, int height)**<br>Draws the outline of the specified rectangle. |
| abstract<br>void | **drawRoundRect(int x, int y, int width, int height,<br>                int arcWidth, int arcHeight)**<br>Draws an outlined round-cornered rectangle using the graphics context's current color. |
| abstract<br>void | **drawString(String str, int x, int y)**<br>Draws the text given by the specified string, using the graphics context's current font and color. |

*(continues)*

**Table 27-2**

*Commonly Used Method the Graphics Class (continued)*

| RETURNS | METHOD/ACTION |
|---|---|
| void | **fill3DRect(int x, int y, int width, int height,**<br>                **boolean raised)**<br>Paints a 3-D highlighted rectangle filled with the current color. |
| abstract<br>void | **fillArc(int x, int y, int width, int height,**<br>            **int startAngle, int arcAngle)**<br>Fills a circular or elliptical arc defined by the specified bounding rectangle. |
| abstract<br>void | **fillOval(int x, int y, int width, int height)**<br>Fills an oval defined by the specified bounding rectangle, using the current color. |
| abstract<br>void | **fillPolygon(int[] xPoints, int[] yPoints, int nPoints)**<br>Fills a closed polygon defined by arrays of x and y coordinates. |
| void | **fillPolygon(Polygon p)**<br>Fills the polygon defined by the specified Polygon object, using the graphics context's current color. |
| abstract<br>void | **fillRect(int x, int y, int width, int height)**<br>Fills the specified rectangle. |
| abstract<br>void | **fillRoundRect(int x, int y, int width, int height,**<br>                **int arcWidth, int arcHeight)**<br>Fills the specified rounded corner rectangle using the current color. |
| void | **finalize()**<br>Disposes of this graphics context once it is no longer referenced. |
| abstract<br>Shape | **getClip()**<br>Gets the current clipping area. |
| abstract<br>Rectangle | **getClipBounds()**<br>Returns the bounding rectangle of the current clipping area. |
| abstract<br>Color | **getColor()**<br>Gets this graphics context's current color. |
| abstract<br>Font | **getFont()**<br>Gets the current font. |

*(continues)*

**Table 27-2**

*Commonly Used Method the Graphics Class (continued)*

| RETURNS | METHOD/ACTION |
|---|---|
| boolean | **hitClip(int x, int y, int width, int height)**<br>Returns true if the specified rectangular area intersects the bounding rectangle of the current clipping area. |
| abstract void | **setClip(int x, int y, int width, int height)**<br>Sets the current clip to the rectangle specified by the given coordinates. |
| abstract void | **setClip(Shape clip)**<br>Sets the current clipping area to an arbitrary clip shape. |
| abstract void | **setColor(Color c)**<br>Sets this graphics context's current color. |
| abstract void | **setFont(Font font)**<br>Sets this graphics context's font. |
| abstract void | **setPaintMode()**<br>Sets the paint mode of this graphics context to overwrite the destination with this graphics context's current color. |
| abstract void | **setXORMode(Color c1)**<br>Sets the paint mode of this graphics context to alternate between this graphics context's current color and the new specified color. |
| String | **toString()**<br>Returns a String object representing this Graphics object's value. |
| abstract void | **translate(int x, int y)**<br>Translates the origin of the graphics context to the point (x, y) in the current coordinate system. |

# Vector-Based Drawing

Several methods of the Graphics class allow drawing straight and curved lines on a graphics object. For example, to draw a filled oval you can use the fillOval() method. The method draws a solid ellipse or circle, as follows:

```
g.fillOval(50, 60, 200, 100);
             _  _  __  __
             |  |  |    |__ height of bounding rectangle
             |  |  |_____ width of bounding rectangle
             |  |_____ y of upper left corner
             |_____ x of upper left corner
```

Other methods that take similar parameters are:

```
fillPolygon()
fillRect()
fillRoundRect()
```

Methods that start with the word "draw" do not fill the interior of figures. For example:

```
drawRect()
drawOval()
```

The drawLine() method allows drawing a straight line defined by its end points. The line attributes are those defined in the device context. For example:

```
drawLine(int x1, int y1, int x2, int y2)
                 _____   _____

                     |             |___ x/y of end point
                     |_____ x/y of start point
```

Some vector-drawing methods of the Graphics class take arrays of coordinates as a parameter. For example:

```
int[] xCoords  =  {350, 500, 500, 350};
int[] yCoords  =  {50, 150, 50, 150};
...
g.drawPolygon(xCoords, yCoords, 4);
                 ____-  ____-  _
                   |       |        |__ number of points
                   |       |_____ array of y coordinates
                   |_____ array of x coordinates
```

Other methods that take similar parameters:

```
drawPolyline()
fillPolygon()
```

The drawArc() method is used to draw an arc of an ellipse, as follows:

```
g.drawArc( 50,          // x of start point
           280,         // y of start point
           150,         // width
           100,         // height
           45,          // start angle
           180);        // arc angle
```

All line drawing methods use lines that are one pixel thick. This is a great limitation of the AWT which was supposed to be fixed in later versions.

## Transformations

One of the most powerful features of vector graphics is the possibility of transforming an image by manipulating its coordinate points. Suppose you create a rectangular-shaped polygon defined by the $x$- and $y$-coordinates of its four screen points. If you add a constant value to each of the $x$ coordinates of this image, the result is a rectangle translated along the $x$-axis by the amount added to each coordinate point. By the same token, you can translate a vector image to any desired screen location by adding or subtracting a constant value to each of its $x$ and $y$ coordinates.

Figure 27-2 shows the translation of a rectangular polygon by adding a constant to its x and y coordinates.

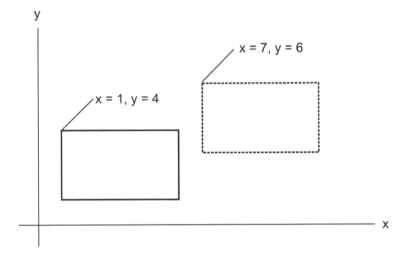

**Figure 27-2** *Translation of a Polygon*

In Figure 27-2 the rectangle in solid lines is translated to the position of the rectangle in dashed lines by manipulating its coordinate points. In this case a value of 6 was added to the $x$ coordinate of each point and a value of 2 to each of the $y$ coordinates.

Other geometrical transformations that can be performed on vector images are scaling and rotation. In scaling each coordinate point is multiplied by a scaling factor, which can be different for each coordinate plane. In the rotation transformation the vector-based object is made to move along a circular arc by applying a trigonometric function to each coordinate point. Objects can be made to appear larger or smaller, can be stretched and shrunk, and even animated, by applying translation, scaling, and rotation transformation. For example, the vector-based arms of a graphical clock can be made to move by applying a series of rotation transformations. An object can be made to move diagonally across the screen by consecutively applying a translation transformation. In either case the graphics application would have to follow a cycle of drawing, transforming, erasing, and redrawing each image.

The sample program named VGraphics, listed below, shows some of the fundamental manipulations in Java vector graphics.

```
//**********************************************************
//**********************************************************
// Project: Java for Engineers
// Program: VGraphics
// Reference: Chapter 27
// Topics:
//        1. Translating the frame origin to the client area
//        2. Creating and using colors
//        3. Vector graphics
//**********************************************************
//**********************************************************
// Requires: ActiveFrame class in the current directory
//**********************************************************
//**********************************************************

import java.awt.*;

//*********************************************
//*********************************************
//               driving class
//*********************************************
//*********************************************

public class VGraphics extends ActiveFrame
{
    // Class data
    int[] xCoords =  {350, 500, 500, 350};
    int[] yCoords =  {50, 150, 50, 150};

    //********************************
    //      redefinition of paint()
    //********************************

    public void paint(Graphics g)
    {
        // Adjust the frame origin to the client area
        g.translate(getInsets().left, getInsets().top);

        // Select a font
        Font f = new Font("Monospaced", Font.BOLD, 16);
        g.setFont(f);
```

```
// Create and set a bright shade of red
Color brightRed = new Color(200, 0, 0);
g.setColor(brightRed);
// Display a message
g.drawString("Demonstrating vector graphics in Java",
            30, 25);
// Create and set a shade of blue
Color aBlue = new Color(0, 0, 255);
g.setColor(aBlue);
// Draw a filled oval
g.fillOval(50, 60, 200, 100);

// Draw a black-border rectangle
Color aBlack = new Color(0, 0, 0);
g.setColor(aBlack);
g.drawRect(30, 180, 200, 50);

// Draw a green polygon
Color aGreen = new Color(0, 180,0);
g.setColor(aGreen);
g.drawPolygon(xCoords, yCoords, 4);

// Translate the image by adding 120 to the
// y coordinates of the polygon
for(int x = 0; x < 4; x++)
   yCoords[x] = yCoords[x] + 120;

// Fill the translated polygon
g.fillPolygon(xCoords, yCoords, 4);

// Translate image again
for(int x = 0; x < 4; x++)
   yCoords[x] = yCoords[x] + 120;

// Draw a magenta polyline. Note that the
// drawPolyline() does not close the figure
Color aMagenta = new Color(180,0 ,180);
g.setColor(aMagenta);
g.drawPolyline(xCoords, yCoords, 4);

// Restore the original values in the array of
// y coordinates
yCoords[0] = 50;
yCoords[1] = 150;
yCoords[2] = 50;
yCoords[3] = 150;

// Draw a cyan arc
Color aCyan = new Color(0, 120 ,120);
g.setColor(aCyan);
g.drawArc( 50,          // x of start point
           280,         // y of start point
           150,         // width
           100,         // height
```

```
                  45,              // start angle
                  180);            // arc angle

  }

  //****************************
  //          main
  //****************************
  public static void main(String[] args)
  {
    // Create an object of the class VGraphics
    VGraphics aframe = new VGraphics();

    // Use methods in superclasses to modify object's defaults
    aframe.setSize(550, 500);                // Set frame size
    aframe.setLocation(200, 100);            // Set frame location
    aframe.setTitle("Vector Graphics Demo");   // Title bar text

    // Display frame calling the show() method of the Window
    // class
    aframe.show();

  }
}
```

Figure 27-3 is a screen snapshot of the VectorGraphics program.

**Figure 27-3** *Screen Snapshot of the VGraphics Program*

**On the Web**

The program VGraphics.java is located in the Chapter 27 folder at www.crcpress.com.

# Raster Graphics

Raster or bitmap graphics is not based on geometrical figures but on images stored dot-by-dot. Raster images are a rectangle of individually colored dots. Raster images can be stored in GIF or JPEG format and displayed in Java programs. This technology is suitable for displaying photographs or other images defined in a pattern of individual dots.

## The image object

In order to display an image stored in a Java-compatible file the application must first create an Image object. This is accomplished by first retrieving the default Java AWT toolkit and then using the getImage() method of the Toolkit class. For example, if you wish to display an image stored in a file named "stars.gif" you start by creating the image object, as follows:

```
Image hstImage =
        Toolkit.getDefaultToolkit().getImage("stars.gif");
```

## Displaying the bitmap

You can display an image called HST_1(of the class Image) using the drawImage() method of the Graphics class, for example:

```
g.drawImage(HST_1, 120, 350, 200, 200, this);
                    |        |        |        |___ image observer
                    |        |        |_____ scaling rectangle
                    |        |_____ x/y location
                    |_____ image object
```

The fifth parameter in the call to drawImage() is an ImageObserver interface. When the call to drawImage() takes place Java starts a new program thread to load the requested image. The image observer is notified by the thread when the image data is acquired. Since the Component class implements the ImageObserver interface, we can use the "this" operator as an image observer in the call to drawImage().

The following program, named RGraphics.java, demonstrates the display of a bitmap file in Java.

```
//****************************************************************
//****************************************************************
// Project: Java for Engineers
// Program: RGraphics
// Reference: Chapter 27
// Topics:
//        1. Creating the image object
//        2. Displaying a raster image
//****************************************************************
//****************************************************************
// Requires: ActiveFrame class in current directory
//           Image file stars.gif in current directory
//****************************************************************
//****************************************************************

import java.awt.*;

//**********************************************
//**********************************************
//              driving class
//**********************************************
//**********************************************

public class RasterGraphics extends ActiveFrame
{
    // Class data

    Image hstImage =
         Toolkit.getDefaultToolkit().getImage("HST_1.JPG");


    //*********************************
    //     redefinition of paint()
    //*********************************

    public void paint(Graphics g)
    {
      // Adjust the frame origin to the client area
      g.translate(getInsets().left, getInsets().top);

      // Display an image in .jpg format
      g.drawImage(hstImage, 20, 20, 440, 400, this);
    }


    //***************************
    //         main
    //***************************
    public static void main(String[] args)
    {
      // Create an object of the class RasterGraphics
      RasterGraphics aframe = new RasterGraphics();

      // Use methods in superclasses to modify object's defaults
      aframe.setSize(488, 470);                // Set frame size
```

```
      aframe.setLocation(200, 100);          // Set frame location
      aframe.setTitle("Raster Graphics");     // Titlebar text

      // Display frame calling the show() method of the Window
      // class
      aframe.show();

   }
}
```

Figure 27-4 is a screen snapshot of the RGraphics program.

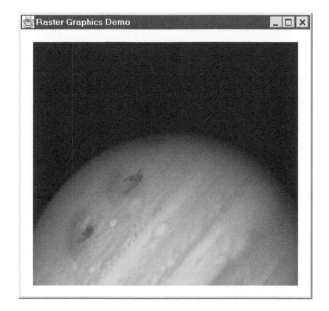

**Figure 27-4** *Screen Snapshot of the RGraphics Program*

# On the Web

The program RGraphics.java is found in the Chapter 27 folder at www.crcpress.com.

# *Index*